OFFICIAL
KNOWLEDGE

OFFICIAL KNOWLEDGE

DEMOCRATIC EDUCATION IN A CONSERVATIVE AGE

Michael W. Apple

ROUTLEDGE
NEW YORK •
LONDON

Published in 1993 by

Routledge
29 West 35th Street
New York, NY 10001

Published in Great Britain by

Routledge
11 New Fetter Lane
London EC4P 4EE

Library of Congress Cataloging-in-Publication Data

Apple, Michael W.
    Official knowledge : democratic education in a conservative age / Michael W. Apple.
        p.   cm.
    Includes bibliographical references (p.   ) and index.
    ISBN 0–415–90748–9—ISBN 0–415–90749–7 (pbk.)
    1. Education—Political aspects—United States.   2. Critical pedagogy—United
States.   3. Education—United States—Philosophy   4. Education—Social aspects—
United States.   I. Title.
    LC89.A815   1993
    370.19′34—dc20   92-35829
                                                                                          CIP

British Library Cataloguing-in-Publication Data also available.

Contents

Acknowledgments

Official Knowledge is volume four of what has come to be called "the Apple trilogy": *Ideology and Curriculum, Education and Power,* and *Teachers and Texts.* In a cute play on historical concepts, perhaps it should now be called the "quadrivium," an idea that also concerned itself—as all these books have—with the relationship between knowledge and power in education. Each volume has built on the ones preceding it, often correcting and extending arguments or striking out for new ground. Taken as a whole, they document my struggle (with the help of many others) to understand the limits and possibilities of democratic educational action.

The roots of these concerns go very far back, as I say in the interview with me published as an appendix to this book. Among the things that influenced me were the years I spent as a young teacher (I was only 19 years old when I began) in the inner-city schools of one of the poorest cities in the United States. It was made strikingly clear to me then that unless we acted politically—both inside the school and in the larger society—to get less racist, sexist, and class-biased curricula, more critically oriented teaching practices, and closer relationships between schools and the local community, neither I nor my students and colleagues would have much of a chance of widespread success. Later on, when I became president of a teachers' union, the structural nature of these problems—in our local, state, and national economic priorities, in our murderous health policies, in the sometimes-conscious destruction of our cities, and so on—became even clearer. My sense of the nature, sources, and complexity of the causes of the oppressive conditions so many people experience has grown; but one thing has not changed: the anger. If we cannot get angry at what this society is doing to its children, what can we get angry about?

Anger can of course make it difficult to concentrate. It can block one's ability to understand complex situations. On the other hand, it is a marvelous motivator to keep going, to try to get to the heart of the matter, in a time when critical educational work is under attack from the Right.

I mentioned in the first paragraph that I have had help from many others. The list is very long and I am certain it could (and should) be longer. But I have a bad character flaw. I like to listen to people; I appreciate their criticisms of my efforts, even when it makes me uncomfortable. Our task is *collective*, and unless we respect others' right to challenge us, we aren't following through on the politics we supposedly hold.

Among the people who have taught me some important things about what I say in this book are: Petter Aasen, Alicia de Alba, Peter Apple, Madeleine Arnot, Shigeru Asanuma, Jim Beane, Basil Bernstein, Lanny Beyer, Nick Burbules, Kathleen Casey, Lourdes Chehaibar, Somphong Chitradub, Linda Christian-Smith, John Clarke, John Codd, Bob Connell, Roger Dale, Linda Darling-Hammond, Gabriela Delgados, Ann De Vaney, Patricia Ducoing, Liz Ellsworth, Mariano Enquita, Steven Fain, Paulo Freire, Edgar Gonzales, Liz Gordon, Beth Graue, Maxine Greene, Stuart Hall, Ove Haugalokken, Allen Hunter, David Hursh, Alison Jones, Didacus Jules, Susan Jungck, Harvey Kantor, Koji Kato, Jane Kenway, Ki Seok Kim, Herbert Kliebard, Colin Lankshear, Ann Lieberman, Dan Liston, Alan Lockwood, Allan Luke, Carmen Luke, Marisol Martinez, Cameron McCarthy, Peter McLaren, Sue Middleton, Isamu Mizutani, Akio Nagao, Susan Noffke, Jeannie Oakes, Michael Olneck, Bertha Orozco, Bu Kwon Park, Paige Porter, Gary Price, Adriana Puiggros, Fazal Rizvi, Leslie Roman, Judyth Sachs, Francis Schrag, Chris Searle, Steven Selden, Tomas Tadeu da Silva, Einar Skaalvik, Graham Smith, Linda Smith, Richard Smith, Jonas Soltis, Alfred Telhaug, Sumlee Thongthew, Carlos Torres, Bonnie Trudell, Lois Weis, Philip Wexler, Geoff Whitty, Paul Willis, and Kenneth Zeichner.

Drafts of the chapters of this book have been worked through at a number of institutions where I was in residence for various periods of time. The University of Auckland in New Zealand, the Pontifical University of São Paulo in Brazil, the University of Trondheim in Norway, and UNAM in Mexico are special places in this regard.

Jayne Fargnoli, friend and editor at Routledge, provided the kind of assistance that demonstrates why she is such a talented editor. Diane Falkner, the secretary with whom I work, has worked with me on a number of books. Her care, skill, and commitment are much appreciated, as are the efforts of Patricia Martin.

In each of my books, I have given a special "thank you" to the Friday

Seminar at the University of Wisconsin, Madison. Whenever visitors come to Madison to spend time with me, they are often amazed at what we at Wisconsin perhaps take for granted too easily—that there can be a time and place where politically and educationally committed folks can come together to support each other, argue like crazy, and sometimes even have fun. I talk about this in chapter eight in this book. But the scores of people who have participated in the Friday Seminar over the past twenty years, and the current group of doctoral students (and friends), continually remind me of the silences and weaknesses of my (our) ideas and the ways they are expressed.

This book is dedicated to Rima D. Apple, historian of medicine, of women, and of the politics of consumption. We also happen to be married to each other. The last few years could have been and often were hell, with a son who is seriously ill and with the protracted decision concerning whether we would move to another university. Through all of these difficulties, she has continued to be the one I rely on most in so many ways. Also, if she thinks something is "bullshit," it often is.

Support for this volume came from the Graduate School Research Fund at the University of Wisconsin, Madison and The Spencer Foundation. Of course, the conclusions of my research are mine, not theirs.

1 Introduction: The Politics of Official Knowledge

THE CHILD AND THE CRITIC

It started right after lunch. The children finished eating in the school cafeteria and went outside to play until it was time to go back in for their afternoon classes. No one saw exactly how it started, but two kids began glaring at each other. Words were exchanged, insults were thrown back and forth. A circle formed. Other kids tried to separate the original two, but soon the fight was on (really only a wrestling match; no punches having been thrown). The principal had been outside, talking to a few teachers who had playground duty that day. He (it could have been a she, but not in this case) separated the now nearly exhausted and crying kids. (He was more than a little angry himself. It had been a tough day so far.) He grabbed them by their collars and took them into his office. But not just the original two. He pointed to another child who, like all the other kids in that circle, had excitedly and a little worriedly watched the fight, and yelled at all three to get to his office, NOW!

The scene in the office wasn't so pleasant: nine-year-old kids sullen or crying, the principal lacing into them. The parents of all three were called to take them home. This behavior won't be tolerated. If this occurs again, suspensions will be forthcoming.

This is the second time the parents of one of the children have been called. He was usually one of the watchers, but had tried to intervene to stop this fight. The first time his parents had been called, two weeks before, he himself had been involved in a serious scuffle. His parents and teacher did what they thought was the right thing. Fighting doesn't solve

1

anything, they said. He learned the lesson well and tried to stop the others from fighting. Now, for the second time, he was in trouble.

The first time he had "lost it" because a larger boy had been taunting him for weeks and it had finally gotten beyond what he could take. The larger boy was white; the child under discussion here is black. The taunt was usually one word, said over and over again. The word was nigger. Just ignore it; just ignore it. Finally an explosion. He is the one berated, too angry to speak in defense of himself; the other boy having, again, lied convincingly about who "started it." Then on the playground, the other scuffle ensued (later on we find out it's over whose turn it is to bat in a softball game) and the boy who learned his lesson about not fighting is pulled in again. He was seen in the midst of it; he's fought recently; he's black; he's got something to do with it.

This is not an apocryphal story. The boy's name is Paul. He is African-American. And he is my son.

This may seem like an odd way to begin a book on the way differential power works in education. Yet, I believe it is usually better to start in one's gut, so to speak, to constantly remind ourselves that the large-scale social forces such as racism and sexism many of us rightly condemn are not abstractions. Their effects are visceral. They are not far removed from daily practices, but constitute, and are constituted, by them.

In this case, racism is reconstituted in daily life in subtle (and not so subtle) ways. It is a small case, one that seems almost inconsequential next to the brutalizing conditions in the schools captured so well by Jonathan Kozol in *Savage Inequalities*[1] and in the highly publicized trauma of the riots in Los Angeles this year. (Of course, we must always remember that the *real* looting of that community had at least a twelve-year history during the conservative attack on cities and the poor. The policies carried out by the Reagan administration and continued by Bush were so destructive that the later actions of poor people in the streets of Los Angeles and elsewhere hardly register on the scale of violence compared to the destruction of hopes, dreams, opportunities, and even bodies brought about by the Right and its allies.) But a child—who this time happens to be my son—over a period of years of experiences in institutions in which racial meanings and power play so large a part is nearly destroyed in the process. How things like this happen, and especially how they come to be legitimated in our daily lives, is part of the story I wish to tell here. It deeply involves the politics of our knowledge in and about many of our institutions.

While issues of race play a considerable role in my account[2]—especially in my discussion of the current rightist restoration—race is not the "only" way differential power operates in education. Gender and class relations, as well as sexuality, and the contradictions within and among them, are crucial as well.

Much of what I say here is critical, for I position myself in opposition to much of what is becoming institutionalized as official policy in this society. The program of criticism and renewal I avow interprets education relationally, as having intimate connections both to the structures of inequalities in this society and to attempts to overcome them. It is based on an ethical and political principle that "no inhuman act should be used as a shortcut to a better day," and especially that at each step of the way any social act—be it in the economy, education, or elsewhere—"will be judged against the likelihood that it will result in linking equity, sharing, personal dignity, security, freedom, and caring."[3] This implies that we need to assure ourselves that the course we follow, inquire into, and analyze "will dignify human life, recognize the playful and creative aspects of people," and see others not as objects to be manipulated or to be "freed" to follow the dictates of the "invisible hand" of the market, but as *co-responsible subjects* involved in the process of democratically deliberating over the ends and means of *all* of their institutions.[4]

The current conservative agenda in education has little interest in this position. As I show later on, it has cleverly transformed the very meaning of democracy so that it is disconnected from the sentiments I express in the previous paragraph. In this regard, one of the hallmarks of the conservative agenda is its unremitting attack on education.

One of the major causes of educational failure is seen to be the supposedly nearly complete control over policy and practice by teachers and other "professional educators." Such autonomy "has left the educational system both unaccountable to consumers (parents and communities) and open to precisely the sort of curriculum initiatives associated with" liberal ideas.[5]

National curricula and assessment, greater opportunities for "parental choice," tighter accountability and control, the marketization and privatization of education—all of these proposals may be internally contradictory as a set of "reforms," but all are part of the conservative package that has been formed by the neo-liberal and neo-conservative wings of this movement.[6] Some of these criticisms leveled by conservatives are partly correct. But, the political and educational response of the Right leads in exactly the wrong direction, not only for children such as Paul but for the majority of people in this society.

For example, the conservative restoration is based on a *de-integrative strategy* that has as one of its results the creation of a "divided and amoral political community."[7] The de-integrative character is visible in the withdrawal of the Right from corporatist arrangements which at least provided safeguards and limited financial and political benefits to people. It is also very visible in the Right's attempts to disenfranchise those groups that it considers outside the "mainstream" (e.g., African-Americans, the poor, people on welfare, etc.). These are groups who, through years of struggle, were actually only recently even partly integrated into national politics. Part of its strategy of de-integration is to make it "far more difficult for women, ethnic minorities, gay [and lesbian] people, the unemployed and even those in non-union jobs to engage in meaningful participation." This is accompanied by a "clear rejection of the universalist and redistributive ethos of the welfare state, repudiation of the pursuit of full employment goals through state intervention, and decisive appeals to specific sectional interests.[8] Even with the election in 1992 of a more "moderate" Democrat as president, the Right has had a truly major and damaging impact on our policies, on our daily lives, and on how we understand ourselves and our responsibilities to each other. The growth in power of conservative groups at the local, county, and state levels continues.

While in the next chapter I call this (following Stuart Hall) *authoritarian populism,* it might be just as accurate to call it *arithmetical particularism* in that it relies on making appeals to specific sectors of a population; e.g., appeals based on questions about race and affirmative action, entrepreneurial values, anti-union sentiment, standards, sacred knowledge and authority based on fundamentalist religious principles, the family, and so forth. It is thus not a mobilization around a unified program,[9] but an attempt to divide people along particularist lines and then bring them under the umbrella of leadership provided by powerful rightist groups.

Yet, we need always to remember that the New Right faces contradictions that it not only does not recognize but that it can't easily solve. This creates opportunities as well as losses for those of us who oppose its arrogant tendencies.[10] In chapter two, I trace this out in much more detail, but I return to it often throughout the book.

It is not unusual for the powerful to challenge the patriotism or good will of those who take our countries to task for their failings. They ask, Is it all bad? Don't you have anything nice to say? Why criticize our society for its economic degradations and its sexual, class, and racial politics? Aren't other countries as bad or worse? Of course it's not "all bad," largely because there is such a strong tradition here of citizens saying, in essence, "you can't do this to me." But what the powerful do not seem to understand is the utter import of maintaining the voices of social conscience in a time when conditions conspire to stain those values and goals we should hold most dear. What they also do not understand is that critique—perhaps especially in its most powerful forms—as Henry Louis Gates says, is itself an affirmation. It is a form of commitment, "a means of laying a claim." In essence, it is one of the ultimate gestures of citizenship, for it is a profoundly important way of saying that I am not "just passing through." I (we) *live* here.[11] Criticism then is one of the most important ways we have of demonstrating that we expect more than rhetorical promises and broken dreams, because we take certain promises seriously.

This is one of the major reasons why, for all of the highly publicized failures of state bureaucratic socialism, it is still essential that we keep in the very forefront of our consciousness what *our* economic and cultural system does. At the cultural level, capitalism establishes a metric that measures everything—including persons like any of us—by the ability to produce wealth and by the success in earning it. This seems to lead "naturally" to the moral condemnation of those who fail to contribute to the production of profit. It also "mystifies" the exploitative relations that allow some to prosper so well at the expense of so many.[12] It was Adam Smith— surely no socialist for temporal as well as ideological reasons—who said that for every rich man there must be five hundred poor ones.[13] This is no small insight into the realities of our society and what is happening to our schools. It is an insight that guides the questions I ask throughout this volume.

Like many others, my investigations here have required that I simultaneously take account of both intellectual developments and cultural, political, and economic conditions. Thus, I have had to keep a dual focus: one on theoretical debates and the other on actual or potential political and educational practices and tendencies.

Yet, being critical means something more than simply fault-finding. It involves understanding the sets of historically contingent circumstances and contradictory power relationships that create the conditions in which we live.[14] History plays a large part here, as will be evident in my analysis of the conservative restoration and in my reconstruction of how the government has intervened in the process of defining official knowledge in the past and how it became a site of conflict over the relations between culture and power in class, race, gender, and religious terms.

As I argue later on, however (in my chapter on how we should think about texts as sites for the reproduction and production of power relations) power is not only a negative concept. It can of course be used to dominate, to impose ideas and practices on people in undemocratic ways. Yet, it also signifies the concrete and material ways all of us attempt to build institutions that respond to our more democratic needs and hopes. This is especially the case for power relations that exist at the level of the "popular" and at the level of common-sense. It is "common sense" that partly legitimates what the Right is currently doing and makes it more likely that many children will experience what my son did.

I focus in part on the groundings of common-sense because popular culture is one of the most important sites where the construction of our everyday lives can be examined. I do this not only for academic reasons, though there is some pleasure in doing that (sometimes only for the writer, of course). Rather, there is a political sensitivity behind this. I examine the shifting power relations that constitute some of our understanding of everyday life and the Right's role in reshaping this in order to both reveal the constellation of interests its construction serves and to rigorously criticize it.[15] In order to do this, I stand on the shoulders of so many women and men who have come before me, those who have struggled to embody critical perspectives in their daily practices in schools (and there are many teachers who are damn good at this) and those who have the luxury of time to be able to step back and write critically about the positives and negatives of what is happening to education in this society.

In stressing the continuing importance of critical work in education, however, I want to suggest a caution for those with that luxury of time for reflection. I have spent considerable time elaborating this elsewhere,[16] but it is worth restating some of my points here.

Perhaps the most important to note is the danger of losing our political soul on the altar of grand theorizing. A large part of what is called "critical educational studies" has tended to be all too trendy. It moves from theory to theory as each new wave of elegant meta-theory (preferably French) finds its way here. Sometimes this is decidedly necessary. For example, the traditions that dominated a good deal of critical educational work needed to be deconstructed because of their marginalization of gender and race, the body and sexuality, and so on. Thus, the growth of feminist work organized around postmodernism and poststructuralism, deconstruction, and others has had a salutary effect. However, at times the perspectives of, say, postmodernism and poststructuralism have been appropriated in ways that make them into simply the cultural capital of a new elite within the academy; so concerned about academic mobility and prestige that some individuals have lost any sense of "real" political issues over culture and power in schools.[17] For some, it is almost as if elementary, middle, and secondary schools hardly exist at all. Everything becomes so "meta-meta." And in the meantime, the Right has a field day.

Don't read this as a diatribe against theory. I've inflicted my share of theoretical labors on audiences throughout the world and am not so laden with guilt about this that I wish to cease doing it. Critical theoretical tools and concepts peek around every page in this book. Indeed, ideas about the continuing importance of political economy, the state, and class relations[18] are connected here to traditions of analysis drawn from theories of patriarchal and racial relations, cultural studies, discourse analysis, and (believe it or not) postmodern theories of the importance of consumption, identity politics, and the politics of pleasure,[19] though, as you will see, I have some reservations about postmodern theory. I have chosen to embed the theory within the text. It not only makes for easier reading, but most importantly, it shows these approaches *at work,* thinking about schools, teachers, curricula, and students, not cut off from the stuff of education.

I also choose to follow this path because of my belief that—as a political actor myself, as someone whose political and educational activity extends beyond writing and speaking about it—this says something important about people like myself.

It means that critical work needs to be done in an "organic" way. It needs to be connected to and participate in those progressive social movements and groups that continue to challenge the multiple relations of exploitation and domination that exist. The role of the "unattached intelligentsia" seems a bit odd here.

I realize that this is a very complicated issue, both theoretically and politically, in itself. We should not assume that there aren't contradictions here. Some challenges to dominant relations may have contradictory effects. After all, an important and expanding literature has effectively argued against essentializing uses of such concepts as "progressive," class, race, gender, and so on, as if all people of color, or women, or working-class groups think alike. Not only are there tensions within and among these groups, but individuals themselves are internally contradictory. Reality is more like listening to many radio stations at the same time, each one sometimes playing different things, than it is like listening to only one station. There are no guarantees that something or someone is eternally "progressive."

To take but one example, some women teachers may be very conservative in class politics, supporting policies that can extend the expansion of powerful economic influences in all our lives. However, at the same time, these same teachers—as women—may actively work against sexist policies and curricula that harm their female students. Or, if the teacher is an African-American woman, she may be an activist in the struggle against racism, but may believe that many feminist issues are largely those of white, middle-class women.

The same may be the case for educators who are men. Some may be deeply committed to radical changes in class relations and in how schools operate to reproduce them. But at the same time, they may believe that patriarchal or racial relations aren't "real" issues until class power is changed or that the immense discrimination against gays and lesbians is "not important." Thus, people may simultaneously hold "progressive" and "retrogressive" positions. As Gramsci reminded us, there will be elements of "good sense" and "bad sense" in our complex ideological experiences. Given this, while I shall continue to use the word "progressive" in my own accounts throughout this book to signify a broad commitment toward democratizing our lives and institutions, whenever I use it, I would hope that the reader also asks "Are there contradictions here?" "Are there ways that these tendencies can detract from other movements for equality?"

I am making this point not only as a caution, but also to show that the project and tools of critical educational studies are still in formation. It is not a finished project. Just as our social and discursive conditions change—with transformations in the internal and international divisions of paid and unpaid labor; in class relations; in a new politics of gender, race, and sexuality; in the attacks on education by the Right; and so on— so too are our theories and practices changing in response to all of this. There is a politics, then, to the ways we understand the world. This too involves the connections between power and forms of knowing.[20]

As I reflect on this, it provides a way of thinking about the roles critical work can play in education and elsewhere. One of the major roles of "critique" is "the self clarification of the struggles and wishes of the age."[21] This actually refers to three ways in which critical theory and political practice are connected. First, it valorizes "historically specific, conjunctural struggles as the agenda setters for critical theory." Second, it puts social movements as the most important shapers of such conjunctural struggles and as the subjects of critique. Third, it "implies that it is in the crucible of political practice that critical theories meet the ultimate test of viability."[22] All three of these—historical specificity, social movements, and political (and cultural) practice—are crucial to my arguments throughout this book.

Nancy Fraser, whose analyses have been so important in helping us think through how, say, gender and power operate in society, articulates my position well. She suggests what people would need to do for their "intellectual" work to be "viable."

How would we think of such a role? First and foremost, they (or we) would be:

> members of social groups and . . . participants in social movements.
> Think of them, in other words, as occupying specifiable locations in
> social space rather than as free-floating individuals who are beyond
> ideology.[23]

Yet, this is not all, for they (or we) also need to recognize that—also because of this location and not another—they (or we) may have something important to offer to those social movements. Thus, think of them . . . as having acquired as a result of the social division of labor some politically useful occupational skills: for example, the ability to show how the welfare system institutionalizes the feminization of poverty or how a poem orientalizes its subject. Think of them as potentially capable of utilizing these skills both in specialized institutions like universities and in the various larger cultural and political public spheres. Think of them, as participants on several fronts in struggles [over] cultural hegemony.[24]

These are the positive aspects of such a role. However, it needs constant correction through lived political (broadly conceived) experience. Therefore,

think of them, also alas, as mightily subject to delusions of grandeur and as needing to remain in close contact with their political comrades who are not intellectual *by profession* in order to remain sane, level-headed, and honest.[25]

This seems correct to me, both in its recognition of the dangers of arrogance and in its sensing of the important (though limited) role critical work can play. Of course, everyone involved in education can and often does play this role continuously, since there is no theory-less action and we are constantly, though not always consciously, making decisions on the consequences of our actions. What is necessary is to connect these decisions both to a wider sense of creating caring communities and social justice and to larger movements whose ends and means embody this. Any critically engaged author hopes to create a fuller understanding of these connections with her or his readers and I am no exception in this book.

THE POLITICS OF OFFICIAL KNOWLEDGE

As I noted, no matter what political party is in the White House, this is a time of rightist resurgence in education. What education is *for,* what and whose knowledge is considered legitimate, and who has the right to answer these questions; all of this is now being reconstructed during the conservative restoration. These transformations are occurring at the level of official policy and in the Right's ability to convince a significant portion of the population that what is private is now good and what is public is bad inside and outside of education. They are witnessed in the increasingly effective attacks on teaching and the curriculum, on the needs of business and industry being seen as more and more the primary, if not the only, goals of schooling, the tighter control of teaching in many states, and in the increasing integration of education into the conservative project.

While the current situation clearly documents that education has become deeply politicized, this is not something new. As I have demonstrated in the three volumes that have preceeded this one (*Ideology and Curriculum, Education and Power,* and *Teachers and Texts*)[26] education and differential cultural, economic, and political power have always been terms of an indissoluble couplet. The means and ends involved in educational policy and practice are the results of struggles by powerful groups and social movements to make their knowledge legitimate, to defend or increase their patterns of social mobility, and to increase their power in the larger social arena.

Yet the powerful are not *that* powerful. The politics of official knowledge are the politics of *accords* or *compromises*. They are usually not impositions, but signify how dominant groups try to create situations where the compromises that are formed favor them. These compromises occur at different levels: at the level of political and ideological discourse, at the level of state policies, at the level of the knowledge that is taught in schools, at the level of the daily activities of teachers and students in classrooms,[27] and at the level of how we are to understand all of this.

These, of course, are not compromises between or among equals. Those in dominance almost always have more power to define what counts as a need or a problem and what an appropriate response to it should be.[28] But, these compromises are never stable. They almost always leave or create space for more democratic action. I shall be at pains to show this throughout this book.

Official Knowledge analyzes the struggles over curriculum, teaching, and policy at a variety of levels and points to possibilities—not only limitations—in the current situation. It argues that the forms of curricula, teaching, and evaluation in schools are always the results of such accords or compromises where dominant groups, in order to maintain their dominance, must take the concerns of the less powerful into account. This accord is always fragile, always temporary, and is constantly subject to threat. There will always be openings for counter-hegemonic activity.

In chapter two, "The Politics of Common-Sense," I show how the Right has been able to build a new hegemonic accord, a new compromise, that integrates the perspectives of various groups under its leadership. A tense coalition around the politics of race, gender, class, religion, and sexuality is formed in such a way that conservative tendencies dominate public discourse over education. Even within this compromise, however—and this is a crucial message throughout this book—there are contradictory outcomes. There is space for a more democratic cultural politics in education and elsewhere.

We should not romanticize these "spaces," however. The conservative restoration is quite powerful. It has been able to create a new politics of official knowledge, especially around the curriculum itself.

The effects of this are seen on the artifact that constitutes the "real curriculum" in most schools: the textbook. How should we look at texts during this period? What is happening to them? Chapter three focuses on the politics of the text, showing once again that while the Right has had a considerable impact, the very nature of texts *themselves*—their contradictory and open meanings, their many possible readings and interpretations, etc.—is never a guarantee that hegemonic knowledge is the outcome.

Chapter four, "Regulating Official Knowledge" continues on from the previous chapter's examination of the textbook. One of the ways the Right is able to exert its growing power is through the control of the governmental mechanisms that grant official legitimacy to particular groups' knowledge. Perhaps the most important of these in the United States is the process of state textbook adoption. Looking historically, we can see that struggles over official knowledge have often centered exactly on these adoption policies and programs. How did they come about in such a way that now they offer conservatives a mechanism of control? What can we learn from this history about getting more progressive texts and curricula in schools? My argument is that this history demonstrates that organized popular struggles from below have had an impact in the past. This continues to be critical for contesting the rightist agenda today.

Textbooks and the mechanisms of official state control are not the only ways the agendas of the Right enter into the school. There are now even more creative, interesting, and radically different interventions that are occurring, ways that are transforming the very nature of how we think about the school itself.

New forms of business involvement and privatization are major forces at work here. A paradigm case, one that has already been institutionalized well before America 2000 and the plans to have a large number of private for-profit schools come to fruition, is the rapid growth of Channel One, the for-profit school news broadcast with commercials that now reaches over one-third of all middle school and high school students in the United States. Here, students are *sold* as an audience to advertisers who market their products directly within the school. This is exactly what chapter five, "Creating the Captive Audience," devotes its attention to. Situating the growth of Channel One within the fiscal crisis now being experienced by so many school districts, the chapter examines the discursive strategies business uses to "penetrate" schools, why schools allow themselves to become lucrative markets, the ideological creation of the news by Channel One, and the effects on and responses by teachers and students. Channel One is seen as a harbinger of things to come, as the "ethic" of privatization and profit reconstruct education. Yet, it too may offer possibilities of critical educational practice for committed teachers.

We should not assume—even given the growing power of rightist social movements and business in our discourse, policies, and practices—that their agenda finds its way into classrooms without being altered in significant ways. Chapter Six, "Whose Curriculum Is This Anyway?" follows another part of the business agenda into the classroom. It provides a detailed look at what teachers and students actually do with many of the pressures they are now under. By focusing on mandated curricula in computer literacy that aim at creating more linkages between education and the "new world of technological work," it demonstrates how teachers and students in turn are partly controlled and yet still partly transform this agenda to their own ends. This is not always successful, but it does give us reason for hope.

In the last section of this book, I purposely change to a more personal style. This may require some explanation. In previous books of mine, I certainly wasn't "invisible." In fact, I was at pains to show that there was a person—with particular visions, particular commitments, sensibilities and values—behind the analyses. Thus, both editions of *Education and Power* begin in part with an essay in self-criticism and the additional material in the recent second edition of *Ideology and Curriculum* is guided by a similar impulse. I continue to be committed to building upon and criticizing my previous positions. After all, we are not in a church, and therefore should not be worried about heresy. However, I only rarely described some of my own practices as an educator where I work. To be sure, I pointed to some of the political and educational (an odd separation at best) action in schools, offices, and factories that I and others have engaged in and that we urged others to engage in as well. This still is crucial. However, here I want to go further, to also point to a few examples of activity that are political and educative in my own home, so to speak.

The struggle for democracy in education does not only take place "out there." We should be deeply concerned about what is happening in our elementary, middle, and secondary schools and, as I show in many chapters in this volume, part of our task is to question what is wrong in these institutions and to make linkages with progressive teachers there who have tried to teach the entire community of educators how to singly or collectively challenge and alter these relations.[29] Yet this is not sufficient.

Those of us who are educators at colleges and universities need also to be held accountable for what we do with our own students and colleagues in the institutions in which *we* work. I am speaking not only about those who, like myself, work in the field of education per se. All "academics"—be they in physics, nursing, sociology, literature, cultural studies, law, medical school, and the list goes on and on—are first and foremost educators, *teachers*. What do we do in our own practices, to follow through on our commitments? These more democratic practices may be partly flawed; after all, like most people, we too are human beings caught in the multiple and sometimes contradictory relations of power in our institutions. Yet, even when flawed or not totally successful, these practices indicate what should be the constant pressure to take seriously the implications of our critical theories.[30]

I provide two stories of what I do. The first talks about a course on curriculum development that I teach every year and about working with children in difficult circumstances. (As some people know, there is a very practical side to me, a side that constantly pushes me to work at what I also enjoy, working with children and with other educators at a local level to help create conditions that might enable their experiences to be more personally and politically interesting.) The second story details a personal reading of the Friday Seminar, the attempt to build a collective and caring environment at the University of Wisconsin where critical educational and cultural work can go on in supportive ways, even in the face of the conservative restoration.

I hasten to add that these are my narratives. There are undoubtedly multiple interpretations, multiple readings, of what goes on in these two settings. I do not present them as "evidence," in any scientific sense, of the power of a different kind of practice. Nor are they meant to demonstrate what a good person Michael Apple supposedly is. Indeed, I am all too aware of many of the possible criticisms of my own pedagogic and curricular practices, an awareness that is constantly (thankfully) brought home to me by the suggestions and criticisms (and support) from my students. Rather, these stories are there to stimulate a dialogue with you, the reader. What seems right and wrong in what I am doing? If you had the opportunity to teach me how to go further, how would you do it? How could these practices be made even more powerful in their challenges to the larger relations of dominance in our society?

I am certain that we all have much to learn in this regard from each other as critical educators. I welcome letters that criticize me, make suggestions, affirm what seems right, provide descriptions of your own efforts, or some combination of these. Just write or call to begin the dialogue. My address is University of Wisconsin, Department of Curriculum and Instruction, 225 N. Mills St., Madison, Wisconsin, 53706, U.S.A. The phone number is (608) 263-4592.

I also add as an appendix to this volume a conversation, in the form of an interview with me, that I had with Carlos Torres and Raymond Morrow. The logic of this book has been to start with personal experience (Paul, my son, and his struggles as an African-American child in a society riven with racial antagonisms), to then move outward to the level of larger current and historical ideological movements and institutions, and then steadily to work our way toward the level of classroom practice, to the experiences of teachers and students during a time of intense pressure on schools to meet the rightist agenda. What begins with the personal should end with the personal, not simply because of symmetry, but because that is where questions of power and knowledge always end.

When thoughtful educators remind us that curriculum and teaching always end in an act of personal knowing, they also tacitly remind us that no matter how grounded our critical investigations are (and *must be*) in an equally critical understanding of the larger relations of dominance and subordination of this society and in the micropolitics of our institutions, it ultimately comes down to a recognition that we, as persons, participate in these relations. We have the responsibility to say "no" to as many of them that are antidemocratic as we can and to act to affirm what is less dominative and more caring. Thus, as the conclusion to this volume, the conversation with Carlos and Raymond returns us to that level: to personal history, biography, and power. Of no less importance, it also reminds us that the analyses published here are embodied; they are written from a particular position. This should be made available for scrutiny, so that you can see where you stand in relationship to them.

Let us begin with the larger story, with the conservative reconstruction that is now having tragic consequences on the lives of millions of people in so many nations.

2 The Politics of Common-Sense: Why the Right Is Winning

INTRODUCTION

The conventional approach to understanding how ideology operates assumes by and large that ideology is "inscribed in" people simply because they are in a particular class position. The power of dominant ideas is either a given in which dominance is guaranteed, or the differences in "inscribed" class cultures and ideologies will generate significant class conflict. In either case, ideology is seen as something that somehow makes its effects felt on people in the economy, in politics, in culture and education, and in the home, without too much effort. It is simply *there*. The common-sense of people becomes common-sense "naturally" as they go about their daily lives, lives that are prestructured by their class position. If you know someone's location in the class structure, you know her/his set of political, economic, and cultural beliefs and you don't really have to inquire into how dominant beliefs actually become dominant. It is usually not assumed that these ideas "should positively have to *win* ascendancy (rather than being ascribed it) through a specific and contingent (in the sense of open-ended, not totally determined) process of ideological struggle."[1]

Yet the current political situation in many Western capitalist nations presents us with evidence that such a conventional story is more than a little inadequate in understanding the shifts that are occurring in people's common-sense. We are seeing a pattern of conflicts within dominant groups that has led to significant changes in their own positions and, even more importantly, we are witnessing how elements of ideologies of groups in dominance become truly *popular*. There is a rupture in the accepted beliefs of many segments of the public who historically have been less powerful,[2] a rupture that has been worked upon and expanded by economically and politically strong forces in the society. And these ideo-logical shifts in common-sense are having a profound impact on how a large portion of the public thinks about the role of education in that soci-ety, to say nothing of its effects on millions of children like my son, Paul.

In this chapter, I shall describe and analyze a number of these most important changes in popular conceptions. A particular concern will be how ideologies actually become a part of the popular consciousness of classes and class fractions who are not among the elite. In order to under-stand this, I shall employ theoretical work on the nature of how ideology functions that has developed over the past decade. I don't want to do this because of some disembodied commitment to the importance of "grand theory." Indeed, as I have argued in *Teachers and Texts* and in chapter one, we have been much too abstract in our attempts to analyze the role of education in the maintenance and subversion of social and cultural power.[3] Rather, I intend to provide an instance in the use of theories to uncover the limits and possibilities of cultural and political action by ac-tually applying them to a concrete situation that is of major importance today, the New Right's reconstruction of our ideas about equality.

Stuart Hall stresses exactly this point in his criticisms of the abstract-ness of much critical literature on culture and power in the last two dec-ades. After a period of "intense theorization," a movement has grown that has criticized "the hyperabstraction and overtheoreticism that has char-acterized theoretical speculation, since . . . the early 1970s." As he puts it, in what seemed to be the pursuit of theory for its own sake, "we have abandoned the problems of concrete historical analysis."[4] How do we counteract this tendency? Theoretical analysis should be there to allow us to "grasp, understand, and explain—to produce a more adequate knowledge of—the historical world and its processes; and thereby to in-form our practice so that we may transform it."[5] This is what I shall do here.

RECONSTRUCTING EDUCATION

Concepts do not remain still very long. They have wings, so to speak, and can be induced to fly from place to place. It is this context that de-fines their meaning. As Wittgenstein so nicely reminded us, one should look for the meaning of language in its specific contextual use. This is especially important in understanding political and educational con-cepts, since they are part of a larger social context, a context that is constantly shifting and is subject to severe ideological conflicts. Education itself is an arena in which these ideological conflicts work themselves out. It is one of the major sites in which different groups with distinct political, economic, and cultural visions attempt to define what the socially legitimate means and ends of a society are to be.

In this chapter, I want to situate the concern with "equality" in education within these larger conflicts. I place its shifting meanings both within the breakdown of the largely liberal consensus that guided much educational and social policy since World War II, and within the growth of the New Right and conservative movements over the past two decades that have had a good deal of success in redefining what education is *for* and in shifting the ideological texture of the society profoundly to the right.[6] In the process, I document how new social movements gain the ability to redefine—often, though not always, in retrogressive ways—the terms of debate in education, social welfare, and other areas of the common good. At root, my claim is that it is impossible to comprehend fully the shifting fortunes of the assemblage of concepts surrounding equality (equality of opportunity, equity, etc.) unless we have a much clearer picture of the society's already unequal cultural, economic, and political dynamics that provide the center of gravity around which education functions.

As I have argued at considerably greater length elsewhere, what we are witnessing today is nothing less than the recurrent conflict between *property rights* and *person rights* that has been a central tension in our economy.[7] Gintis defines the differences between property rights and person rights in the following way:

> A *property right* vests in individuals the power to enter into social relationships on the basis and extent of their property. This may include economic rights of unrestricted use, free contract, and voluntary exchange; political rights of participation and influence; and cultural rights of access to the social means for the transmission of knowledge and the reproduction and transformation of consciousness. A *person right* vests in individuals the power to enter into these social relationships on the basis of simple membership in the social collectivity. Thus, person rights involve equal treatment of citizens, freedom of expression and movement, equal access to participation in decision-making in social institutions, and reciprocity in relations of power and authority.[8]

The attempts to enhance person rights partly rest on a notion of what is best thought of as positive liberty, "freedom to" as well as "freedom from." In industrial nations, this has grown stronger over the years as many previously disenfranchised groups of women and men demanded suffrage.

The right to equal political participation would be based on being a person rather than on ownership of property (or later on being a white male). Further, person rights have been extended to include the right of paid workers to form unions, to organize a common front against their employers. At the same time, claims about the right to have a job with dignity and decent pay have been advanced. And, finally, there have been demands that economic transactions—from equal treatment of women and people of color in employment, pay, and benefits to health and safety for everyone—are to be governed by rules of due process and fairness, thereby restricting management powers of unrestricted use and "free contract."[9]

This last point is important since it documents a growing tendency to take ideas of civil equality and apply them to the economic sphere. Thus, "the right to equal treatment in economic relationships, which directly expresses the dominance of person over property rights, has been an explicit demand of women, racial minorities, immigrant workers, and others."[10] This, too, has been accompanied by further gains in which the positive rights of suffrage and association that have been won by women and by minority and working-class groups have been extended to include what increasingly became seen as a set of minimum rights due any individual simply by the fact of citizenship. These included state-supported services in the areas of health, education, and social security, consumer protection laws, lifeline utility guarantees, and occupational safety and health regulations. In their most progressive moments, these tendencies led to arguments for full workplace democracy, democratic control over investment decisions, and the extension of the norms of reciprocity and mutual participation and control in most areas of social life, from the paid workplace and the political life of local communities and schools to the home.[11] Taken together, these movements did constitute at least a partial restructuring of the balance between person rights and property rights, one that would soon be challenged by powerful groups.

It is not surprising that in our society dominant groups "have fairly consistently defended the prerogatives of property," while subordinate groups on the whole have sought to advance "the prerogatives of persons."[12] In times of severe upheaval, these conflicts become even more intense and, given the current balance of power in society, advocates of property rights have been able once again to advance their claims for the restoration and expansion of their prerogatives not only in education but in all of our social institutions.

The United States economy is in the midst of one of the most powerful structural crises it has experienced since the depression. In order to solve it on terms acceptable to dominant interests—since as many aspects of the society as possible need to be pressured into conforming with the requirements of international competition, reindustrialization, and (in the words of the National Commission on Excellence in Education) "rearmament"—the gains made by women and men in employment, health and safety, welfare programs, affirmative action, legal rights, and education must be rescinded because "they are too expensive" both economically and ideologically.

Both of these latter words are important. Not only are fiscal resources scarce (in part because current policies continue to transfer them to the military or to tax breaks), but people must be convinced that their belief that person rights come first is simply wrong or outmoded given current "realities." Thus, intense pressure must be brought to bear through legislation, persuasion, administrative rules, and ideological maneuvering to create the conditions right-wing groups believe are necessary to meet these requirements.[13]

In the process, not just in the United States, but in Britain, Australia, and elsewhere as well, the emphasis on public policy has materially changed from issues of employing the state to overcome disadvantage. Equality, no matter how limited or broadly conceived, has become redefined. No longer is it seen as linked to past *group* oppression and disadvantagement. It is now simply a case of guaranteeing *individual choice* under the conditions of a "free market."[14] Thus, the current emphasis on "excellence" (a word with multiple meanings and social uses) has shifted educational discourse so that underachievement once again increasingly is seen as largely the fault of the student. Student failure, which was at least partly interpreted as the fault of severely deficient educational policies and practices, is now being seen as the result of what might be called the biological and economic marketplace. This is evidenced in the growth of forms of Social Darwinist thinking in education and in public policy in general.[15]

In a similar way, behind a good deal of the rhetorical artifice of concern about the achievement levels in, say, inner-city schools, notions of choice have begun to evolve in which deep-seated school problems will be solved by establishing free competition over students. These assume that by expanding the capitalist marketplace to schools, we will somehow compensate for the decades of economic and educational neglect experienced by the communities in which these schools are found.[16] Finally, there are concerted attacks on teachers (and curricula) based on a profound mistrust of their quality and commitments.

All of this has led to an array of educational conflicts that have been instrumental in shifting the debates over education profoundly to the right. The effects of this shift can be seen in a number of educational

policies and proposals now gaining momentum throughout the country:
1) proposals for voucher and choice plans and tax credits to make
schools more like the idealized free-market economy; 2) the movement
in state legislatures and state departments of education to "raise standards" and mandate both teacher and student "competencies" and basic
curricular goals and knowledge, thereby centralizing even more at a state
level the control of teaching and curricula; 3) the increasingly effective
assaults on the school curriculum for its supposedly antifamily and anti-
free enterprise bias, its "secular humanism," its lack of patriotism, and its
neglect of the "Western tradition"; 4) the growing pressure to make the
needs of business and industry into the primary goals of the educational
system.[17] These are major alterations, ones that have taken years to show
their effects. Although I paint in rather broad strokes here, an outline of
the social and ideological dynamics of how this has occurred still will be
visible. Clinton's presidency may slow the pace of these dynamics, but in
many ways he too—for reasons of ideology and economics—will be a
participant in some of their development.

THE RESTORATION POLITICS OF AUTHORITARIAN POPULISM

The first thing to ask about an ideology is not what is false about it, but
what is true. What are its connections to lived experience? Ideologies,
properly conceived, do not dupe people. To be effective, they must connect to real problems, real experiences.[18] As I document, the movement
away from social democratic principles and an acceptance of more right-
wing positions in social and educational policy occur precisely because
conservative groups have been able to work on popular sentiments, to
reorganize genuine feelings, and in the process to win adherents.

Important ideological shifts take place not only by powerful groups
"substituting one, whole, new conception of the world for another." Often,
these shifts occur through the presentation of novel combinations of old
and new elements.[19] Let us take the positions of the Reagan administration, positions that by and large provided the framework for the Bush administration's policies and created the economic conditions that will
make it exceedingly difficult, no matter what party is in power, to act on
person rights in more than a rhetorical way in the future, as a case in
point. For as Clark and Astuto have demonstrated in education, and Piven
and Cloward and Raskin have shown in the larger areas of social policy,
significant and enduring alterations have occurred in the ways policies
are carried out and in the content of those policies.[20]

The "success" of the policies of the Reagan administration, like that of Thatcherism and then Major in Britain, should not simply be evaluated in electoral terms. They also need to be judged by their success in disorganizing other more progressive groups, in shifting the terms of political, economic, and cultural debate onto the terrain favored by capital and the Right.[21] In these terms, there can be no doubt that the current right-wing resurgence has accomplished no small amount in its attempt to construct the conditions that will put it in a hegemonic position.

The Right in the United States and Britain has thoroughly renovated and reformed itself. It has developed strategies based on what might be best called an *authoritarian populism*.[22] As Hall has defined this, such a policy is based on an increasingly close relationship between government and the capitalist economy, a radical decline in the institutions and power of political democracy, and attempts at curtailing "liberties" that have been gained in the past. This is coupled with attempts to build a consensus, one that is widespread, in support of these actions.[23] The New Right's authoritarian populism[24] has exceptionally long roots in the history of the United States. The political culture here has always been influenced by the values of the dissenting Protestantism of the seventeenth century. Such roots become even more evident in periods of intense social change and crisis.[25] As Burnham has put it:

> Whenever and wherever the pressures of "modernization"—secularity, urbanization, the growing importance of science—have become unusually intense, episodes of revivalism and culture-issue politics have swept over the social landscape. In all such cases since at least the end of the Civil War, such movements have been more or less explicitly reactionary, and have frequently been linked with other kinds of reaction in explicitly political ways.[26]

The New Right works on these roots in creative ways, modernizing them and creating a new synthesis of their varied elements by linking them to current fears. In so doing, the Right has been able to rearticulate traditional political and cultural themes and because of this has effectively mobilized a large amount of mass support.

As I noted, part of the strategy has been the attempted dismantling of the welfare state and of the benefits that working people, people of color, and women (these categories are obviously not mutually exclusive) have won over decades of hard work. This has been done under the guise of antistatism, of keeping government "off the backs of the people," and of "free enterprise." Yet, at the same time, in many valuative, political, and economic areas, the current government is extremely state-centrist both in its outlook and very importantly in its day-to-day operations, in large part because of the sometimes competing neo-liberal and neo-conservative wings of the movement.[27]

One of the major aims of a rightist restoration politics is to struggle in not one but many different arenas at the same time, not only in the economic sphere but in education and elsewhere as well. This aim is grounded in the realization that economic dominance must be coupled to "political, moral, and intellectual leadership" if a group is to be truly dominant and if it wants genuinely to restructure a social formation. Thus, as both Reaganism and Thatcherism recognized so clearly, to win in the state you must also win in civil society.[28] As the noted Italian political theorist Antonio Gramsci would put it, what we are seeing is a war of position. "It takes place where the whole relation of the state to civil society, to 'the people' and to popular struggles, to the individual and to the economic life of society has been thoroughly reorganized, where 'all the elements change.'"[29]

The Right, then, has set itself an immense task, to create a truly "organic ideology," one that seeks to spread throughout society and to create a new form of "national popular will." It seeks to intervene "on the terrain of ordinary, contradictory common-sense," to "interrupt, renovate, and transform in a more systematic direction" people's practical consciousness. It is this restructuring of common-sense, which is itself the already complex and contradictory result of previous struggles and accords, which becomes the object of the cultural battles now being waged.[30]

In this restructuring, Reaganism and Thatcherism did not create some sort of false consciousness, creating ways of seeing that had little connection with reality. Rather, they "operated directly on the real and manifestly contradictory experiences" of a large portion of the population. They did connect with the perceived needs, fears, and hopes of groups of people who felt threatened by the range of problems associated with the crises in authority relations in culture, in the economy, and in politics.[31]

What has been accomplished has been a successful translation of an economic doctrine into the language of experience, moral imperative, and common-sense. The free-market ethic has been combined with a populist politics. This has meant the blending together of a "rich mix" of themes that have had a long history—nation, family, duty, authority, standards, and traditionalism—with other thematic elements that have also struck a resonant chord during a time of crisis. These latter themes include self interest, competitive individualism (what I have elsewhere called the possessive individual),[32] and antistatism. Many of these themes are now echoed by both major parties in the United States. In this way, a reactionary common-sense is partly created.[33]

The sphere of education has been one of the most successful areas in which the Right has been ascendant. The social democratic goal of expanding equality of opportunity (itself a rather limited reform) has lost much of its political potency and its ability to mobilize people. The "panic" over falling standards and illiteracy, the fears of violence in schools, the concern with the destruction of family values and religiosity, all have had an effect. These fears are exacerbated, and used, by dominant groups within politics and the economy who have been able to move the debate on education (and all things social) onto their own terrain, the terrain of "tradition," standardization, productivity, and industrial needs.[34] Since so many parents *are* justifiably concerned about the economic futures of their children—in an economy that is increasingly conditioned by lowered wages, unemployment, capital flight, and insecurity[35]—rightist discourse connects with the experiences of many working-class and lower-middle-class people.

However, while this conservative conceptual and ideological apparatus does appear to be rapidly gaining ground, one of the most critical issues remains to be answered. How *is* such an ideological vision legitimated and accepted? How was this done?[36]

UNDERSTANDING THE CRISIS

The right-wing resurgence is not simply a reflection of the current crisis. Rather, it is itself a response to that crisis.[37] Beginning in the immediate post–World War II years, the political culture of the United States was increasingly characterized by American imperial might, economic affluence, and cultural optimism. This period lasted for more than two decades. Socially and politically, it was a time of what has been called the *social democratic accord,* in which government increasingly became an arena for a focus on the conditions required for equality of opportunity. Commodity-driven prosperity, the extension of rights and liberties to new groups, and the expansion of welfare provisions provided the conditions for this compromise both between capital and labor and with historically more dispossessed groups such as African-Americans, Latinos and Latinas, and women. This accord has become mired in crisis since the late 1960s and early 1970s.[38]

Allen Hunter gives an excellent sense of this in his own description of this accord:

> From the end of World War II until the early 1970s world capitalism experienced the longest period of sustained economic growth in its

history. In the United States a new "social structure of accumulation"—"the specific institutional environment within which the capitalist accumulation process is organized"—was articulated around
several prominent features: the broadly shared goal of sustained economic growth, Keynesianism, elite pluralist democracy, an imperial
America prosecuting a cold war, anti-communism at home and
abroad, stability or incremental change in race relations and a stable
home life in a buoyant, commodity-driven consumer culture. Together these crystallized a basic consensus and a set of social and
political institutions which was hegemonic for two decades.[39]

At the very center of this hegemonic accord was a compromise reached
between capital and labor in which labor accepted what might be called
"the logic of profitability and markets as the guiding principles of resource allocation." In return they received "an assurance that minimal living standards, trade union rights and liberal democratic rights would be
protected."[40] These democratic rights were further extended to the poor,
women, and people of color as these groups expanded their own
struggles to overcome racially and sexually discriminatory practices.[41]
Yet, this extension of (limited) rights could not last, given the economic
and ideological crises that soon beset American society, a set of crises
that challenged the very core of the social democratic accord.

The dislocations of the 1960s and 1970s—the struggle for racial and
sexual equality, military adventures such as Vietnam, Watergate, the resi-
lience of the economic crisis—produced both shock and fear. "Mainstream culture" was shaken to its very roots in many ways. Widely shared
notions of family, community, and nation were dramatically altered. Just
as importantly, no new principle of cohesion emerged that was sufficiently compelling to recreate a cultural center. As economic, political,
and valuative stability (and military supremacy) seemed to disappear, the
polity was itself "balkanized." Social movements based on difference—
regional, racial, sexual, religious—became more visible.[42] The sense of
what Marcus Raskin has called "the common good" was fractured.[43]

Traditional social democratic "statist" solutions, which in education,
welfare, health, and other similar areas took the form of large-scale attempts at federal intervention to increase opportunities or to provide a
minimal level of support, were seen as being part of the problem and not
as part of the solution. Traditional conservative positions were more easily dismissed as well. After all, the society on which they were based was
clearly being altered. The cultural center could be *built* (and it had to be
built by well-funded and well-organized political and cultural action)
around the principles of the New Right. The New Right confronts the

"moral, existential, [and economic] chaos of the preceding decades" with a network of exceedingly well-organized and financially secure organizations incorporating "an aggressive political style, on outspoken religious and cultural traditionalism and a clear populist commitment."[44]

In different words, the project was aimed at constructing a "new majority" that would "dismantle the welfare state, legislate a return to traditional morality, and stem the tide of political and cultural dislocation which the 1960's and 1970's represented." Using a populist political strategy (now in combination with an aggressive executive branch of the government), it marshalled an assault on "liberalism and secular humanism" and linked that assault to what some observers have argued was "an obsession with individual guilt and responsibility where social questions are concerned (crime, sex, education, poverty)" with strong beliefs against government intervention.[45]

The class, racial, gendered, and sexual specificities here are significant. The movement to create a conservative cultural consensus in part builds on the hostilities of the working and lower middle classes toward those above and below them and is fueled as well by a very real sense of antagonism against the new middle class. State bureaucrats and administrators, educators, journalists, planners, and so on, all share part of the blame for the social dislocations these groups have experienced.[46] Race, gender, and class themes abound here, a point to which I return in the next section of my analysis.

This movement is of course enhanced within academic and government circles by a group of policy-oriented neo-conservatives who have become the organic intellectuals for much of the rightist resurgence. A society based on individualism, market-based opportunities, and the drastic reduction of both state intervention and state support: these are the currents that run deep in their work.[47] They provide a counterpart to the New Right and are themselves part of the inherently unstable alliance that has been formed.

BUILDING THE NEW ACCORD

Almost all of the reform-minded social movements—including the feminist, gay and lesbian, student, and other movements of the 1960s—drew upon the struggle by African-Americans "as a central organizational fact or as a defining political metaphor and inspiration."[48] These social movements infused new social meanings into politics, economics, and culture. These are not separate spheres. All three of these levels exist simultaneously. New social meanings about the importance of person rights infused individual identity, family, and community, and penetrated state institutions and market relationships. These emerging social movements expanded the concerns of politics to all aspects of the "terrain of everyday life." Person rights took on ever more importance in nearly all of our institutions, as evidenced in aggressive affirmative-action programs, widespread welfare and educational activist programs, and so on.[49] In education this was very clear in the growth of bilingual programs and in the development of women's, black, Hispanic, and Native American studies in high schools and colleges.

There are a number of reasons the state was the chief target of these earlier social movements for gaining person rights. First, the state was the "factor of cohesion in society" and historically had maintained and organized practices and policies that embodied the tension between property rights and person rights.[50] As such a factor of cohesion, it was natural to focus on it. Second, "the state was traversed by the same antagonisms which penetrated the larger society, antagonisms that were themselves the results of past cycles of [social] struggle." Openings in the state could be gained because of this. Footholds in state institutions dealing with education and social services could be deepened.[51]

Yet even with these gains, the earlier coalitions began to disintegrate. In the minority communities, class polarization deepened. The majority of barrio and ghetto residents "remained locked in poverty," while a relatively small portion of the black and brown population was able to take advantage of educational opportunities and new jobs (the latter being largely within the state itself).[52] With the emerging crisis in the economy, something of a zero-sum game developed in which progressive social movements had to fight over a limited share of resources and power. Antagonistic rather than complementary relationships developed among groups. Minority groups, for example, and the largely white and middle-class women's movement had difficulty integrating their programs, goals, and strategies.

This was exacerbated by the fact that, unfortunately, given the construction of a zero-sum game by dominant groups, the gains made by women sometimes came at the expense of blacks and browns. Furthermore, leaders of many of these movements had been absorbed into state-sponsored programs that, while the adoption of such programs *was* in part a victory, had the latent affect of cutting off leaders from their grass-roots constituency and lessened the militancy at this level. This often resulted in what has been called the "ghettoization" of movements within state institutions as movement demands were partly adopted in their most moderate forms into programs sponsored by the state. Militancy is transformed into constituency.[53]

The splits in these movements occurred as well because of strategic divisions, divisions that were paradoxically the results of the movements' own successes. Thus, for example, those women who aimed their work within existing political/economic channels *could* point to gains in employment within the state and in the economic sphere. Other, more radical, members saw such "progress" as "too little, too late."

Nowhere is this more apparent than in the black movement in the United States. It is worth quoting one of the best analyses of the history of these divisions at length:

> The movement's limits also arose from the strategic divisions that befell it as a result of its own successes. Here the black movement's fate is illustrative. Only in the South, while fighting against a backward political structure and overt cultural oppression, had the black movement been able to maintain a *de*-centered unity, even when internal debates were fierce. Once it moved north, the black movement began to split, because competing political projects, linked to different segments of the community, sought either integration in the (reformed) mainstream, or more radical transformation of the dominant racial order.
>
> After initial victories against segregation were won, one sector of the movement was thus reconstituted as an interest-group, seeking an end to racism understood as discrimination and prejudice, and turning its back on the oppositional "politics of identity." Once the organized black movement became a mere constituency, though, it found itself locked in a bear hug with the state institutions whose programs it had itself demanded, while simultaneously isolated from the core institutions of the modern state.[54]

In the process, those sectors of the movement that were the most radical were marginalized or, and this must not be forgotten, were simply repressed by the state.[55]

Even though there were major gains, the movements' integration into the state latently crated conditions that were disastrous in the fight for equality. A mass-based, militant, grass-roots movement was defused into a constituency, dependent on the state itself. *And very importantly, when the neo-conservative and right-wing movements evolved with their decidedly anti-statist themes, the gains that were made in the state came increasingly under attack and the ability to recreate a large-scale, grass-roots movement to defend these gains was weakened considerably.*[56] Thus, when there are right-wing attacks on the more progressive national and local educational policies and practices that have benefitted people of color, it becomes increasingly difficult to develop broad-based coalitions to counter these offensives.

In their failure to consolidate a new "radical" democratic politics, one with majoritarian aspirations, the new social movements of the 1960s and 1970s "provided the political space in which right wing reaction could incubate and develop its political agenda."[57] Thus, state reforms won by, say, minority movements in the 1960s in the United States, and the new definitions of person rights embodied in these reforms, "provided a formidable range of targets for the 'counter-reformers' of the 1970s." Neoconservatives and the New Right carried on their own political "project." They were able to rearticulate particular ideological themes and to restructure them around a political movement once again.[58] And these themes *were* linked to the dreams, hopes, and fears of many individuals.

Let us examine this in somewhat more detail. Behind the conservative restoration is a clear sense of loss: of control, of economic and personal security, of the knowledge and values that should be passed on to children, of visions of what counts as sacred texts and authority. The binary opposition of we/they becomes very important here. "We" are law abiding, "hard working, decent, virtuous, and homogeneous." The "theys" are very different. They are "lazy, immoral, permissive, heterogenous."[59] These binary oppositions distance most people of color, women, gays, lesbians, and others from the community of worthy individuals. The subjects of discrimination are now no longer those groups who have been historically oppressed, but are instead the "real Americans" who embody the idealized virtues of a romanticized past. The "theys" are undeserving. They are getting something for nothing. Policies supporting them are "sapping our way of life," most of our economic resources, and creating government control of our lives.[60]

These processes of ideological distancing make it possible for anti-black and anti-feminist sentiments to seem no longer racist and sexist because they link so closely with other issues. Once again, Allen Hunter is helpful:

> Racial rhetoric links with anti-welfare state sentiments, fits with the push for economic individualism; thus many voters who say they are not prejudiced (and may not be by some accounts) oppose welfare spending as unjust. Anti-feminist rhetoric is articulated around defense of the family, traditional morality, and religious fundamentalism.[61]

All of these elements can be integrated through the formation of ideological coalitions that enable many Americans who themselves feel under threat to turn against groups of people who are even less powerful than themselves. At the very same time, it enables them to "attack domination by liberal, statist elites."[62]

This ability to identify a range of "others" as enemies, as the source of the problems, is very significant. One of the major elements in this ideological formation has indeed been a belief that liberal elites within the state "were intruding themselves into home life, trying to impose their values." This was having serious negative effects on moral values and on traditional families. Much of the conservative criticism of textbooks and curricula rests on these feelings, for example, a feeling that goes back many years as we shall see in chapter four.[63] While this position certainly exaggerated the impact of the "liberal elite," and while it certainly misrecognized the power of capital and of other dominant classes,[64] there was enough of an element of truth in it for the Right to use it in its attempts to dismantle the previous accord and build its own.

While racist and anti-feminist sentiment and the mistrust of "urban elites" play such a large part in the current conservative restoration, it is not totally new by any means. These elements have strong roots in our past. And, as I mentioned above and in chapter one, they are the results of contradictory ideological impulses. Take the anti-feminist and racist stance of many right-wing women today.[65] This provides some women room for activism at the very same time as it does so at the expense of many other women and people of color. Let me take one historical example here, that of a famous (or, better, infamous) ultra-right-wing organization.

It is important not to assume that activist women who challenged male dominance "have always belonged to a left-wing tradition of social equality and ethnic tolerance." One of the best counterexamples can be found in the Women of the Ku Klux Klan (WKKK). Recent historical work demonstrates that, with chapters in over two-thirds of the states and a membership that rivaled its male counterpart in the early years of this century, the WKKK encompassed thousands of women who saw the organization as furthering Prohibition, woman suffrage, and "a moral housecleaning of public life." In many ways, these are often the same reforms that many self-described progressives also favored. These Klanswomen viewed their very real hostility toward ethnic and religious groups "as a necessary means of self-defense against a decadent, anti-maternal threat." In the process, under "the sometimes uneasy supervision" of the men of the KKK, these Klanswomen "articulated a language of rights, arguing that vice and immorality denigrated white Protestant women and that they had the right, and the duty, to end it."[66]

I do not wish to excuse in any way the violent racism that stood behind this vision. Klanswomen spearheaded "poison squads" that tried to get consumers to boycott Catholic- and Jewish-owned businesses. Their treatment of African-Americans is too painful to recount one more time.

Yet, Klan life was "mundane," an accepted part of daily life of many main-stream, native-born, white, Protestant congregations. In many ways, this documents how naturally accepted racism always has been in the United States and how the nation's everyday life was (and continues to be) struc-tured around a racial politics. Yet, for many right-wing women activists, the Klan also provided a space for them to be resourceful and vocal *as women,* to act against the "traffic in both liquor and young women" that they saw as evils that could only be fought against through a collective structure. As odd as it seems, for some women, there may have seemed to be "rational and liberating" reasons for them to join the Klan.[67] Similar "rational" reasons may also help explain parts of the current rightist resur-gence.

Historically, in fact, grass-roots movements on the right, even in the 1920s, often shared two themes. These involved an opposition between a longing for and protection of self-governing, pious communities and dec-adent, hypocritical cosmopolitan elites. They also involved a distaste for consumerism and "unearned benefits" such as welfare and the fostering of a morality of hard work, self-control, and self-reliance. Coupled with this as well, especially after the 1930s, was a hostility toward international cooperation and a conviction that force was a necessary tool to achieve "law and order," not only away but at home as well.[68] It is not too long a trip from here to the fusion of the triad of family, church, and "native place" with a vision of "objective" moral values. And from this "creative work"—and it was very creative—another fusion could occur, that linking "the free market" with its emphasis on individual hard work and individ-ual entrepreneurialism with "traditional" values.[69] The enemy that both created was the "haughty" liberal establishment and those who received its "unearned" largesse. And both were and are driven by fears of eco-nomic and moral decline, fears so powerful in the current climate of right-ist triumphalism. Some of this also fueled Ross Perot's emergence as a national figure.

A new hegemonic accord, then, is reached now. It combines dominant economic and political elites intent on "modernizing" the economy, white working-class and middle-class groups concerned with security, the fam-ily, and traditional knowledge and values, and economic and cultural conservatives.[70] It also includes a fraction of the new middle class whose own advancement depends on the expanded use of accountability, effi-ciency, and management procedures which are their own cultural capi-tal.[71] This coalition has partly succeeded in altering the very meaning of what it means to have a social goal of equality. The citizen as "free" con-sumer has replaced the previously emerging citizen as situated in struc-turally generated relations of domination. Thus, the common good is now to be regulated exclusively by the laws of the market, free competition, private ownership, and profitability. In essence, the definitions of freedom and equality are no longer democratic, but *commercial*.[72] This is particularly evident in the proposals for voucher and choice plans as "solutions" to massive and historically rooted relations of economic and cultural inequality.

In sum, then, the Right in both the United States and Britain has succeeded in reversing a number of the historic post–World War II trends.

> It has begun to dismantle and erode the terms of the unwritten social contract on which the social forces settled after the war. It has changed the currency of political thought and argument. Where previously social need had begun to establish its own imperatives against the laws of market forces, now questions of "value for money," the private right to dispose of one's own wealth, the equation between freedom and the free market, have become the terms of trade, not just of political debate . . . but in the thought and language of everyday calculation. There has been a striking reversal of values: the aura that used to attach to the value of the public welfare [that is, the value of the common good], now adheres to anything that is private—or can be privatized. A major ideological reversal is in progress in society at large; and the fact that it has not swept everything before it, and that there are many significant points . . . of resistance, does not contradict the fact that, conceived not in terms of outright victory but more in terms of the mastery of an unstable equilibrium, [the Right] has . . . begun to reconstruct the social order.[73]

This reconstruction is not imposed on unthinking subjects. It is not done through the use of some right-wing attempt at what Freire has called "banking" where knowledge and ideologies become common-sense simply by pouring them into people's heads. The ruling or dominant conceptions of the world and of everyday life "do not directly prescribe the mental content of the illusions that supposedly fill the heads of the dominated classes."[74] However, the meanings, interests, and languages we construct are bound up in the unequal relations of power that do exist. To speak theoretically, the sphere of symbolic production is a contested terrain just as other spheres of social life are. "The circle of dominant ideas does accumulate the symbolic power to map or classify the world for others," to set limits on what appears rational and reasonable, indeed on what appears sayable and thinkable.[75] This occurs not through imposition, but through creatively working on existing themes, desires, and fears and reworking them. Since the beliefs of people are contradictory and have tensions because they are what some have called polyvocal,[76] it is then possible to move people in directions where one would least expect given their position in society.

Thus, popular consciousness can be articulated to the right precisely because the feelings of hope and despair and the logic and language used to express these are "polysemic" and can be attached to a variety of discourses. Hence, a male worker who has lost his job might be antagonistic to the corporations who engaged in capital flight or can blame unions, people of color, or women "who are taking men's jobs." A principal in a school where there are "discipline problems" might blame the racial structuring of this society or see most students of color as probable "at-risk" trouble makers. The response is *constructed,* not preordained, by the play of ideological forces in the larger society.[77] And, though this construction occurs on a contradictory and contested terrain, it is the Right that seems to have been more than a little successful in providing the discourse that organizes that terrain, so much so that even the current Democratic administration has taken on a good deal of its underlying discourse.

WILL THE RIGHT SUCCEED?

So far, I have broadly traced out many of the political, economic, and ideological reasons that the social democratic consensus that led to the limited extension of person rights in education, politics, and the economy slowly disintegrated. At the same time, I have documented how a new "hegemonic bloc" is being formed, coalescing around New Right tactics and principles. The question remains: Will this accord be long lasting? Will it be able to inscribe its principles into the very heart of the American polity?

There are very real obstacles to the total consolidation within the state of the New Right political agenda. First, there has been something of a "great transformation" in, say, racial identities. Omi and Winant describe it thusly:

> The forging of new collective racial identities during the 1950s and 1960s has been the enduring legacy of the racial minority movements. Today, as gains won in the past are rolled back and most organizations prove unable to rally a mass constituency in racial minority communities, the persistence of the new racial identities developed during this period stands out as the single truly formidable obstacle to the consolidation of a newly repressive racial order.[78]

Thus, even when social movements and political coalitions are fractured, when their leaders are coopted, repressed, and sometimes killed, the racial subjectivity and self-awareness that were developed by these movements has taken permanent hold. "No amount of repression or cooptation [can] change that." In Omi and Winant's words, the genie is out of the bottle.[79] This is the case because, in essence, a new kind of person has been created within minority communities.[80] A new, and much more self-conscious, *collective* identity has been forged. Thus, for instance, in the struggles over the past four decades by people of color to have more control of education and to have it respond more directly to their own culture and collective histories, these people themselves were transformed in major ways.[81] Thus,

> social movements create collective identity by offering their adherents a different view of themselves and their world; different, that is, from the world view and self-concepts offered by the established social order. They do this by the process of *rearticulation,* which produces new subjectivity by making use of information and knowledge already present in the subject's mind. They take elements and themes of her/his culture and traditions and infuse them with new meaning.[82]

Even with the political machinations of putting African-American conservatives such as Clarence Thomas on the Supreme Court, these meanings will make it exceedingly difficult for the Right to incorporate the perspectives of people of color under its ideological umbrella and will continually create oppositional tendencies within the communities of people of color. The slow, but steady, growth in the power of people of color at a local level will serve as a countervailing force to the solidification of the new conservative accord.

Added to this is the fact that even within the new hegemonic bloc, even within the conservative restoration coalition, there are ideological strains that may have serious repercussions on its ability to be dominant for an extended period. These tensions are partly generated because of the class dynamics within the coalition. Fragile compromises may come apart because of the sometimes directly contradictory beliefs held by many of the partners in the new accord.

This can be seen in the example of two of the groups now involved in supporting the accord. There are both what can be called "residual" and "emergent" ideological systems or codes at work here. The residual culture and ideologies of the old middle class and of an upwardly mobile portion of the working class and lower middle class—stressing control, individual achievement, "morality," etc.—has been merged with the emergent code of a portion of the new middle class: getting ahead, technique, efficiency, bureaucratic advancement, and so on.[83]

These codes are in an inherently unstable relationship. The stress on New Right morality does not necessarily sit well with an amoral emphasis on careerism and economic norms. The merging of these codes can only last as long as paths to mobility are not blocked. The economy must pay off in jobs and mobility for the new middle class and for angry working-class people or the coalition is threatened. There is no guarantee, given the unstable nature of the economy and the kinds of jobs being created, that this payoff will occur.[84] Thus, another Ross Perot style campaign may be waiting in the wings.

This tension can be seen in another way which shows again that, in the long run, the prospects for such a lasting ideological coalition are not necessarily good. Under the new, more conservative accord, the conditions for capital accumulation and profit must be enhanced by state activity as much as possible. Thus, the "free market" must be set loose. As many areas of public and private life as possible need to be brought into line with such privatized market principles, including the schools, health care, welfare, housing, and so on. Yet, in order to create profit, capitalism by and large also requires that traditional values are subverted. Commodity purchasing and market relations become the norm and older values of community, "sacred knowledge," and morality will need to be cast aside. This dynamic plants the seeds of possible conflicts in the future between the economic modernizers and the New Right cultural traditionalists, between neo-liberals and neo-conservatives, who make up a significant part of the coalition that has been built.[85] Furthermore, the competitive individualism now being so heavily promoted in educational reform movements in the United States may not respond well to traditional working-class and poor groups' somewhat more collective senses.

Finally, there are counter-hegemonic movements now being built within education itself. The older social democratic accord included many educators, union leaders, minority group members, and others. There are signs that the fracturing of this coalition may only be temporary. Take teachers, for instance. Even though salaries have been on the rise throughout parts of the country, this has been countered by a rapid increase in the external control of teachers' work, the rationalization and deskilling of their jobs, and the growing blame of teachers and education in general for most of the major social ills that beset the economy.[86] Many teachers have organized around these issues, in a manner reminiscent of the earlier work of the Boston Women's Teacher's Group.[87] Furthermore, there are signs throughout the country of multiracial coalitions being built among elementary and secondary school teachers, university-based educators, and community members to act collectively on the conditions under which teachers work and to support the democratization of curriculum and teaching and a rededication to the equalization of access and outcomes in schooling. These are important points and I want to specify them even further at the level of policy and practice so that we can see what is possible for—not only the limits of—action today.

PROGRESSIVE POSSIBILITIES

Just as in the past when progressive educational and community activists organized to attempt to counter antidemocratic tendencies,[88] so too are similar things occurring today. I want to describe certain gains that have been made, especially in urban areas, even in the face of the conservative restoration. In the process, I note certain tendencies that can challenge the existing ways the economy, community, and education are linked and/or that provide for more progressive curricula and less deskilled teaching.

New curriculum initiatives have been established that provide significant alternatives to the usually economically conservative models in use in all too many districts. For example, after having won a political victory in Congress with the passage of certain aspects of the Carl D. Perkins Vocational Education Act of 1984, progressive educators have established a number of interesting programs. The 1984 act specifies that states must assess and then meet the need to give all students *"experience in and understanding of all aspects of the industry* in which the student is preparing to enter." It also specifies that states must "enhance the use of problem-solving and basic skills (including mathematics, reading, writing, science, and social studies) in a vocational setting." Finally, the act had the additional requirement that what are called special populations—that is, economically or educationally disadvantaged students, students with handicaps, students with limited English proficiency, and so on—are to be provided with "equal access, individual assessment and planning, and the special services needed to succeed in quality programs."[89]

All this is of great importance. For example, in his supporting statement given on the floor of the Senate, Senator Edward Kennedy (certainly no radical, but often someone who is committed to progressive educational initiatives) gives a particular interpretation to the phrase "all aspects of the industry." As he puts it, the bill is intended to mean that "beyond being given the production skills for one particular job slot, the students will also gain experience and understanding of an *entire* enterprise in which the job exists—such as *planning, management, finances, and labor and community relations.*"[90]

Based on this bill, a legal and educational activist group, the Center for Law and Education, has established the Vocational Education Project.

This is a nationwide effort to assist low-income students and their communities to establish or redirect vocational educational programs "to better meet their own long-term needs for education, employment, and community development." In the words of the Center, the Vocational Education Project "is based on a belief that vocational programs should provide broad, long-term skills which enable students to exercise more control over their lives and participate actively in running their communities' institutions."[91]

The demonstration sites throughout the country, including the Rindge School of Technical Arts in the Boston Area, are guided by three overlapping emphases: *educational opportunity, ongoing employability, and community development.*

1. Educational opportunity—a vocational emphasis on active problem-solving, academic skills, and the skills needed to run an enterprise, instead of tracking certain students away from academic areas and toward limited training for passive narrow skills.

2. Ongoing employability—an emphasis on the broad, transferable skills of mastering all aspects of an enterprise, instead of depending upon the impossible task of accurately predicting precisely how many of which jobs will exist in several years and precisely what skills they will require.

3. Community development—an emphasis on establishing and running enterprises needed by the community and on linking the vocational program to broader development efforts and enterprises, such as worker-owned and worker-managed businesses, instead of dependency only on the job openings generated by current employers, particularly in underemployed communities.[92]

Notice here that the focus is not only on making students more "competitive" as workers, but on community development, employee control, and community and student involvement at every level. This is a far cry from much of the conservative political agenda,[93] and takes the vocational emphasis wanted by some members of the rightist coalition in an entirely new direction, to say the least.

Elsewhere, the Southern Coalition for Educational Equity, begun ten years ago to support work in public education based on the philosophy of the civil rights movement, has aided educators from eleven southern states to develop concrete models of education for poor and minority children. Winifred Green, founder of the Coalition, explains that their work intends to "undo problems caused by racism and sexism in public education." The Southern Coalition is involved in a number of projects. In New Orleans, they have helped organize an "effective schools" effort (but one that has also partly redefined what we *mean* by effective schools, which all too often may serve as an excuse for strengthening administrative control over curriculum) to improve instruction in the lowest achieving inner-city schools. After an initial pilot program proved successful, the district has expanded the program to a number of schools. Managed by four New Orleans teachers, this project includes a summer-school program for developing alternative teaching practices designed to improve the (critical) reading skills of the district's largely African-American population.[94]

In Alabama, Georgia, and North Carolina, the Southern Coalition has also helped develop the Minority Computer Resource Opportunity project (MICRO). The Coalition has recognized that as more and more advances are made by dominant groups through the use of newly developed technologies, the split between the "haves" and "have nots" will only worsen.[95] Begun in 1984 and designed to make certain that African-American children and young women are getting the knowledge and skills needed to gain access to the new technology, MICRO focuses on developing something I take up in more detail in the next chapter: *critical literacy* (both socially and intellectually), through the use of such technology, rather than the all too usual formal and informal tracking systems in schools where working-class and poor children simply get "cooled out" of such experiences early on or are taught low-level skills that often lead to employment in the non-unionized, low-paying, and deskilled sectors of the economy.[96] (It remains to be seen whether the Clinton administration's emphasis on the benefits of "new technology for the 21st century" will actually widen the gap between the haves and the have nots. At the least, it makes projects such as MICRO even more important.)

In other urban areas, significant gains are also being registered. Perhaps one of the most interesting of these experiments in reestablishing a more progressive tradition in urban schools can be found in Milwaukee. One of the most residentially segregated cities in the United States, Milwaukee has also witnessed an increase in racial tensions, complaints that its schools are unconnected to the cultures and aspirations of people of color, and a bureaucratized curriculum and evaluation process that some have argued exacerbates the problem.[97]

Recognizing that changes in the curriculum and pedagogy must be accompanied by alterations in power relations within the school, between central office officials and teachers, and between the schools and the local community, a group of teachers, academics, and community members have begun to challenge taken-for-granted assumptions and procedures. They have founded a progressive newspaper, *Rethinking Schools*, that is mass distributed with a circulation of approximately 20,000 and an increasingly national audience.[98] This has had considerable influence in stimulating the school system's rethinking of its reliance on specific mandated reading programs and standardized testing. Here, the Rethinking Schools group recognized that the politics of information is critical to any gains. Only by *making public* the case for more community-oriented programs and more flexible and democratic curriculum and evaluation models, only by engaging in the difficult and time-consuming work of organizing alternative channels through which curricular, pedagogical, and political arguments could be brought to bear on educational deliberations (in essence creating a new politics of official knowledge), were they able to make a serious impact.

Rethinking Schools did not limit itself to altering the politics of information about schools. It also committed itself to altering the politics of curriculum and teaching within schools. After a long and involved series of negotiations, a number of the group's members were able to get Milwaukee to approve the establishment of the progressive Fratney Street School. Teachers and parents in Milwaukee's integrated Riverwest neighborhood, a mainly African-American, Hispanic, and working-class area, took over the empty Fratney Street School building and have opened a two-way bilingual, multicultural public elementary school. The curriculum and the teaching are markedly different from what one might find elsewhere and are certainly more directly linked to the daily lives, histories, and cultures of the students than one might ordinarily see in our increasingly bureaucratized urban school systems.

Fratney Street School is still in its early stages, but the group's success in establishing a public school that is more democratic in both content and process, and in the way it interacts with its community, demonstrates the very real possibility of further programs of this nature. It also points to something else, however. Such success may have been largely dependent on those who are interested in significant changes in the control of curriculum and teaching, having engaged in a much wider and more organized effort to bring their case before a larger public. Political and educational efforts had to be joined. Thus, the politics of curriculum and teaching in our urban schools extends well beyond the classroom.

In New York City's East Harlem, other educators concerned about the quality of the curriculum and teaching made available to their largely African-American and Latina and Latino students have created a number of alternatives. Among the most well known is of course Central Park East Secondary School, within the city's public education system. Based on a commitment to community involvement, CPES has organized around more personalized styles of teaching, an advisory system that assists students in decision making, academic planning, and social relations, a lower teacher/pupil ratio, and a school/community-service program. In my mind, however, its most important political feature can be found within its core curriculum. The curriculum begins from the crucial political question, "From whose perspective are we seeing, or reading, or hearing?" This repoliticizes the issue of what counts as official knowledge, making it subject to critical scrutiny by students, teachers, and others. Central Park East School, like many of its counterparts in other urban areas, represents a fragile victory, but it clearly deserves our attention.

Finally, though it is not specifically only related to curricula and teaching, the movement in Chicago to decentralize decision making and place more power in the hands of locally elected school councils must be mentioned. I note this not only because of its effects on the politics of curriculum—on whose knowledge is taught and what the power relations over choosing it and teaching it are to be—could possibly be large in some instances, but also because it provides an excellent example of my argument that larger relations of power must always be considered if we are serious in our attempts to understand the complicated politics of education.

The Chicago experiment—the result in part of compromise between rightist politicians and inner-city activists—could result in a great deal more public and especially parental involvement. It could also result in people of color and members of working-class communities learning even more about the skills that are essential to influencing the schools and other institutions in their local communities. And it could lead to other steps that would establish less alienating school experiences for children of groups who have historically been culturally and economically dispossessed.

Yet, the Chicago experiment can also serve less progressive purposes and may indeed lead later on to greater power being given to the conservative alliance. It can cause splits within communities at the school level, pitting one group against another unless we are very cautious. Even more importantly, it is becoming clear that few or no new resources will be made available to a school system that is already in a deep financial crisis. The economics of such urban areas are often being torn asunder as economic inequalities in our cities widen considerably. Thus, we can expect no major changes in job creation, housing, health care, and so on. The gender, class, and race structuring of opportunity will not be altered dramatically.

I say this not to be overly political or perverse, but to ask us to focus realistically on the question of whether more local control of schools, finance, and curricula can compensate for these conditions. If the schools cannot overcome these problems, and achievement scores (usu-

ally and unfortunately the primary measure of the quality of school experience) do not markedly rise, then it is possible that powerful groups will
blame the more democratic policy itself. "We have tried democracy, and
it doesn't work." Educators committed to a more egalitarian educational
system in both means and ends will need to be prepared for such a conservative reaction. Sufficient resources and time are essential to alter the
problematic structures that currently exist.

Each of these examples could be multiplied, of course, since there are
many more. What is important is that they reveal a growing ferment from
below, a growing commitment to the hard day-to-day efforts to build an
education whose commitment to equality is not simply rhetorical but
lived out in daily practice.

CONCLUSION

I have focused on a particular kind of political tension in this chapter.
The conservative alliance has clearly attempted to transform what education is for and what our policies and practices over curriculum and teaching will look like. In opposition to these tendencies, ones that mirror the
larger ideological, political, and economic project of the Right, there are
grass-roots movements that seek to expand the space created by the new
accord and whose educational and social visions suggest a different
course for teachers, administrators, students, and community members
to take. Neither of these tendencies is more nor less political than the
other. After all, as an act of influence, education is profoundly ethical and
political by its very nature.[99] Our task is, then, not to reject the politics of
curriculum and teaching, but to recognize how politics works, to use it,
and to recognize what is at stake for the real teachers and administrators,
children, and parents who now work so hard in such uncertain conditions
to create an education worthy of its name if the conservative restoration
succeeds.

Together, these examples say something very important about the politics of curriculum and teaching. In each case, success required the conscious building of coalitions between the school system and the communities being served. In none of the cases was the impetus generated
from the top. Rather, bottom-up movements, within groups of teachers,
the community, social activists, and so on, provided the driving force for
change. Finally, none of these instances were guided simply by a technical vision. Instead, each is overtly linked to a political project: enhancing
democracy at the grass roots, empowering individuals who had hereto-
fore been largely silenced, creating new ways of linking people outside

and inside of the schools together so that schooling is not seen as an alien institution but something that is integrally linked to the political, cultural, and economic experiences of people in their daily lives.[100]

None of these examples are guaranteed to succeed. In fact, given the economic crisis and the disintegration of our inner cities stimulated by the conservative restoration, many of them may indeed come under threat. However, it is from the experience of attempting to create a new, more democratic politics of school life that we can learn what is possible.

Even given the emerging tensions I noted within the conservative restoration and the increase once again of alliances inside and outside of education to counter its attempted reconstruction of the politics and ethics of the common good, this doesn't mean we should be at all sanguine. It is possible that, both because of these tensions and counter movements and because of the nature of the economic crisis, the Right's economic program will fail. Yet its ultimate success may be in shifting the balance of class, gender, and race forces considerably to the right and in changing the very ways we consider the common good.[101] Privatization, profit, and greed may still substitute for any serious collective commitment, especially if Clinton's more neo-liberal approach fails to deliver on its economic promises in a rapid, striking, and lasting way.

We are, in fact, in danger both of forgetting the decades of hard work it took to put even a limited vision of equality on the social and educational agenda and of forgetting the reality of the oppressive conditions that exist for so many of our fellow Americans. The task of keeping alive in the minds of the people the collective memory of the struggle for equality, for person rights in *all* of the institutions of our society, is one of the most significant tasks educators can perform. In a time of conservative restoration, we cannot afford to ignore this task. This requires renewed attention to important curricular questions. Whose knowledge is taught? Why is it taught in this particular way to this particular group? How do we enable the histories and cultures of the majority of working people, of women, of people of color (again, these groups are obviously not mutually exclusive) to be taught in responsible and responsive ways in schools? Given the fact that the collective memory that *now* is preserved in our educational institutions is more heavily influenced by dominant groups in society,[102] the continuing efforts to promote more democratic curricula and teaching are more important now than ever. For it should be clear that the movement toward an authoritarian populism will become even more legitimate if the values embodied in the conservative restoration are the only ones made available in our public institutions. The widespread recognition that there were, are, and can be more equal modes of economic, political, and cultural life can only be accomplished by organized efforts to teach and expand this sense of difference. Clearly, there is educational work to be done.

This means, of course, that only communicating these perspectives with (notice I said "with," not "to") other educators is not enough. If we are to overcome apathy and cynicism, the effectiveness of the conservative restoration in transforming our discourse, and the rightist agenda in education and elsewhere, many more people need to be involved in articulating and constructively criticizing alternatives. The impressive socialist-feminist and anti-racist arguments about how we might democratically organize and engage in counter-hegemonic activity can teach us all a good deal here.[103] Most importantly, we must keep our feet on the ground, so to speak.

As I argued in chapter one in my discussion of the role of critical educational work, successful ways of countering the rightist reconstruction cannot be fully articulated at the theoretical level. They begin and end in many ways at the level of educational practice. As I just showed, there *are* examples of critical and emancipatory education being built in a number of places. These are occurring in schools and universities, in community development, in many critical literacy programs, and elsewhere.[104] While these are in no way about to radically and immediately shift an entire nation's consciousness in more progressive directions, I for one am certain that they provide ample amounts of insight into what is necessary and possible now. I am just as certain, however, that these principles and practices are not generated or learned from afar. They are learned by engaging in the thoughtful and committed daily activity of working in varied social movements for a more just and caring set of educational, cultural, political, economic, and bodily relations.

There *is* educational work to be done; and, perhaps, by joining in these ongoing struggles for democracy in schools and universities, in local communities, in the race, class, gender, and sexual relations in the multitude of institutions in which we now go about our daily lives, not only can we teach but we can be taught as well. The Right has succeeded in part by listening to (and, as well, manipulating) genuine feelings and in the process has once again demonstrated the power of the cultural and ideological. Here, too, we have much to learn. For only by engaging in the time-consuming, difficult, and sometimes draining (yet ultimately immensely satisfying) work of building communities based on varied but shared sentiments (or as others might put it, "across differences"),[105] and on programs that promise to take honestly the problems people face in their daily lives, can we start again on the path that Raymond Williams has so eloquently called "the journey of hope" toward "the long revolution."[106]

One of the places that journey of hope continues is in the real lives and experiences of those politically active teachers, parents, and students who are now struggling in such uncertain conditions to construct an education worthy of its name. We can join with them, assist them, and be helped by them. In the process, the "we" can become larger, more inclusive, more democratic, a more decentered unity, thereby countering the Right. Perhaps in this way, an education that is grounded not in providing human capital for the profit machine or in a romantic "return" to elite cultural literacy, but in a vision of critical literacy, can be built. Too much is at stake if we don't.

3 Cultural Politics and the Text

INTRODUCTION[1]

For most people, literacy has a nonpolitical function. It is there supposedly to help form the intellectual character of a person and to provide paths to upward mobility. Yet, the process of both defining what counts as literacy and how it should be gained has always had links to particular regimes of morality as well. Literacy was often there to produce economic skills and a shared system of beliefs and values, to help create a "national culture." As the author of a recent volume on newly emerging redefinitions of literacy in education has put it, it served as something of a "moral technology of the soul."[2]

An emphasis on literacy as both "moral technology" and economically driven skills is of course not the only way one could and should approach the issue, no matter what the Right keeps telling us. The value of writing, speaking, and listening should not be seen as access to "refined culture" or to "life skills" for our allotted (by whom?) places in the paid and unpaid labor market, but as a crucial means to gain power and control over our entire lives. In responding to the dangers posed by the conservative restoration, I argued that our aim should not be to create "functional literacy," but *critical* literacy, *powerful* literacy, *political* literacy which enables the growth of genuine understanding and control of all of the spheres of social life in which we participate.[3]

This involves a different vision of knowledge and culture. Neither of these concepts refer to a false universality, a pregiven consensus that is divorced from patterns of domination and exploitation. Rather they refer to the utterly complex struggles over who has the right to "name the world."

Take the word "culture." Culture—the way of life of a people, the constant and complex process by which meanings are made and shared—does not grow out of the pregiven unity of a society. Rather, in many ways, it grows out of its divisions. It has to *work* to construct any unity that it has. The idea of culture should not be used to "celebrate an achieved or natural harmony." Culture is instead "a producer and reproducer of value systems and power relations."[4]

The same is true for the way we think about knowledge. Speaking theoretically, John Fiske reminds us of this:

> Knowledge is never neutral, it never exists in an empiricist, objective relationship to the real. Knowledge is power, and the circulation of knowledge is part of the social distribution of power. The discursive power to construct a commonsense reality that can be inserted into cultural and political life is central in the social relationship of power. The power of knowledge has to struggle to exert itself in two dimensions. The first is to control the "real," to reduce reality to the knowable, which entails producing it as a discursive construct whose arbitrariness and inadequacy are disguised as far as possible. The second struggle is to have this discursively (and therefore sociopolitically) constructed reality accepted as truth by those whose interests may not necessarily be served by accepting it. Discursive power involves a struggle both to construct (a sense of) reality and to circulate that reality as widely and smoothly as possible throughout society.[5]

Fiske's language may perhaps be a bit too abstract here, but his points are essential. They point to the relationship among what counts as knowledge, who has power and how power actually functions in our daily lives, and, finally, how this determines what we see as "real" and important in our institutions in general and in education in particular. In this chapter, I focus on one particular aspect of education that helps define what "reality" is and how it is connected to critical, powerful, and political literacy in contradictory ways, ways the Right has recognized for years.

WHOSE KNOWLEDGE IS OF MOST WORTH?

Reality, then, doesn't stalk around with a label. What something is, what it does, one's evaluation of it—all this is not naturally preordained. It is socially constructed. This is the case even when we talk about the institutions that organize a good deal of our lives. Take schools, for example. For some groups of people, schooling is seen as a vast engine of democracy: opening horizons, ensuring mobility, and so on. For others, the reality of schooling is strikingly different. It is seen as a form of social control, or, perhaps, as the embodiment of cultural dangers, institutions whose curricula and teaching practices threaten the moral universe of the students who attend them.

While not all of us may agree with this diagnosis of what schools do, this latter position contains a very important insight. It recognizes that behind Spencer's famous question about "What knowledge is of most worth?" there lies another even more contentious question, *"Whose* knowledge is of most worth?"

During the past two decades, a good deal of progress has been made on answering the question of whose knowledge becomes socially legitimate in schools.[6] While much still remains to be understood, we are now much closer to having an adequate understanding of the relationship between school knowledge and the larger society than before. Yet, little attention has actually been paid to that one artifact that plays such a major role in defining whose culture is taught: *the textbook.* Of course, there have been literally thousands of studies of textbooks over the years.[7] But, by and large, until relatively recently, most of these remained unconcerned with the politics of culture. All too many researchers could still be characterized by the phrase coined years ago by C. Wright Mills, "abstract empiricists." These "hunters and gatherers of social numbers" remain unconnected to the relations of inequality that surround them.[8]

This is a distinct problem since, as the rightist coalition has decisively shown by their repeated focus on them, texts are not simply "delivery systems" of "facts." They are at once the results of political, economic, and cultural activities, battles, and compromises. They are conceived, designed, and authored by real people with real interests. They are published within the political and economic constraints of markets, resources, and power.[9] And what texts mean and how they are used are fought over by communities with distinctly different commitments and by teachers and students as well.

As I have argued in a series of volumes, it is naive to think of the school curriculum as neutral knowledge.[10] Rather, what counts as legitimate knowledge is the result of complex power relations and struggles among identifiable class, race, gender, and religious groups. Thus, education and power are terms of an indissoluble couplet. It is at times of social upheaval that this relationship between education and power becomes most visible. Such a relationship was and continues to be made manifest in the struggles by women, people of color, and others to have their history and knowledge included in the curriculum. Driven by an economic crisis and a crisis in ideology and authority relations, it has become even more visible in the past decade or so in the resurgent conservative attacks on schooling. Authoritarian populism is in the air and the New Right has been more than a little successful in bringing its own power to bear on the goals, content, and process of schooling.[11]

As I noted in chapter one, the movement to the Right has not stopped outside the schoolroom door as you well know. Current plans for the centralization of authority over teaching and curriculum, often cleverly disguised as "democratic" reforms, are hardly off the drawing board before new management proposals or privatization initiatives are introduced. Similar tendencies are more than a little evident in Britain, and in some cases are even more advanced.

I showed that all of this has brought about countervailing movements in the schools. The slower, but still interesting, growth of more democratically run schools, of practices and policies that give community groups and teachers considerably more authority in text selection and curriculum determination, in teaching strategy, in the use of funds, in administration, and in developing more flexible and less authoritarian evaluation schemes is providing some cause for optimism in the midst of the conservative restoration.

Even with these positive signs, however, it is clear that the New Right has been able to rearticulate traditional political and cultural themes. In so doing, it has often effectively mobilized a mass base of adherents. Among its most powerful causes and effects has been the growing feeling of disaffection about public schooling among conservative groups. Large numbers of parents and other people no longer trust either the institutions or the teachers and administrators in them to make "correct" decisions about what should be taught and how to teach it. The rapid growth of evangelical schooling, of censorship, of textbook controversies, and the emerging tendency of many parents to teach their children at home rather than send them to state-supported schools are clear indications of this loss of legitimacy.[12]

As we saw, the ideology that stands behind this is often very complex. It combines a commitment to both the "traditional family" and clear gender roles with a commitment to "traditional values" and literal religiosity. Also often packed into this is a defense of capitalist economics, patriotism, the "Western tradition," anticommunism, and a deep mistrust (often based on racial undercurrents) of the "welfare state."[13] When this ideology is applied to schooling, the result can be as simple as dissatisfaction with an occasional book or assignment. On the other hand, the result can be a major conflict that threatens to go well beyond the boundaries of our usual debates about schooling.

Few places in the United States are more well known in this latter context than Kanawha County, West Virginia. In the mid-1970s, it became the scene of one of the most explosive controversies over what schools should teach, who should decide, and what beliefs should guide our educational programs. What began as a protest by a small group of conservative parents, religious leaders, and business people over the content and design of the textbooks that had been approved for use in local schools, soon spread to include school boycotts, violence, and a wrenching split within the community that in many ways has yet to heal.

There were a number of important contributing factors that heightened tensions in West Virginia. Schools in rural areas had been recently consolidated. Class relations and country/city relations were increasingly tense. The lack of participation by rural parents (or many parents at all, for that matter) in text selection or in educational decision making in general also led to increasing alienation. Furthermore, the cultural history of the region, with its fierce independence, its fundamentalist religious traditions, and its history of economic depression, helped create conditions for serious unrest. Finally, Kanawha County became a cause celebre for national right-wing groups who offered moral, legal, and organizational support to the conservative activists there.[14]

Though perhaps less violent, many similar situations have occurred since then in a number of districts throughout the country. For instance, the recent experiences in Yucaipa, California—where the school system and largely conservative and fundamentalist protesters have been locked in what at times seemed to be a nearly explosive situation—documents the continuing conflict over what schools are for and whose values should be embodied in them. Here, too, parents and community members have raised serious challenges over texts and over cultural authority, including attacks on the material for witchcraft and occultism, a lack of patriotism, and the destruction of sacred knowledge and authority. And here, too, nationally based conservative organizations have entered the fray.

It is important to realize, then, that controversies over "official knowledge" that usually center around what is included and excluded in textbooks really signify more profound political, economic, and cultural relations and histories. Conflicts over texts are often proxies for wider questions of power relations. They involve what people hold most dear. And, as in the cases of Kanawha County and Yucaipa, they can quickly escalate into conflicts over these deeper issues.

Yet, textbooks are surely important in and of themselves. They signify, through their content *and* form, particular constructions of reality, particular ways of selecting and organizing that vast universe of possible knowledge. They embody what Raymond Williams called the *selective tradition:* someone's selection, someone's vision of legitimate knowledge and culture, one that in the process of enfranchising one group's cultural capital disenfranchises another's.[15]

Texts are really messages to and about the future. As part of a curriculum, they participate in no less than the organized knowledge system of society. They participate in creating what a society has recognized as legitimate and truthful. They help set the canons of truthfulness and, as such, also help recreate a major reference point for what knowledge, culture, belief, and morality really *are.*[16]

Yet such a statement, even with its recognition that texts participate in constructing ideologies and ontologies, is basically misleading in many important ways. For it is not a "society" that has created such texts, but specific groups of people. "We" haven't built such curriculum artifacts in the simple sense that there is universal agreement among all of us and this is what gets to be official knowledge. In fact, the very use of the pronoun "we" simplifies matters all too much.

As Fred Inglis so cogently argues, the pronoun "we":

> smooths over the deep corrugations and ruptures caused precisely by struggle over how that authoritative and editorial "we" is going to be used. The [text], it is not melodramatic to declare, really is the battleground for an intellectual civil war, and the battle for cultural authority is a wayward, intermittently fierce, always protracted and fervent one.[17]

Let me give one example. In the 1930s, conservative groups in the United States mounted a campaign against one of the more progressive textbook series in use in schools. *Man and His Changing World* by Harold Rugg and his colleagues became the subject of a concerted attack by the National Association of Manufacturers, the American Legion, the Advertising Federation of America, and other "neutral" groups. They charged that Rugg's books were socialist, anti-American, antibusiness, and so forth. The conservative campaign was more than a little successful in forcing school districts to withdraw Rugg's series from classrooms and libraries. So successful were they that sales fell from nearly 300,000 copies in 1938 to only approximately 20,000 in 1944.[18]

We, of course, may have reservations about such texts today, not least of which would be the sexist title. However, one thing that the Rugg case makes clear is that the *politics* of the textbook is not something new by any means. Current issues surrounding texts—their ideology, their very status as central definers of what we should teach, even their very effectiveness and their design—echo the past moments of these concerns that have had such a long history in so many countries.

Few aspects of schooling currently have been subject to more intense scrutiny and criticism than the text. Perhaps one of the most graphic descriptions is provided by A. Graham Down of the Council for Basic Education.

> Textbooks, for better or worse, dominate what students learn. They set the curriculum, and often the facts learned, in most subjects. For many students, textbooks are their first and sometimes only early exposure to books and to reading. The public regards textbooks as authoritative, accurate, and necessary. And teachers rely on them to organize lessons and structure subject matter. But the current system of textbook adoption has filled our schools with Trojan horses—glossily covered blocks of paper whose words emerge to deaden the minds of our nation's youth, and make them enemies of learning.[19]

This statement is made just as powerfully by the author of a recent study of what she has called "America's textbook fiasco."

> Imagine a public policy system that is perfectly designed to produce textbooks that confuse, mislead, and profoundly bore students, while at the same time making all of the adults involved in the process look good, not only in their own eyes, but in the eyes of others. Although there are some good textbooks on the market, publishers and editors are virtually compelled by public policies and practices to create textbooks that confuse students with non sequiturs, that mislead them with misinformation, and that profoundly bore them with pointlessly arid writing.[20]

REGULATION OR LIBERATION AND THE TEXT

In order to understand these criticisms and to understand both some of the reasons why texts look the way they do and why they contain some groups' perspectives and not others', we also need to realize that the world of the book has not been cut off from the world of commerce. Books are not only cultural artifacts. They are economic commodities as well. Even though texts may be vehicles of ideas, they still have to be "peddled on a market."[21] This is a market, however, that—especially in the national and international world of textbook publishing—is politically volatile, as the Kanawha County and Yucaipa experiences so clearly documented.

Texts are caught up in a complicated set of political and economic dynamics. Text publishing often is highly competitive. In the United States, where text production is a commercial enterprise situated within the vicissitudes of a capitalist market, decisions about the "bottom line" determine what books are published and for how long. Yet, this situation is not just controlled by the "invisible hand" of the market. It is also largely determined by the highly visible "political" hand of state textbook adoption policies.[22]

Nearly half of the states—most of them in the southern tier and the "sun belt"—have state textbook adoption committees that by and large choose what texts will be purchased by the schools in that state, a process that is itself contradictory in its history. As I shall demonstrate in the next chapter, it too has signified losses and gains at the same time. The economics of profit and loss of this situation makes it imperative that publishers devote nearly all of their efforts to guaranteeing a place on these lists of approved texts. Because of this, the texts made available to the entire nation, and the knowledge considered legitimate in them, are determined by what will sell in Texas, California, Florida, and so forth. This is one of the major reasons the Right concentrates its attention so heavily on these states (though, because of resistance, with only partial success). There can be no doubt that the political and ideological controversies over content in these states, controversies that were often very similar to those that surfaced in Kanawha County, have had a very real impact on what and whose knowledge is made available. It is also clear that Kanawha County was affected by and had an impact on these larger battles over legitimate knowledge.

Economic and political realities structure text publishing not only internally, however. On an international level, the major text-publishing conglomerates control the market of much of the material not only in the capitalist centers, but in many other nations as well. Cultural domination is a fact of life for millions of students throughout the world, in part because of the economic control of communication and publishing by multinational firms, in part because of the ideologies and systems of political and cultural control of new elites within former colonial countries.[23] All of this, too, has led to complicated relations and struggles over official knowledge and the text, between "center" and "periphery," and within these areas as well.[24] Thus, the politics of official knowledge in Britain and the United States, where rightist policies over legitimate content are having a major impact, also can have a significant impact in other nations that also depend on British and U.S. corporate publishers for their material.

I want to stress that all of this is not simply of historical interest, as in the case of newly emerging nations, Kanawha County, or the Rugg textbooks. The controversies over the form and content of the textbook have not diminished. In fact, they have become even more heated in the United States in particular, as Yucaipa demonstrates. The changing ideological climate has had a major impact on debates over what should be taught in schools and on how it should be taught and evaluated. There is considerable pressure to raise the standards of texts, make them more "difficult," standardize their content, make certain that the texts place more stress on "American" themes of patriotism, free enterprise, and the "Western tradition," and link their content to statewide and national tests of educational achievement.

These kinds of pressures are not only felt in the United States. The text has become the center of ideological and educational conflict in a number of other countries as well. In Japan, for instance, the government approval of a right-wing history textbook that retold the story of the brutal Japanese invasion and occupation of China and Korea in a more positive light has stimulated widespread international antagonism and has led to considerable controversy within Japan as well.

Along these same lines, at the very time that the text has become a source of contention for conservative movements, it has stood at the center of controversy for not being progressive enough. Class, gender, and race bias have been widespread in the materials. All too often, "legitimate" knowledge does not include the historical experiences and cultural expressions of labor, women, people of color, and others who have been less powerful.[25]

All of these controversies are not "simply" about the content of the books students find—or don't find—in their schools, though obviously they are about that as well. The issues also involve profoundly different definitions of the common good,[26] about our society and where it should be heading, about cultural visions, and about our children's future. To quote from Inglis again, the entire curriculum, in which the text plays so large a part, is "both the text and context in which production and values intersect; it is the twistpoint of imagination and power."[27] In the context of the politics of the textbook, it is the issue of power that should concern us the most.

The concept of power merely connotes the capacity to act and to do so effectively. However, in the ways we use the idea of power in our daily discourse, "the word comes on strongly and menacingly, and its presence is duly fearful."[28] This "dark side" of power is, of course, complemented by a more positive vision. Here, power is seen as connected to a people acting democratically and collectively, in the open, for the best ideals.[29] It is this dual concept of power that concerns me here, both at the level of theory (how we think about the relationship between legitimate knowledge and power) and practice (how texts actually embody this relationship). Both the positive and the negative senses of power are essential for us to understand these relationships. Taken together, they signify that arguments about textbooks are really a form of *cultural politics*. They involve the very nature of the connections between cultural visions and differential power.

This, of course, is not new to anyone who has been interested in the history of the relationship among books, literacy, and popular movements. Books themselves, and one's ability to read them, have been inherently caught up in cultural politics. Take the case of Voltaire, that leader of the Enlightenment who so wanted to become a member of the nobility. For him, the Enlightenment should begin with the "grands." Only when it had captured the hearts and minds of society's commanding heights, could it concern itself with the masses below. But, for Voltaire and many of his followers, one caution should be taken very seriously. One should take care to prevent the masses from learning to read.[30]

For others, teaching "the masses" to read could have a more "beneficial" effect. It enables a "civilizing" process, in which dominated groups would be made more moral, more obedient, more influenced by "real culture."[31] We can, of course, hear echoes of this today in the arguments of the cultural conservatives. And for still others, such literacy could bring social transformation in its wake. It could lead to a "critical literacy," one that would be part of larger movements for a more democratic culture, economy, and polity.[32] The dual sense of the power of the text emerges clearly here.

Thus, activities that we now ask students to engage in every day, activities as "simple" and basic as reading and writing, can be at one and the same time forms of regulation and exploitation *and* potential modes of resistance, celebration, and solidarity. Here, I am reminded of Caliban's cry, "You taught me language; and my profit on't is, I know how to curse."[33]

This contradictory sense of the politics of the book is made clearer if we go into the classrooms of the past. For example, texts often have been related to forms of bureaucratic regulation both of teachers' lives and those of students. Thus, one teacher in Boston in 1899 relates a story of what happened during an observation by the school principal in her first year of teaching. As the teacher rather proudly watched one of her children read aloud an assigned lesson from the text, the principal was less than pleased with the performance of the teacher or her pupil. In the words of the teacher:

> The proper way to read in the public school in 1899 was to say, "page 35, chapter 4" and holding the book in the right hand, with the toes pointing at an angle of forty-five degrees, the head held straight and high, the eyes looking directly ahead, the pupil would lift up his voice and struggle in loud, unnatural tones. Now, I had attended to the position of the toes, the right arm, and the nose, but had failed to enforce the mentioning of page and chapter.[34]

Here, the text participates in both bodily and ideological regulation. The textbook in this instance is part of a system of enforcing a sense of duty, morality, and cultural correctness. Yet, historically, the standardized text was struggled *for* as well as against by many teachers. Faced with large classes, difficult working conditions, insufficient training, and even more importantly, little time to prepare lessons for the vast array of subjects and students they were responsible for, teachers often looked upon texts not necessarily as impositions but as essential tools. For young women elementary school teachers, the text helped prevent exploitation.[35] It solved a multitude of practical problems. It led not only to deskilling, but led to time to become more skilled as a teacher as well.[36] Thus, there were demands for standardized texts by teachers even in the face of what happened to that teacher in Boston and to so many others.

This struggle over texts was linked to broader concerns about who should control the curriculum in schools. Teachers, especially those most politically active, constantly sought to have a say in what they taught. This was seen as part of a larger fight for democratic rights. Margaret Haley, for instance, one of the leaders of the first teachers' union in the United States, saw a great need for teachers to work against the tendency toward making the teacher "a mere factory hand, whose duty it is to carry out mechanically and unquestioningly the ideas and orders of those clothed with authority of position."[37] Teachers had to fight against the deskilling or, as she called it, "factoryizing" methods of control being sponsored by administrative and industrial leaders. One of the reasons she was so strongly in favor of teachers' councils as mechanisms of control of schools was that this would reduce considerably the immense power over teaching and texts that administrators then possessed. Quoting John Dewey approvingly, Haley wrote, "If there is a single public-school system in the United States where there is official and constitutional provision made for submitting questions of methods, of discipline and teaching, and the questions of curriculum, textbooks, etc. to the discussion of those actually engaged in the work of teaching, that fact has escaped my notice."[38]

In this instance, teacher control over the choice of textbooks and how they were to be used was part of a more extensive movement to enhance the democratic rights of teachers on the job. Without such teacher control, teachers would be the equivalent of factory workers whose every move was determined by management.

These points about the contradictory relationships teachers have had with texts and the way such books depower and empower at different moments (and perhaps at the same time) document something of importance. It is too easy to see a cultural practice or a book as totally carrying its politics around with it, "as if written on its brow for ever and a day." Rather, its political functioning "depends on the network of social and ideological relations" it participates in.[39] Text writing, reading, and use can be retrogressive or progressive (and sometimes some combination of both) depending on the social context. Textbooks can be fought against because they are part of a system of moral regulation. They can be fought for both as providing essential assistance in the labor of teaching or as part of a larger strategy of democratization.

What textbooks do, the social roles they play for different groups, is then *very complicated*. This has important implications not only for the politics of how and by whom textbooks are used, but for the politics of the internal qualities, the content and organization, of the text. Just as crucially, it also has an immense bearing on how people actually read and interpret the text, especially in a time of rightist resurgence. It is to these issues that I now turn.

THE POLITICS OF CULTURAL INCORPORATION

We cannot assume that because so much of education has been linked to processes of gender, class, and race stratification[40] that all of the knowledge chosen to be included in texts simply represents relations of, say, cultural domination, or only includes the knowledge of dominant groups. This point requires that I speak theoretically and politically in this section of my argument, for all too many critical analyses of school knowledge— of what is included and excluded in the overt and hidden curricula of the school—take the easy way out. Reductive analysis comes cheap. Reality, however, is complex. Let us look at this in more detail.

It has been argued in considerable detail elsewhere that the selection and organization of knowledge for schools is an ideological process, one that serves the interests of particular classes and social groups.[41] How-ever, as I just noted, this does not mean that the entire corpus of school knowledge is "a mirror reflection of ruling class ideas, imposed in an unmediated and coercive manner." Instead, "the processes of cultural in-corporation are dynamic, reflecting both continuities and contradictions of that dominant culture and the continual remaking and relegitimation of that culture's plausibility system."[42] Curricula aren't imposed in coun-tries like the United States. Rather, they are the products of often intense conflicts, negotiations, and attempts at rebuilding hegemonic control by actually incorporating the knowledge and perspectives of the less power-ful under the umbrella of the discourse of dominant groups.

This is clear in the case of the textbook. As disenfrachised groups have fought to have their knowledge take center stage in the debates over cul-tural legitimacy, one trend has dominated in text production. In essence, little is usually dropped from textbooks. Major ideological frameworks do not get markedly changed. Textbook publishers are under considerable and constant pressure to include more in their books. Progressive *items* are perhaps mentioned, then, but are not developed in depth.[43] Domi-nance is partly maintained here through compromise and the process of "mentioning." Here, limited and isolated elements of the history and cul-ture of less powerful groups are included in the texts. Thus, for example, a small and often separate section is included on "the contributions of women" and "minority groups," but without any substantive elaboration of the view of the world as seen from their perspectives. Neo-conserva-tives have been particularly good at doing this today.

Tony Bennett's discussion of the process by which dominant cultures actually become dominant is worth quoting at length here.

> Dominant culture gains a purchase not in being imposed, as an alien
> external force, onto the cultures of subordinate groups, but by reach-
> ing into these cultures, reshaping them, hooking them and, with
> them, the people whose consciousness and experience is defined in
> their terms, into an association with the values and ideologies of the
> ruling groups in society. Such processes neither erase the cultures of
> subordinate groups, nor do they rob "the people" of their "true cul-
> ture": what they do do is shuffle those cultures on to an ideological
> and cultural terrain in which they can be disconnected from whatever
> radical impulses which may (but need not) have fuelled them and be
> connected to more conservative or, often, downright reactionary cul-
> tural and ideological tendencies.[44]

In some cases, "mentioning" may operate in exactly this way, integrat-ing selective elements into the dominant tradition by bringing them into close association with the values of powerful groups. Thus, for instance, we will teach about AIDS, but only in the context of total abstinence or the sacredness of particular social constructions of the "traditional family." There will be times, however, when such a strategy will not be successful. Oppositional cultures may at times use elements of the dominant culture against such groups. Bennett goes on, describing how oppositional cultures operate, as well.

> Similarly, resistance to the dominant culture does not take the form of launching against it a ready-formed, constantly simmering oppositional culture—always there, but in need of being turned up from time to time. Oppositional cultural values are formed and take shape only in the context of their struggle with the dominant culture, a struggle which may borrow some of its resources from that culture and which must concede some ground to it if it is to be able to connect with it—and thereby with those whose consciousness and experience is partly shaped by it—in order, by turning it back upon itself, to peel it away, to create a space within and against it in which contradictory values can echo, reverberate and be heard.[45]

Some texts may, in fact, have such progressive "echoes" within them. There are victories in the politics of official knowledge, not only defeats.

Sometimes, of course, not only are people successful in creating some space where such contradictory values can indeed "echo, reverberate, and be heard," but they transform the entire social space. They create entirely new kinds of governments, new possibilities for democratic political, economic, and cultural arrangements. In these situations, the role of education takes on even more importance, since new knowledge, new ethics, and a new reality seek to replace the old. This is one of the reasons that those of us committed to more participatory and democratic cultures inside and outside of schools must give serious attention to changes in official knowledge in those nations that have sought to overthrow their colonial or elitist heritage. Here, the politics of the text takes on special importance, since the textbook often represents an overt attempt to help create a new cultural reality. The case of the creation of more democratic textbooks and other educational materials based on the expressed needs of less powerful groups in Granada during the years of the New Jewel Movement provides a cogent example here,[46] even though it was partly destroyed by Reagan's invasin of Granada.

New social contexts, new processes of text creation, a new cultural politics, the transformation of authority relations, and new ways of reading texts, all of this can evolve and help usher in a positive rather than a negative sense of the power of the text. Less regulatory and more emancipatory relations of texts to real people can begin to evolve, a possibility made real in many of the programs of critical literacy that have had such a positive impact in nations throughout the world. Here people help create their own "texts," ones that signify their emerging power in the control of their own destinies.

However, we should not be overly romantic here. Such transformations of cultural authority and mechanisms of control and incorporation will not be easy.

For example, certainly, the ideas and values of a people are not directly prescribed by the conceptions of the world of dominant groups and just as certainly there will be many instances where people have been successful in creating realistic and workable alternatives to the culture and texts in dominance. Yet, we do need to acknowledge that the social distribution of what is considered legitimate knowledge *is* skewed in many nations. The social institutions directly concerned with the "transmission" of this knowledge, such as schools and the media, *are* grounded in and structured by the class, gender, sexual, and race inequalities that organize the society in which we live. The area of symbolic production is not divorced from the unequal relations of power that structure other spheres.[47]

Speaking only of class relations (much the same could be said about race, sex, and gender), Stuart Hall, one of the most insightful analysts of cultural politics, puts it this way:

> Ruling or dominant conceptions of the world do not directly prescribe the mental content of the illusions that supposedly fill the heads of dominated classes. But the circle of dominant ideas *does* accumulate the symbolic power to map or classify the world for others; its classifications do acquire not only the constraining power of dominance over other modes of thought but also the initial authority of habit and instinct. It becomes the horizon of the taken-for-granted: what the world is and how it works, for all practical purposes. Ruling ideas may dominate other conceptions of the social world by setting the limit on what will appear as rational, reasonable, credible, indeed sayable or thinkable within the given vocabularies of motive and action available to us. Their dominance lies precisely in the power they have to contain within their limits, to frame within their circumference of thought, the reasoning and calculation of other social groups.[48]

In the United States, as I showed in chapters one and two, there has been a movement of exactly this kind. Dominant groups—really a coalition of economic modernizers, what has been called the old humanists, and neo-conservative intellectuals—have attempted to create an ideological consensus around the return to traditional knowledge. The "great books" and "great ideas" of the "Western tradition" will preserve democracy. By returning to the common culture that has made this nation great, schools will increase student achievement and discipline, increase our international competitiveness, and ultimately reduce unemployment and poverty.

Mirrored in the problematic educational and cultural visions of volumes such as Bloom's *The Closing of the American Mind* and Hirsch's *Cultural Literacy,*[49] this position is probably best represented in quotes from former Secretary of Education William Bennett. In his view, we are finally emerging out of a crisis in which "we neglected and denied much of the best in American education." For a period, "we simply stopped doing the right things [and] allowed an assault on intellectual and moral standards." This assault on the current state of education has led schools to fall away from "the principles of our tradition."[50]

Yet, for Bennett, "the people" have now risen up. "The 1980's gave birth to a grass roots movement for educational reform that has generated a renewed commitment to excellence, character, and fundamentals." Because of this, "we have reason for optimism."[51] Why? Because

> the national debate on education is now focused on truly important matters: mastering the basics; . . . insisting on high standards and expectations; ensuring discipline in the classroom; conveying a grasp of our moral and political principles; and nurturing the character of our young.[52]

Notice the use of "we," "our," and "the people" here. Notice as well the assumed consensus on "basics" and "fundamentals" and the romanticization of the past both in schools and the larger society. The use of these terms, the attempt to bring people in under the ideological umbrella of the conservative restoration, is very clever rhetorically. However, as many people in the United States, Britain, and elsewhere—where rightist governments have been very active in transforming what education is about—have begun to realize, this ideological incorporation is having no small measure of success at the level of policy and at the level of whose knowledge and values are to be taught.[53]

If this movement has its way, the texts made available and the knowledge included in them will surely represent a major loss for many of the groups who have had successes in bringing their knowledge and culture more directly into the body of legitimate content in schools. Just as surely, the ideologies that will dominate the official knowledge will represent a considerably more elitist orientation than what we have now.

Yet, perhaps "surely" is not the correct word here. The situation is actually more complex than that, something we have learned from many of the newer methods of interpreting how social messages are actually "found" in texts.

Allan Luke has dealt with such issues very persuasively. It would be best to quote him at length here.

> A major pitfall of research in the sociology of curriculum has been its willingness to accept text form as a mere adjunct means for the delivery of ideological content: the former described in terms of dominant metaphors, images, or key ideas; the latter described in terms of the sum total of values, beliefs, and ideas which might be seen to constitute a false consciousness. For much content analysis presumes that text mirrors or reflects a particular ideological position, which in turn can be connected to specific class interests. . . . It is predicated on the possibility of a one-to-one identification of school knowledge with textually represented ideas of the dominant classes. Even those critics who have recognized that the ideology encoded in curricular texts may reflect the internally contradictory character of a dominant culture have tended to neglect the need for a more complex model of text analysis, one that does not suppose that texts are simply readable, literal representations of "someone else's " version of social reality, objective knowledge and human relations. For texts do not always mean or communicate what they say.[54]

These are important points for they imply that we need more sophisticated and nuanced models of textual analysis. While we should certainly *not* be at all sanguine about the effects of the conservative restoration on texts and the curriculum, if texts don't simply represent dominant beliefs in some straightforward way and if dominant cultures contain contradictions, fissures, and even elements of the culture of popular groups, then our readings of what knowledge is "in" texts cannot be done by the application of a simple formula.

We can claim, for instance, that the meaning of a text is not necessarily intrinsic to it. As poststructuralist theories would have it, meaning is "the product of a system of differences into which the text is articulated." Thus, there is not "one text," but many. Any text is open to multiple readings. This puts into doubt any claim that one can determine the meanings and politics of a text "by a straightforward encounter with the text itself." It also raises serious questions about whether one can fully understand the text by mechanically applying any interpretive procedure. Meanings, then, can be and are multiple and contradictory and we must always be willing to "read" our own readings of a text, to interpret our own interpretations of what it means.[55] It seems that answering the questions of "whose knowledge" is in a text is not at all simple, though clearly the Right would very much like to reduce the range of meanings one might find.

This is true of our own interpretations of what is in textbooks. But it is also just as true for the students who sit in schools and at home and read (or in many cases don't read) their texts. I want to stress this point, not only at the level of theory and politics as I have been stressing here, but at the level of practice.

We cannot assume that what is "in" the text is actually taught. Nor can we assume that what is taught is actually learned. As I show when I take us inside some classrooms in chapters five and six, teachers have a long history of mediating and transforming text material when they employ it in classrooms. Students bring their own classed, raced, religious, and gendered biographies with them as well. They, too, accept, reinterpret, and reject what counts as legitimate knowledge selectively. As critical ethnographies of schools have shown, and as later chapters will document, students (and teachers) are not empty vessels into which knowledge is poured. Rather than what Freire has called "banking" education going on,[56] students are active constructors of the meanings of the education they encounter.[57]

We can talk about three ways in which people can potentially respond to a text: dominant, negotiated, and oppositional. In the dominant reading of a text, one accepts the messages at face value. In a negotiated response, the reader may dispute a particular claim, but accept the overall tendencies or interpretations of a text. Finally, an oppositional response rejects these dominant tendencies and interpretations. The reader "repositions" herself or himself in relation to the text and takes on the position of the oppressed.[58] These are, of course, no more than ideal types and many responses will be a contradictory combination of all three. But the point is that not only do texts themselves have contradictory elements, but that audiences *construct* their own responses to texts. They do not passively receive texts, but actively read them based on their own class, race, gender and religious experiences.

An immense amount of work needs to be done on student (and teacher) acceptance, interpretation, reinterpretation, or partial and/or total rejection of texts. While there is a tradition of such research, much of it quite good, most of this in education is done in an overly psychologized manner. It is more concerned with questions of learning and achievement than it is with the equally-as-important and prior issues of whose knowledge it is that students are learning, negotiating, or opposing and what the sociocultural roots and effects are of such processes. Yet we simply cannot fully understand the power of the text, what it does ideologically and politically (or educationally, for that matter) unless we take very seriously the way students actually read them—not only as individuals but as members of social groups with their own particular cultures and histories.[59] For every textbook, then, there are multiple texts—contradictions within it, multiple readings of it, and different uses to which it will be put. Texts—be they the standardized, grade-level specific books so beloved by school systems, or the novels, trade books, and alternative materials that teachers either use to supplement these books or simply to replace them—are part of a complex story of cultural politics. They can signify authority (not always legitimate) or freedom. And critical teachers throughout many nations have learned a good deal about how we can employ even the most conservative material into a site for reflexive and challenging activity that clarifies with students the realities they (teachers and students) experience and construct. They can search out, as so many of them have, material and experiences that show the very possibility of alternative and oppositional interpretations of the world that go well beyond mere mentioning.[60] This act is the core of the programs to which I pointed in chapter two.

To recognize this, then, is also to recognize that our task as critically and democratically minded educators is itself a political one. We must acknowledge and understand the tremendous capacity of dominant institutions to regenerate themselves "not only in their material foundations and structures but in the hearts and minds of people." Yet, at the very same time—and especially now with the Right being so powerful and with their increasing attention to politics at the local, county, and state levels—we need never to lose sight of the power of popular organizations, of real people, to struggle, resist, and transform them.[61] Cultural authority, what counts as legitimate knowledge, what norms and values are represented in the officially sponsored curriculum of the school, all of these serve as important arenas in which the positive and negative relations of power surrounding the text will work themselves out, something I demonstrate in chapter four. And all of them involve the hopes and dreams of real people in real institutions, in real relations of inequality.

From all that I have said here, it should be clear that I oppose the idea that there can be one textual authority, one definitive set of "facts" that is divorced from its context of power relations. A "common culture" can never be an extension to everyone of what a minority mean and believe. Rather, and crucially, it requires not the stipulation and incorporation within textbooks of lists and concepts that make us all "culturally literate," *but the creation of the conditions necessary for all people to participate in the creation and recreation of meanings and values.* It requires a democratic process in which all people—not simply those who see themselves as the intellectual guardians of the "Western tradition"—can be involved in the deliberation of what is important.[62] It should go without saying that this necessitates the removal of the very real material obstacles (unequal power, wealth, time for reflection) that stand in the way of such participation.[63] Whether a more "moderate" administration can provide substantial spaces for countering the New Right and for removing these obstacles will take some time to see.

The very idea that there is one set of values that must guide the "selective tradition" can be a great danger, especially in contexts of differential power. Take, as one example, a famous line that was printed on an equally famous public building. It read, "There is one road to freedom. Its milestones are obedience, diligence, honesty, order, cleanliness, temperance, truth, sacrifice, and love of country." Many people may perhaps agree with much of the sentiment represented by these words. It may be of some interest that the building on which they appeared was in the administration block of the concentration camp at Dachau.[64]

We must ask, then, are we in the business of creating dead texts and dead minds? If we accept the title of educator—with all of the ethical and political commitments this entails—I think we already know what our answer should be. Critical literacy demands no less.

These struggles over the politics of official knowledge—over the text as both a commodity and a set of meaningful practices—are grounded in the history of previous conflicts and accords. Here, too, compromises were made. And here, too, dominant groups attempted to move the terms of the compromise in their direction. Yet, once again, the accord had cracks, spaces for action, but ones that were always in danger of being coopted as this history will show. Perhaps the best way to document this is to go even deeper into the politics of the text by focusing our attention on the growth of the activist state, on how the government—as a site of conflicting power relations and social movements—entered into the regulation of official knowledge. Conservatives (and even some of those upwardly mobile "cosmopolitan elites") may have dominated here, but as we shall see, this is *not* the entire story

4 Regulating Official Knowledge

INTRODUCTION

As I noted in the preceding chapter, nearly half of the states in the United States have some process by which curricular materials, usually textbooks, are evaluated and endorsed at a state level. Publishers differentiate between two kinds of states. In what is called "open territory"—most of the East, Midwest, and Far West—publishers sell directly to school districts or individual schools. In "closed territory"—mostly in the South and Southwest—centralized adoption policies prevail.[1] Individual districts in the "closed territory" can usually buy nearly any book, but state funds can only be used to purchase approved texts. Of all the states in the "closed territory," Texas and California (and now increasingly perhaps Florida) have the most power over what counts as official knowledge.

The influence of such state adoption policies should not be underestimated. The sheer economics of it is quite important. Take Texas as an example. Texas spends tens of millions of dollars on instructional materials and has a rather narrow policy of approving five textbooks or less (the minimum is two) for each subject. This puts it in an exceptionally strong position to influence the content of texts as publishers compete to gain their share of what is obviously a lucrative part of the market.[2] The various factions of the Right understand this all too well.

Texas has other characteristics that make it powerful besides the stringent limits it places on the number of texts it approves. Texas not only has a rapidly growing population that puts it second only to California in the "closed territory" in sheer numbers of students for which it buys books, but it adopts for both elementary and secondary schools. Furthermore, purchase contracts between the state and textbook publishers are for eight years, thereby guaranteeing that large market for a considerable length of time. Finally, and not unimportantly, Texas uses a method of payment that is in many ways a publisher's delight. It has a single-payment system in which one large check pays for the state's entire purchase of particular textbooks. To quote one publisher, "The money we get from sales in Texas is fast and clean."[3]

While Texas may be the most visible economically, the recent choice by California to reject all of the submitted textbooks in one subject area—and the shock waves that rippled through the educational and publishing communities—demonstrates its own considerable ability to exert pressure on the content and form of official knowledge. Along with Texas, it controls nearly 25% of the market in textbooks.[4] In the process, both have an immense impact on what gets published for schools in the entire nation.

In my discussion here, I want to begin to illuminate one major element in this process of making knowledge official: the complicated politics of the text that is seen in such state adoption policies. Part of my task here will be theoretical. How do we think about this process? This will require that I make some arguments about the role of government (the "State")[5] in making some groups' "cultural capital" more legitimate than others'. And other parts of my task will be political, historical, and empirical. What happens within this process? What are its roots in the past? What can we learn about this that can help us challenge the newly emerging hegemonic accord? This will require that we examine some of the previous and current conflicts over state adoption policies. Let us turn to some initial theoretical points about the role of the State first. However, those readers who have less tolerance for such theoretical labors can turn to the section on "'Incompetent' Teachers, 'Unethical' Publishers" that follows the next three sections without jeopardizing too much of the historical story I wish to tell.

SYMBOLIC CONTROL AND THE STATE

While there is a formal right for everyone to be represented in the debates over whose cultural capital, whose knowledge "that," "how," and "to," will be declared legitimate for transmission to future generations of students, it is still the case that, as I noted in the preceding chapter, a *selective tradition* operates in which only specific groups' knowledge becomes official knowledge.[6] Thus, the freedom to help select the formal corpus of school knowledge is bound by power relations that have very real effects. Perhaps a sense of how this formal right operates in real material conditions can best be seen in another area of the cultural apparatus of a society, the press.

Freedom can be defined in two different ways, negatively and positively. Speaking specifically about freedom of the press, Ernest Mandel puts the negative case this way.

> The negative definition of freedom means the absence of censorship and of institutions a priori denying average citizens (or organizations of citizens) the opportunity of printing and diffusing their opinions. In that negative sense, freedom of the press means the formal right of all to publish whatever they wish, at least in the field of beliefs, opinions, commentary on events, and general information.[7]

Mandel goes on, now turning to the positive sense of freedom.

> The positive definition of a free press means the effective material capacity of individuals or groups of individuals to have their opinions printed and circulated. If it costs $10 million to found a daily newspaper, and many more millions to run it, the abstract "right" to do this—that is the absence of any law or institution prohibiting it—will be of little avail for the overwhelming majority of citizens. It will be like the right to become a millionaire, when in fact less than 0.5% of the population accumulate such wealth.[8]

These points are significant. Notice that the positive sense of freedom is linked to existing relations of power. The right of cultural distribution is partly dependent on economic and political conditions, no matter what the Right would like us to think about the supposed neutrality of the "free market." This means that one cannot simply assert that all parties have a "right" to make their knowledge public. The question of the right to determine what counts as legitimate content cannot be answered in the abstract. We need to focus on the actual economics and politics of regulation. What counts as legitimate knowledge and one's right to determine it is lodged in a complicated politics of symbolic control of public knowledge. Since it is public, that is, since it is declared to be "knowledge for all," it is subject to scrutiny by official bodies (and is subject to the drives and tendencies of a market). In most countries, this means that some level of government is officially charged with the duty of creating a selective tradition.

In fact, one of the most interesting historical dynamics has been the extension—gradually but still graphically—of the direct or indirect State authority over the field of symbolic control. Education has become a crucial set of institutions through which the State attempts to "produce, reproduce, distribute, and change" the symbolic resources, the very consciousness of society.[9] These institutions of course have often been sites of intense conflict over whose symbols should be transmitted and over whose principles should organize this transmission.[10] At the center of these conflicts, however, sits the State.

In the past, as critical work on the curriculum began to emerge as a serious force in educational research, all too many people assumed that the State would uniformly support only the knowledge of dominant groups. In a capitalist economy, only the knowledge required by economically powerful groups would become legitimate in publicly supported schools. However, as Carnoy, myself, and others have documented, this is far too simplistic and is historically inaccurate.[11] The State is *not* guaranteed to serve the interests of a unified dominant class. Instead of this "instrumentalist" view, the State, like civil society, is a site of *interclass* struggle and negotiation, "a sphere of political action where the interests of dominant classes [and gendered and racial groups] can be partially institutionalized and realized" as well.[12]

It is not only the case, however, that the State acts as an arena of interclass, race, and gender conflict and negotiation. It also, and very importantly, serves as a site for *interclass* conflict and compromise. That is, there is a second logic which informs State action. The State tends to balance the opposing interests of different segments of dominant groups.[13]

To further complicate matters, but also to be true to the historical record, as I have argued earlier, since the State is the arena where the conflict over the dominance of property rights vs. person rights in government comes to the fore—the conclusion of which cannot always be known in advance—there will be times when State educational policy will be genuinely progressive. Because the State *is* a site of conflict, compromises or accords will have to be formed that will sometimes signify at least partial victories for progressive or less powerful groups.[14]

In essence, historically there often has been something of a trade-off between the meeting of State-sponsored goals and the wishes of groups outside the State itself. Economic, political, and cultural elites will seek a maximum amount of support from other groups for their educational policies "in return for conceding a minimum amount of diversification."[15] Thus, there will always be pressure from above to gain support for decisions made by government bodies; but such support is very difficult to obtain if State policies do not also incorporate some of the other diverse perspectives both within other elements of elite groups and from those groups with less economic, cultural, and political power. As I noted, the key is to form an accord that acts as an umbrella under which many groups can stand but which basically still is under the guiding principles of dominant groups.

Yet, because of this, the content of curricula and the decision-making process surrounding it cannot simply be the result of an act of domination. The "cultural capital" declared to be official knowledge, then, is *compromised* knowledge, knowledge that is filtered through a complicated set of political screens and decisions before it gets to be declared legitimate. This affects what knowledge is selected and what the selected knowledge looks like as it is transformed into something that will be taught to students in school. In this way, the State acts as what Basil Bernstein would call a "recontextualizing agent" in the process of symbolic control as it creates accords that enable the creation of "knowledge for everyone."

This process of transformation, in which knowledge is taken out of its original social or academic context and "recontextualized" and changed by the political rules which govern its new setting, is elaborated on in even greater theoretical detail by Bernstein. Agents such as textbook publishing houses, content consultants, and state and local educational authorities—all those whose task it is to *reproduce,* not produce, knowledge—together act as recontextualizing agents. The original knowledge from academic disciplines, differing social groups, and so on is appropriated by those groups of people who have power in the new context. The "text," as Bernstein calls it, "undergoes a transformation prior to its relocation" in the new context. As the text is "de-located" from its original location and "re-located" into the new pedagogic situation, the logic and power relations of the recontextualizing agents ensure that "the text is no longer the same text." [16] Political accords and educational needs can radically alter the shape and organization of the knowledge.

This occurs in three distinct ways. First, "the text has changed its position in relation to other texts, practices, and positions." It is no longer part of the professional discourse of researchers or part of the cultural discourse of oppressed groups, for example. This, thereby, alters power relations. In the new context, the knowledge *re*producers have more power and the knowledge is integrated around a different set of political and cultural needs and principles. Second, the text itself has been modified by "selection, simplification, condensation, and elaboration." Thus, for example, dominant pedagogical approaches and the economics of publishing will both influence textbook writers and adopters to order knowledge into bite-sized chunks that can be easily understood and mastered (and which are politically safe). In the process, the knowledge is transformed. Third, "the text has been re-positioned and re-focused." [17] Not only is the knowledge organized around different principles, but its *use* changes. It may be there for socialization purposes now, not to expand our intellectual horizons; or as I demonstrate in the second half of this chapter, it may now signify a way to maintain the unstable equilibrium that has been established by the accord over whose knowledge will have gained the official imprimatur.

Thus, when knowledge is made into content for school, certain principles are embodied in identifiable agents who bring these principles into play. In Bernstein's words, "The de-contextualizing principle regulates the new ideological positioning of the text in its process of re-location in one or more levels of the field of reproduction."[18] Of prime import here are agents in the State and agents in the economy, textbook publishers in particular. The decontextualizing and recontextualizing principles are built through the interaction of the political and educational needs represented in state adoption policies and by the need for profitable operation by publishers.

These points about the State and about how knowledge is altered by the politics of symbolic control may seem rather abstract, but while theoretical, their import is great. They do support my claim that curricula are rooted in differential power, in a set of social relationships that ultimately play a large part in determining whose cultural capital is made available and "relocated" in our schools. Only by understanding the interaction between the forces acting on government regulation and on the economics of textbook publishing can we determine how such decontextualizing and relocating works.

REFORM FROM ABOVE

The reasons for the increasingly powerful State regulation of symbolic control are tied up both with larger patterns of differential political and economic power as well as more specific issues that arise within the educational system itself. In understanding both these external and internal reasons, we need to be sensitive to the fact that not all parts of the United States are the same. There are different patterns of regulation, different class, race, gender, and religious relations, and different articulations between, say, the ways official knowledge is chosen and the textbook publishing industry. Perhaps the best way of demonstrating this is to delve more deeply into the history of state adoption policies and the conflicts and compromises that they generated.

Even given the interest by state governments in extending their control over what counts as legitimate knowledge, there were decidedly different plans for centralizing text selection and rationalizing adoption procedures. Not all plans gave power to the state. Thus, for instance, in 1933, while twenty-five states empowered the state board of education or a special textbook committee to select texts for use in the public schools, another group of five states left that decision at a county level. Still others did not intervene in local decisions at all.[19] Why the difference?

Why would the South be the area in which one finds most of the centralized state adoption procedures, as well as the longest history of rightist populism? This is a very complicated question since it requires not only that we think about the causes within education that could lead to the centralization of "re-contextualizing agents" at the top, but also a firmer understanding of the larger relations of power in which educational "reforms" of this type took place. Even a brief glimpse at, say, class and economic conditions that differed from region to region shows the significance of such power relations.

We need to remember some of the peculiarities of American political history. Unlike many European nations, for example, the United States educational system grew out of a federation of relatively independent states. Thus, the power of national controls, and the pattern of state control over curriculum and teaching, is dependent on this history. While it is possible to speak of a national curriculum here currently—one whose content is determined largely by Texas and California and by the competitive market in textbooks—the situation is still one of a very different articulation between the power of the state and the school than in those nations with homogeneous school systems.[20]

These differences can be readily seen in the politics of school governance. Historically, while the stereotype exists that all states had similar patterns of school governance, a closer look reveals clear patterns of regional variation.

> The model of state-level appointments and local-level elections characterized northeastern states and is reasonably defined as bureaucratic. Yet the southern model was the reverse, with state officers elected and local levels appointed. Both levels were elective across midwestern states. The divergence of southern and midwestern states from the bureaucratic model of the Northeast sufficiently jeopardizes the claim that there was a single, national model of school governance.[21]

Some of the political and economic reasons for these regional differences are noted by Richardson in his own discussion of the class and race relations underlying the different strategies used for "reforming" education.

> Although the architects of public school systems in the northeastern and southern states were from similar social backgrounds and were members of the weakly established new middle class, they differed significantly in the broader context of relations. The presence of a landed, planter class and its potential for antagonistic relations to poor white farmers underlay the essentially conservative intentions of southern educational reform. . . . "The small professional middle class that included a number of important southern reformers allied itself with the landed upper class that sponsored industrialization and, after 1900, expanded the range of state activity, thereby exchanging the right to rule for the right to teach school." For southern educational reform, the systematization of schooling was entrapped by the politics of class and race which led inexorably to the construction of dual systems separating whites and blacks.[22]

It is not as if class and race dynamics were absent in other regions of the country. Of course they were present. Yet, because of the specific differences in the regional political economies and class structures, the power of the state was articulated in diverse ways. Richardson is again helpful here.

> While the design and content of both northeastern and southern school systems were motivated by pressing needs for social [and symbolic] control, the "universal educational movement" of the South spoke more openly of the need to design a common education in the service of industrialization. . . . In this respect, the content of school reform differed between the Northeast and the South. The absence of a landed class in the North enlarged the flexibility of school reformers. Educational systems in the Northeast originated from substitutive strategies where school reformers were able to erect an institutional structure upon already established *local instructional networks*. This enabled them to link more closely the conduct of instruction to the character and occupational futures of the new middle class, evident in curricula stressing a denial or escape "from the ethos of the industrial system and its traditional asceticism." . . . In contrast, southern educational reform originated from partial restrictive strategies, restrained by the continuity of political power based in a landed, planter class. Here educational reform was "*from above*," defining the public realm by the extension of common schooling to the broad base of poor whites.[23]

In the South, then, as I show in more detail shortly, an accord is formed between a somewhat less powerful but still emergent white middle class with its own professionalizing and rationalizing interests and those of the landed planter class in which the "needs" of poor whites are taken into account. "Reform from above" rather than a greater emphasis on "reform from below" is established because of different educational conditions (a longer tradition of local educational networks in the North, for instance) and because of both the class and race antagonisms and the perceived need by powerful groups for industrialization in the South. A tradition of state intervention and control, hence, is established very early on in the history of the accords which govern how and whose knowledge is recontextualized.

Though I have focused my attention on the South and Northeast here, similar data are available on the Midwest and Far West regions of the country. While I shall not go into detail about this, there too specific differences emerge that help us explain the reasons behind centralized or decentralized models of curricular decision making.[24] The important point is to recognize not only the differences but the connections between these varied traditions and the specific conditions of economic and political power within each region.

Yet the attention one might give to such economic and political conditions is not sufficient. There were serious regional *ideological* differences as well that need to be taken into account and which also contributed to further regulation of the text. Historically, there was strong sentiment after the Civil War, for example, for textbooks to reflect the perspectives of either the North or the South; but in the South this became integrated more readily into "reform from above" strategies. Thus, in one instance, in Texas a Scott, Foresman arithmetic text was pressured to make certain that its arithmetic problems featured "the victories of southern generals." In another instance, an advertisement in 1867 for books published by the New York firm of E. J. Hale and Son claimed that the publishing house printed textbooks that were specifically "prepared for southern schools, by southern authors, and therefore free from matter offensive to southern people."[25] The power of the politics of adoption policies and the economics of publishing are already more than a little visible here as the principles of ideological screening become institutionalized.

CONTESTED REFORM

We need to be careful not to overextend these arguments. State control over the text may appear to be total and can, from the outside, seem to be an example of strong top down power. Yet, this may not always be the case. It is not preordained that state institutions always influence others more than these institutions are influenced by them. The fact that a centralized administrative framework for making decisions exists "does not automatically make it the leading part."[26] In fact, if my earlier arguments about the State being a site of conflict both within dominant groups and between dominant and less powerful groups is correct, then we should expect that even though such top down mandates were instituted they were undoubtedly subject to intense debate and conflict. When we look more specifically at the history of state adoption policies in these primarily southern regions, we shall see that this is exactly the case.

My discussion of the nature of the accord over knowledge and of the historical roots of state adoption policies has so far stressed the larger relations of power and the political/economic (and ideological) history of regions. While these relations are important in that they provide the structural boundaries within which educational decisions were made, there were reasons internal to the educational system for such centralized policies as well. Here, too, these reasons were continually contested. As we shall see, such policies resulted not only from pressure from above but again from pressure from below. Furthermore, there were partly progressive elements interwoven with the more conservative bureaucratic tendencies in the actual policies that were instituted. The history of such progressive elements should give us some reason for hope in today's conservative climate, if we take their limits and possibilities seriously.

The conflict over state adoption policies that we are currently witnessing is not new by any means. The controversy over whether such policies are wise has had an extensive history, at least as far back as 1850.[27] A deeper analysis of this is essential if we are to more fully understand how the politics of official knowledge—with all of its contradictory tendencies—has operated.

"INCOMPETENT" TEACHERS, "UNETHICAL" PUBLISHERS

As I noted, state adoption policies and the overall tendency to centralize control of educational policy and content in general that they represent did not spring full grown. They have a distinctive history and grew out of a multitude of social and educational conditions. While my focus in this part of the chapter will continue to be mostly on the larger socio/historical conditions that led to such a tendency, it is important to first understand the overt educational arguments for such policies.

Historically, the arguments for state adoption policies and for statewide uniformity in texts centered around four basic points: 1) such policies tend to ensure that books will be purchased at the lowest price; 2) instead of the all too real dangers of selecting poor textbooks that are associated with local school district control, state adoption guarantees that selections will not be done by relatively naive people but by experts; 3) state adoption of uniform texts ultimately lowers the costs associated with a mobile population in which parents (often looking for work) move their children from district to district; 4) uniformity of textbooks at a state level enables the establishment of a minimum and standard course of study throughout the state.[28]

Certain historical themes emerge here: the overpricing of texts due to what were seen as profit-hungry publishers, control by experts, a particular vision of school populations, and a statewide curriculum. As we shall see, each of these had its roots in wider social movements and conflicts.

Yet this history of internal problems doesn't exhaust the reasons for turning to statewide solutions in the South. The perception on the part of some government officials that teachers themselves were by and large incompetent played a part here as well. Speaking in 1874, the superintendent of schools of South Carolina, for instance, complained vociferously that county examiners awarded teaching certificates "to persons whose ignorance was glaringly apparent to the most careless observer." As he went on to say, "our schools never will and never can become deservedly popular so long as the evil of employing so many incompetent, inefficient and worthless teachers continues." All too many teachers taught "from motives of personal convenience, and in many instances, from a consciousness of being unfit for anything else."[29] Though similar complaints were heard throughout the country,[30] its effects in the South were more powerful.

This "incompetence" of teachers was a continuing concern that supported the power of state textbook commissions. As one educator summarizing decades of criticism of teachers and reviewing the status of Kentucky's adoption policy put it, "We must recognize that our teachers are not . . . well prepared professionally." Given such a "poorly prepared corps of teachers," there is only one hope if we are to improve instruction. We must place the best textbook possible in the hands of the students. "The poorer the teacher, the better the textbooks need to be."[31] (Does all this sound familiar?)

We need to be careful about accepting this interpretation of teachers as largely "incompetent and worthless" at face value, however. Most teachers were neither stupid and uncaring, nor were they passive "victims" of this situation with no voice. In fact, one of the first interpreters of the origins of state adoption plans understood that in earlier periods of schooling in the United States it was not unusual for teachers to have to rely on either whatever books students might have available at home or whatever books or texts a local store had in stock. Because of this, pressure to institute state laws that required uniform textbooks also *"had its origin in the complaints of disheartened teachers* against this incongruous situation."[32] Teacher pressure, based on the conditions they faced every day, takes center stage here, mirroring the points I raised in the previous chapter.

Yet, while I want to stress the importance of teachers' self-formative activity here, this did not seem to have an effect on those who saw teachers as a major part of the problem. In many ways, they intensified their attacks. Thus, to the claim that teachers were so poorly prepared was added the claim that teachers could be too easily influenced by textbook agents who worked their ways through the state. A new group of recontextualizers—"disinterested" experts, not naive teachers—was required.

Commenting on the situation in 1918, when state adoption policies developed in the late nineteenth and early twentieth century were being questioned, Charles Judd lays out this part of the case for statewide adoption.

> It is because teachers are showing so little wisdom in the selection of books that the public has in many states safeguarded the situation by laws removing from the teacher all power of choice. The writer recalls a letter from a public official responsible for the choice of textbooks who was moved by criticisms made of his selections to a sharp retort. He said that there was no justification for criticisms of the state selections, that school people were for the most part wholly unreliable in their choices. He asserted that it was entirely possible to map out the route followed by certain book agents through the state by the stream of letters recommending certain books that came to the state text-book commission.[33]

Teachers were not the only ones focused upon. Linked to the distrust of teachers was a concern that is of great significance here: the vision of textbook publishers as more than a little rapacious and corrupt. Money motivated them, not educational issues. And while many publishers expressly argued against such stereotyping,[34] this view of textbook publishers was still widespread even as late as the 1930s. It had its beginnings much earlier.

For example, throughout the later part of the nineteenth century and the early decades of the twentieth, serious questions were raised about "the control of text-books by private individuals and commercial publishing houses."[35] As long as the textbook was produced by commercial concerns whose motive was profit, and as long as teachers had such limited educational experience, the textbook unfortunately was "removed from institutional control."[36]

Of course, many publishers disputed the arguments about their rapaciousness, preferring to be seen as "constructive workers in the field of education" who were partners in enhancing the cultural life of the nation. A representative of one of the largest textbook publishers waxes eloquent about just this point.

> [The publisher] is not merely a manufacturer of and distributor of books for material gain. He is an idealist, a constructive worker in the field of education, ambitious to do his share in putting into the schools of the nation the ideas and ideals which express the nation's best thought now and which should later be wrought into the national life through the influence of schools.[37]

Publishers did not deny they were in a business, but they were organized in fact to act as the agents that would test out and improve American life. The publisher:

> represents a large business organization, which he is ready to place at the service of any author who can convince him that he has a message for the schools, and through the schools for the nation. And, finally, he stands ready to risk his reputation and financial resources to test the validity of approved ideals and methods in textbooks as a means to the constant improvement of the nation's educational life.[38]

Not all people agreed with such a positive portrayal of textbook publishers. For many people, they were still not to be trusted. That such concerns about the motives of publishers continued to be widespread and influenced the development of state adoption policies can readily be seen in a questionnaire that J. B. Edmonson sent out to school superintendents and other educators and representatives of textbook publishers in preparation for his chapter on "The Ethics of Marketing and Selecting Textbooks" in the famous *NSSE Yearbook* on the textbook. Among the questions that seemed important to ask about the ethics of publishing and publishers' representatives were the following:[39]

1. Would it be ethical for a representative to try to influence the election or appointment of persons to teaching or administrative positions in order to secure adoptions of certain books?
2. Would it be ethical for a representative to try to stimulate dissatisfaction among teachers with the textbooks adopted for use in schools?

3. Would it be ethical for a representative to bring to the attention of a board of education unethical practices of a superintendent in the selection of textbooks?

4. Would it be ethical for a representative to bring to the attention of the superintendent unethical practices of a committee in the selection of textbooks?

5. Would it be ethical for a representative to try to secure confidential information regarding secret committees for textbook adoption?

6. Would it be ethical for a representative to circulate criticism of superintendents who have made decisions adverse to the representative's company?

7. Would it be ethical for a representative to take an active interest in the election of school board members in a community other than his own?

8. Would it be ethical for a representative to circulate petitions among teachers calling for changes in textbooks?

9. Would it be ethical for a textbook company to employ attorneys to influence the adoption of textbooks?

10. Would it be ethical for a representative to influence the appointment of persons to selecting committees?

The fact that questions such as these had such prominence documents the fear that the politics and economics of textbooks had been and still could easily get out of control. The answer across the South was to regulate and centralize to keep this from happening.[40]

However, there are a multitude of responses that could be made to this situation. One response could be to heighten accountability through enhanced local control as many northern and midwestern states did. Another would be simply to bring the sales practices of publishers under the ethically regulated codes of state departments of commerce and industry or leave it up to the Better Business Bureau. These and other solutions may not be adequate, but it is not preordained that the *state* should set up an elaborate machinery to specifically "police'" the practices of publishers and the content of the textbook. Yet this is exactly what many southern states did.

What conditions caused such a response? The roots lie not in the immediacy of decisions to regulate texts but further back. As I argued in the discussion of regionalism in the first part of this chapter, these roots lie in the establishment throughout many areas of the South of strong centralized regulatory dynamics that set off the South historically from the North. Without a more thorough understanding of these dynamics, we will miss

29

the larger social movements that generated such centralizing responses, for as I show, these regulatory urges—as in the case of the teachers who wanted less random and better curriculum material—again came not only from above but from *below* as well. Finally, in a manner very much like today, we will miss the role that the government has played in forming accords or compromises that incorporate certain progressive tendencies over knowledge and power while at the same time recontextualizing them so that they do not threaten the overall basis of power over culture and economy. In many ways, it is the equivalent of "mentioning" that I discussed in chapter 5, though it plants seeds that have the potential for going much further.

TOWARD A REGULATORY STATE

From the late nineteenth century to the early years of the twentieth century, American governance went through a fundamental transition. As Wiebe has described it, what emerged was "a government broadly and continually involved in society's operations."[41] Instead of a government dominated by the legislature, the executive branch enlarged its power. Even more importantly, increasing power became vested in what was essentially a new branch of government made up of administrative boards and agencies. Through these administrative mechanisms, government agencies became increasingly involved in mediating clashing interests. These agencies assumed greater responsibility for mitigating conflicts through planning, administration, and regulation. Toward the end of the nineteenth century, government was not deeply involved in "recognizing and adjusting group differences." Yet, by the time the second decade of the twentieth century closed, "innumerable policies committed officials to that formal purpose and provided the bureaucratic structures for achieving it."[42]

Scandals at local, state, and national levels had created a furor against politico/business corruption. Among the most glaring offenses that were uncovered were the many ways corporations corrupted politicians to secure government subsidies, public privileges, and benefits.[43] In California, legislative hearings uncovered fresh scandals. In many southern states, the divided Democratic party and the other less powerful parties and alliances brought their rivalries into the public eye by extolling their own virtues and telling tales of each other's corruption by business interests.[44] Muckraking helped, of course, to bring these scandals center stage and business corruption of politics soon became a leading theme in public halls.[45]

Out of this situation emerged a commitment to a particular type of government, one that would restrain privileged corporations, protect the weaker elements of the community, establish formal mechanisms for new interest groups to have a voice in government, and "acknowledge and adjust group differences."[46] At the state level in particular, the late 1890s and early 1900s were years that were characterized by experiments with a variety of methods of regulation and administration.[47] These experiments soon solidified into a body of practices and a particular approach to reform.

While these types of scandals were not new to the American political and economic system by any means, and many people had a vague understanding of the pervasiveness of some of the corrupting practices, something important was very new here. A new understanding had begun to emerge, one in which an awareness of the *process* of corruption was central. No longer was corruption seen largely as the result of a few "bad men." Rather, the problem was *systemic* and could only be solved by enlarged government action that altered the system itself.[48] An onslaught of legislation ensued, regulating lobbying, outlawing special favors given by business to public officials, and establishing and/or strengthening the regulatory and administrative arms of government in a wide array of areas from commerce and transportation to health, welfare, and education.[49]

In the process, government involvement and direction shifted. The forces of localism and opposition to government authority (forces that were very strong in the South) slowly but surely lost ground to the forces of centralization, bureaucratization, and expanded governmental authority.[50] This had a special impact on education in general and ultimately on the state regulation of texts. Throughout the South, a coalition of businessmen, professionals, and the urban middle class—assisted by turmoil and pressure from below as we shall see—formed an important element in the push for greater state responsibility, one that combined efficiency with limited social reforms in education and social welfare.[51]

For progressive reformers from dominant economic groups and within the upwardly mobile, new middle class, one succeeded in bringing more efficient and effective schooling throughout the South by relying on objective information, on "the facts," and by employing experts in public administration for dealing with social problems.[52] Industrialization, economic development, material progress, the transformation and conservation of elements of southern culture, the "race problem," and the social conflicts that were threatening stability throughout the region—all of these could be solved through limited social reforms.[53] The public sphere must be organized around knowledge, expertise, and efficient administration. The disinterested expert could be counted upon to promote the general interest. While municipal and countywide reforms were focused upon as well, it was in the growth of state functions that one sees the largest changes. As a commentator argued in 1912, "A realization of the greater efficiency that central state departments have . . . has, during the past decade, caused the people to delegate all new functions, and some old ones, to state departments or commissions."[54] In all of this, however, the most striking development of state services and state authority occurred in education.

Other actors were important here besides the spokespeople for the "new South" such as modernizing business people, professionals, and the urban middle class. Given the largely agrarian nature of the South, movements among farmers were also significant in focusing attention on areas that were crying out for reform from credit and monetary policy to elections and education. The "old South," with its history of a powerful landed, planter class, had already established a tradition of educational reform *from above* and the newer calls for reform by small farmers and others often moved in that direction as well.[55]

Small farmers in the South, who were being squeezed by sagging prices, mounting interest charges, and unfavorable laws, joined together to form organizations such as the Farmers' Alliance which soon began searching for answers to their problems.[56] With their way blocked by policies within the resurgent Democratic party in southern states such as Texas, agrarian movements spawned calls for reform.[57] While radical about class politics, the Alliance consistently focused on the resolution of differences through the ballot.[58] The individual sovereignty of a more *politically educated* public electorate would vote into office a government whose actions would serve "the greatest good for the greatest number." Armed with feelings of the political and moral superiority of the small farmer, they stressed a vision in which the State was to be used as an instrument supporting the weak against the strong.[59] While adult education centering around radical political and economic issues played a very strong part in their program, public education and the kinds of knowledge taught (and not taught) to farmers and their children in schools were important areas of interest and political work for the Alliance.[60] For Alliance members, what was going on was *miseducation* in which "those who labor are educated to be abject slaves and the rich are educated to be tyrannical, presumptuous, and vicious. . . . All the people have been educated to bow submissively at the feet of Mammon."[61]

Some of the reconstructed lyrics to the song "My Country tis of Thee" give a good indication of their anticorporate sentiment.

> My Country tis of thee
> Land of lost Liberty,

Of thee I sing.
Land where the Millionaires,
Who govern our affairs
Own for themselves and heirs,
Hail to thy King.[62]

Since the capitalist, "Mammon," also controlled "the channels of information," only miseducation could result. In opposition to this, Alliance
spokespersons mounted attacks on newspapers, the publishing industry,
and the public schools.[63]

Leaders of the Alliance were not loath to criticize the public schools as
being controlled by the exact same "plutocratic" groups that dominated
the other elements of government. They argued against both monopolies
in textbook publishing and partisan political control of educational governance. At the same time, they supported creating a more effective system of public education in Texas and in other southern states.[64]

In 1890, the national leadership of the Alliance levelled charges against
a group of textbook publishers. They accused the publishers of "conspir-
ing to consolidate markets, control competition, and raise prices in the
schoolbook market through the creation of a holding company, the American Book Company." For the Alliance, this had the effect of raising the
prices of texts, a cardinal sin for the hard-pressed farmers of the South.
Just as bad, however, was the fact that the textbooks themselves seemed
to teach exactly the ideological perspectives the Alliance so strongly opposed, the virtues both of industrialization and the industrial giants. At
the same time, the Alliance argued that this publishing "trust" had guaranteed its economic and ideological power "through an intricate and secret system of kickbacks to local and state superintendents."[65]

The Alliance's arguments about education and about the economic and
political situation small farmers and workers found themselves in struck
a responsive chord throughout the region. The fact that many of the economic, political, and cultural interests they fought against originated in
the North helped bind their supporters together; but it also helped bind
otherwise opposing groups within the South together as well.

The strength of sentiment against the North was something that united
most white southerners of all stations. The waving of "the bloody shirt"—
the traditional symbol of white southern solidarity—wrapped race, party,
and region tightly together as the wounds of the Civil War and the Reconstruction period proved very slow to heal. This left a scar across the southern landscape uniting many southerners in a dislike and distrust of things
northern.[66] What happened in school content was not immune from these
emotions.

The issue of race plays an important role here. Racism and racial antagonism helped determine a significant part of the cultural politics of the entire region at the same time as it so effectively shaped the consciousness of southerners,[67] including the small farmers. Like today, racism, and racial politics, helped split the Populist movement and the Alliance in the South. It divided people against each other and helped to hide their common interest against dominant economic groups.[68] The ultimate result, as we shall see, was limited reform and a strong state dominated by conservative and "moderate" interests.

Other factors, too, split the Populist and Alliance forces, a split that enabled centralizing reformers to take up some of the educational and social issues they raised and to transform these issues into problems to be solved not by the more radical proposals coming from the Alliance, but by the methods of "experts."

The defeat of the Populists in 1892 "broke the spirit of the Alliance."[69] As it became more and more difficult to maintain its status as a mass-based, grass-roots organization, in later years many of its members were easily recruited into the educational crusade of the late nineteenth and early twentieth century to rebuild southern schools and to bring them under the more centralized governance of a strong network of experts sponsored by Rockefeller and other northern industrialists and strongly supported by many southern industrialists, a rising, new middle class who also were interested in southern economic development, university intellectuals, and others. The Alliance's faith in education later led many of its members to support policies that they would have been more than a little skeptical of earlier.[70] In the process, they too became actors in the historic dynamic to centralize and bring education under the control of recontextualizing "experts."

"Expert" regulation and administration had a number of advantages. It appeared sane and moderate at the same time that it transferred responsibility out of the hands of the business and political figures who seemed to be at the root of the problems. It gave a (*limited*) voice to varied factions of the public. Even more importantly perhaps, it primarily focused on the *state* level, thereby effectively removing politically volatile elements from possibly exercising power. Thus, by shifting the passion for reform from the local, and often more insurgent, level, it isolated groups that might have called for more radical solutions.[71] As McCormick puts it, "In gaining a statewide hearing for reform, the accusations of politico-business corruption actually increased the likelihood that conservative solutions would be adopted."[72]

How and why did this happen? What were the deeper economic, political, and ideological conditions that led to centralization in the South?

This requires that we look again at the more general context in which education and the politics of symbolic control functioned.

THE CLASS AND RACIAL ROOTS OF CONSERVATIVE COMPROMISE

We need to understand that in the late nineteenth century, despite a regional trend toward diversification and industrialization, the South still retained important elements of what can only be called a colonial economy. It was characterized by undeveloped resources and an abundance of unskilled labor, low-wage industries, outside domination by railroads, and large timber and mining interests, as well as external control of much of its banking and industrial wealth. Class resentments and racial antagonisms were exceptionally strong.[73] Poverty became increasingly institutionalized on both the farm and in the cities. And the schooling system of many states was more than a little underdeveloped and underfinanced. It was an inherently unstable and tense situation, one that fostered a concern for social order, stability, and efficiency among many groups.[74]

Because of this, across the South during this period, the state was increasingly looked upon as the source of regulatory action and as an important provider of new services.[75] Throughout the South, the crusaders to improve schooling were influenced by the belief that it was essential to try to create a situation in which educational leaders were less vulnerable to pressure from an electorate and legislatures that were often less than enthusiastic about spending large sums of money for education[76] or who would interfere in decisions better left to experts.

The reformers were bound together by a set of assumptions that favored increasingly centralized control to "balance" the tradition of local autonomy that was so powerful in the South. First, the educational reformers believed in the very correctness of their vision. Their own success as individuals gave them the right to lead. As Charles Dabney, one of the leaders of the educational crusade put it, "The people need leaders to show them the way."[77] In Theodore Mitchell's compelling words, these reformers "saw public opinion as a mass to be shaped and molded, convinced to accept their notions of education and schooling."[78] Second, their vision combined a progressive commitment to "clean government," one that was unpolluted by the taint of scandal and political interference, with an equally strong commitment to social control. The role of the public school in both its content and pedagogy was to "develop a broad and efficient system of drilling the children . . . to the habits of discipline and the customs of obedience which make for the public order." Sound moral training and obedience were to be combined with the third element: the reformers' belief that the South would only grow economically with the help of an enlarged and efficient school system, but again one that was insulated from political parties and politics in general.[79]

This was to be a society that was "democratic," but for whites only. However, while seeking to preserve white solidarity in the face of tensions and conflicts, not all whites were seen as being equal. All too many well-to-do and middle-class, white southerners, including the bulk of the reformers, held a profound mistrust of the masses of people they were seeking to help. Because of this, mechanisms were developed that "cleansed" the governance of education and other services and at the same time limited participation in decision making to include only "those who were prepared for responsible citizenship."[80] State-level experts who could stand above the corrupt or overly political processes of educational governance and text and curriculum selection were clearly more "responsible" than others.

The evolving class structure of the South—"the presence of a depressed mass of rural and urban working people and an emerging middle class increasingly conscious of the need for social control and restraint"—is not an inconsequential element in this equation.[81] Yet, as I hinted at earlier, educational efficiency experts and reformers did not ignore the black population in their plans for centralization of authority over schools and texts. Their approach to what was called the "race problem" mixed paternalism, social efficiency, guidance, and protection in separate schools in exchange for the values of the new South that were emerging: thrift, industriousness, "self respect for the 'good negro'," and continued subservience.[82]

There were differences between states, of course. Texas, for instance, had a smaller black population and somewhat less of a tradition of corruption common to many southern regimes.[83] Yet, it is quite clear that behind certain of the reforms that the Democratic party enacted in the first decade of this century was a concern with the Latino/Latina and black citizens of the state.[84] Thus, as with all movements for reform in the South, the racial undercurrent here undoubtedly played no small part in the growth of centralized control over schooling and the text.

Both whites and blacks were focussed on by the reformers. For the more liberal reformers, a more efficient and effective school system—one organized by reformers and experts—was essential not just to "elevate the inferior race," but also to "save whites from the blighting influences of narrow mindedness, intolerance and injustice."[85] Rigid racial separation could be guaranteed by the state and could be fostered by state regulation and inspection of education and texts. Furthermore, by educating the masses of poor whites, and instilling in them "appropriate" morality and codes of behavior, it would make them more tolerant of blacks. Order and tranquility would reign supreme.[86]

All of this was not only due to the politics of class and race. Gender politics played a role here as well. While white women in the South may seemingly not have been as overtly militant as in other areas of the country, in part because of the particular ways patriarchal relations operated in the South, they did actively seek educational reforms and organized around a variety of issues of social justice. One woman put it this way, perhaps more than a little wryly: "We have to go slow in the South. . . . We may not at first do very big things and we are perfectly certain not to do spectacular things, but . . . *we are not dead!*"[87] Thus, importantly, added impetus for the educational crusade came from the involvement of women. Organized groups of mostly middle-class, white women became deeply involved in social reform movements including prohibition, women's suffrage, the regulation of child labor, and the expansion of education.[88] These all required an expansion of the role of the state. And while the women's movements ultimately helped spawn processes that over the next decades solidified state control over education and the text, they also led to major gains in the self-formative power of women.[89]

Given these kinds of contradictory class, race, and gender pressures, in the largely one-party politics of the region, southern Democrats in many states themselves increasingly accepted what had originally been an idea generated out of the Populist movement: the concept of the positive State in which government played a much more active role in promoting growth and stabilizing and protecting the economic, cultural, and moral fiber of society.[90] And these movements dovetailed easily with some of the anticorporate and proregulatory sentiments I mentioned earlier in this chapter.

When the anticorporate attack came as expected from farmers and labor, it also included small manufacturers, warehousemen, local merchants, and others who supported public regulation of large business concerns,[91] thereby creating quite complicated alliances among groups. Texas provides a good example of the complicated social alliances and ideologies that stood behind the movement toward more state regulation and control in a number of areas. It also shows how regional differences and antagonisms played a crucial role in the State's activity as a recontextualizer.

As in other southern states, funding for schools had always been a problem in Texas. Class, ideological, and ethnic differences made it an even more difficult situation. A relatively decentralized system, but one in which railroads, land sales, and school funding were tied together,

evolved that favored church and private schools and often left little resources for public schools. After the devastation of the Civil War, with the
economics of railroads and land in disarray and with reformers from the
North holding greater control of state governments, a more centralized
system was established.

One early commentator who was sympathetic to "the cause of the
South" points to the increasing power of the state board in this context.

> The reformers from the North in 1881 established an autocratic,
> centralized system of schools with a state board and districts in
> charge of local trustees under the direction of a state superintendent
> of schools assisted by thirty-five supervisors. . . . The lands for the
> school fund were donated and put under the control of the state
> board, the lost funds were reappropriated, one-fourth of the state's
> annual revenue from general taxation was appropriated. . . . The state
> board invested school funds and allotted income according to law,
> made the regulations for the control of the schools, examined and
> appointed teachers, laid down the courses of study and selected text-
> books.[92]

These centralizing tendencies were enforced by a state superintendent
of schools who, while he served in the Federal Army, had not taught
school. Over a good deal of conservative opposition, he often overruled
school district decisions, appointed inspectors, set up schools, appointed teachers, and selected textbooks many of which, according to
Dabney's early history, were "written by Northern authors, made statements and expressed opinions offensive to southerners."[93]

Whatever Dabney's sentiments, there can be no doubt that this system
did in fact generate considerable controversy, and soon the state, now
under the control of Democrats, returned to a more locally oriented model
of governance and funding in which central guidance was almost "non-
existent" in the mid-1870s.[94] This soon led to frequent and bitter controversies and rivalries over political favoritism, incompetence, inefficiency,
and racism.[95] A slow return to a somewhat more centralized system began. By 1900 or so, pressure for an activist state had grown again.

In Texas, the major campaign in the early years of the century concerned efforts to deal with corporate wealth and with the fact that the
foremost corporations were of "foreign" (i.e., northern) origin. The rapaciousness of capital and the influence of "foreign" corporations fed into
the other concerns. Not only was there "foreign" control of the economy
through northern railroads, banks, and so on, but anger at "foreign"
ideas—an anger that had been simmering since the Civil War—was un-

leashed against northern publishers as well, not only by the Farmers' Alliance, but by many groups. The same regulatory impulse that was now impacting on banking, food, medicine, and so many other areas again ultimately worked its way out in the state regulation of textbooks.[96]

In Texas, organized labor and farmers' unions were more influential than elsewhere and for a time at the beginning of the century were able to work together to try to influence the state to support their cause. Support for increased state power again came from professional groups and organized business people whose own influence grew as well.[97] Texas reforms, probably to a greater extent than other southern states, represented a response to the state's very diverse economic, geographic, and cultural interests. Its very diversity fostered the formation of groups to pressure the state. The pattern of Texas reforms was highlighted by "well-organized urban middle class pressure groups loosely coordinated at times with farmer, labor, business, or professional organizations."[98] Thus, this newly emerging, middle-class group played a major part. It was this group from which experts employed within the state would be drawn. Support for increased state intervention in education and elsewhere would guarantee their own mobility and give them a controlling interest in an expanded State. Motivated by a contradictory bundle of sentiments including altruism, optimism, expanding economic opportunity, social control, and a search for order and efficiency in a time of very real uncertainty, they provided important support for the power of "the expert." As members of a reforming coalition, their increasing power within the emerging state bureaucracy helps explain the historic pattern of tight state control of texts in Texas.

Politicians were not blind to these issues. In fact, in many states they were quick to sense the advantages that could be gained in supporting (and leading) campaigns against corporations. No matter what their commitments, which may or may not have been quite laudatory, many state politicians were talented enough "to capture the liveliest issues in sight."[99] In the first decade of the century, campaigns to establish regulatory commissions quickly grew. They soon spilled out over the borders of transportation and commerce and extended into other areas such as education. In the context of these concerns, the state assumed more and more of the functions of resolving and regulating conflicts, business practices, and social behavior.[100]

Yet it is important to realize that many southern conservatives feared that the anticorporate sentiments would discourage northern economic and cultural investment in the region. The answer was not to drive northern corporations out, but to regulate them so that they helped economic development in the South.[101] Education was part of this program of economic development and textbooks—recontextualized and organized around southern but less overtly regional and more *modernizing* themes—were essential to such progress.

Grantham provides one of the most coherent summaries of the ideological tendencies that lay behind much of the centralizing movement. The southern reformers that ultimately led the movement for state control:

> shared a yearning for a more orderly and cohesive community. Such a community, they believed, was a prerequisite for economic development and material progress. Its realization depended upon the effective regulation of society in the interest of ethical business practices and good government, and in the elimination of political corruption, machine politics, and the insidious power of large corporations and other special interests. This meant that the regulatory power of the state must be expanded. Social controls were also indispensable for the preservation of moral values, for the purification of social institutions, and for the protection of men and women from their own weaknesses. Underlying this coercive reformism was a substantial vein of self-righteousness and moral apprehension. Optimistic about future prospects but alarmed by the tensions and conflicts that pervaded the South in the late nineteenth century, southern [reformers] looked toward the creation of a clearly defined community that would accommodate a society differentiated by race and class, but one that also possessed unity, cohesion, and stability.[102]

The result was what I have earlier called an *accord,* a historic compromise in which dominant groups maintain much of their economic, political, and cultural power by incorporating under their own leadership parts of the perspectives of competing or dispossessed groups.[103] Top-down models *would* incorporate greater public control. They would offer new services to the poor, the farmer, and the laborer. They would "cleanse" the government in general and the control of education and texts from the taint of corruption and would expand schooling extensively. Yet, they would also effectively disempower the more democratically inclined movements for public control of economic, political, and educational institutions by keeping them in the hands of "experts" and elites. Many elements of this position, with all of its positive and negative possibilities, can be found in the moderate to conservative Democratic administration in Washington. The underlying politics of the accord or compromise that developed is nicely summarized by Grantham:

> There was room in this [compromise] for material progress, efficiency, ethical standards, social order, a more vigorous regulatory state, social justice, public services, and especially the vision of a

revitalized southern community. The [reformers] were able to effect a synthesis of the antithetical approaches of the Bourbons and populists. They attracted support from diverse social elements, including the section's civic-commercial elites and upwardly mobile urban groups. But [they] also drew on the swirling protest of the 1890s, and agrarian radicalism flowed in a somewhat attenuated but distinct current into the politics of the progressive era, helping to account for the anticorporation sentiment, party insurgency, and morality oriented campaigns that followed. In the early twentieth-century setting the [reformers] were able to function both as agents of modernization and as guardians of southern tradition.[104]

There was progress to be sure. But the reforms were still characterized by paternalism and a hierarchical view of society, by a class consciousness that distrusted the masses of people in the South, by basic acceptance of racial stereotypes and a racist social order, and by a search for social consensus and social stability that would be guaranteed by a "disinterested" state.[105] The politics of state regulation, then, is—in microcosm—the politics of the South as a whole.

OLD PROBLEMS RENEWED

While I have painted a picture of the social, ideological, and educational context out of which state control over official knowledge emerged, of how the state became the prime recontextualizing agent, it would be wrong to assume that the growth of state intervention completely dealt with the problems they were meant to solve. Accords are compromises. As I argued in chapter two, they provide *temporary* "solutions" at a variety of levels; but, almost always, they also spawn further conflicts at the level of the State or in the daily practices and policies involved in the politics of school knowledge. The example of state textbook adoption provides a case in point here. While it did establish "expert" mechanisms for partially dealing with the complicated ideological differences concerning class and race in the South (again, and very much like today, usually on the terrain favored by dominant groups), it also created an arena for older conflicts to emerge again in a new form.

Take the case of the accusations of governmental corruption and the rapaciousness of textbook publishers, issues that had been among the important internal educational reasons for the adoption of state control in the first place. Even after the adoption of state control, this controversy continued nationwide, especially over questions of expertise and political/economic favoritism. Thus, in the 1930s, Edmonson reports that a considerable number of people throughout the country regarded "baleful influences" that could "undermine standards of good practice in the selecting of textbooks" were most likely to occur in connection with state adoption policies. The possibility of "scandal" was enhanced "when political appointees who are laymen are able, directly or indirectly, to influence the selection of texts for the public schools, and thus control the distribution of considerable sums of money."[106]

This situation was not lost on textbook publishers. Many publishers also recognized both the politics and the economics that may have lay behind some of the original state adoption models. One textbook publisher, reflecting on the history of state adoption policies, argued that "bookmen" wanted to "salt down" business for a number of years at a time, especially in those geographical areas where "schools gave all of their business to their favorite bookman." Some superintendents and boards of education "were not above sharing in the profits of the adoption." In the process, state officials and legislators were turned to in order to "sew up" the business for five-year periods, and finally the state adoption was conceived."[107] Here, state control was specifically *used* as a mechanism for guaranteed profits and to squeeze out competition, even at the same time that it was meant to protect schools from some of these same problems.

The pressure that local districts, administrators, teachers, and later state textbook boards were put under became legendary. Even as late as the 1920s, what was called an "insidious form of bribery" was practiced to insure the adoption of particular texts by state boards. Here, the textbook agent retains a well-known attorney who is located in the state and attempts to exert influence on board members through the intervention of the attorney, interventions that would be prohibited on the part of the publisher's representative. Numerous reports surfaced of attorneys having direct relations with the board. More egregiously, other reports indicated cases in which the attorney had so much political clout that his entreaties for particular books were hard to resist because of "cronyism" or in other cases because of "the most brazen threats of political or personal punishment to members of the adopting board or their agents."[108]

Again, publishers responded to this criticism. While admitting that there was corruption in textbook publishing, the situation had gotten considerably better according to them. While they did not totally approve of many of the existing programs of state adoption, even they did not want a return to a totally unregulated system. One of their major criticisms of those who put the blame totally on publishers was that the critics failed to see that it was often not the publishers' supposed hunger for profits that was at fault. Often, it was the profit motive behind local business concerns within states that had uniform adoption policies that was at the root of the problem.

> We do not find uniform adoptions in the states that are most pro-gressive educationally but rather in the states which are far distant from central sources of supply. The laws inaugurating these state adoptions were in most cases engineered by a concern in the capital city in the state which hoped to profit by being assigned the distribu-tion of the books in that state . . . which means 10 percent more out of the pupils' pockets into the pocket of the unnecessary middle-man.[109]

This comment is fascinating since it points to the multiple uses of state power over official knowledge. In a compromise among old and new elites, experts from the emerging middle class, and populist forces such as the Farmers' Alliance, multiple agendas are brought together, some in-ternal and some external to educational policy and practice. Yet, some-how out of this complex set of relations and even with the growth of the regulatory state, "Mammon" enters in again through the back door. Thus are the seeds of conflict and even further state intervention sown again.

CONCLUSION

In this chapter, I have explored what is seemingly a simple question: Why the South? What made this region more inclined to accept state-centered solutions to the regulation and control of textbooks in particular and education in general? How did what is usually the most conservative region of the country come to be so powerful in the politics of official knowledge, in the political economy of the textbook? In answering these questions, I have purposely focused our attention on larger social move-ments and on economic, political, and ideological forces that differen-tiated the South from other areas, rather than on the internal educational justifications given by educators at the time.[110] Not that I believe that such internal arguments had no weight. Of course they did. However, they would not have been made or accepted if these larger social movements and race and inter- and intra-class forces had not been so powerful. The justifications for state educational control and recontextualization did not stand alone, isolated either from the conflicts in the larger society or from attempts to solve these conflicts on terms acceptable to groups with power.

While I have highlighted the complex nexus of historical forces out of which the centralizing tendencies arose in the South, this story should interest us not only because it is a fascinating part of the history of the growth of educational regulation in this country. The story says something of great import to those interested in the politics of official knowledge and of educational policy in general. It was large-scale social movements, organized groups, stimulated from above *and below,* that made a difference. State regulation and control came about because of a complicated politics of social ferment. Organized social movements and alliances among them, then and now, are *crucial* if "Mammon" is not to be in control. *Altering what we now have will undoubtedly require the same.* As we saw earlier, this is something the Right has clearly recognized.

How something becomes "official knowledge" is always a political process. If we are to understand how the primary carrier of such official knowledge—the textbook—comes to look the way it does and if we are to understand how to alter it, we cannot afford to ignore the historic politics of social movements. History has a way of not always remaining in the past, especially if we rely only on waiting for the State to act in a time of conservatism. This realization becomes even more pressing when we turn in the next chapter to an analysis of more current rightist victories, victories that have been able to sidestep even the politics and regulations of state adoption policies. For, sometimes, dominant groups see that eliminating the State, rather than strengthening its forms of control, can bring more people under their ideological umbrella.

5 Creating the Captive Audience: Channel One and the Political Economy of the Text

INTRODUCTION

Nearly two decades ago, a number of individuals within the critical educational community warned that movements then taking hold in education in the United States would soon become the norm not only there but in many other nations as well. Movements toward reductive, mechanistic, and industrialized accountability systems, tighter control over the curriculum and pedagogy, the complex dynamics of deskilling and reskilling of teachers, an increasingly close relationship between economic rationality and educational means and ends.[1] The list could go on. It is with no great sense of glee that I note that these predictions have not been proven wrong. Of course, economic, political, and ideological conditions and the educational traditions and balance of power within each nation have mediated these movements and have created specific configurations of them that are not mirror reflections of their original impulses. Yet, no matter how detailed and conjunctural our analyses, it is difficult to miss the international transformations that have occurred.

In *Teachers and Texts*,[2] and in my introductory chapter here, I argued that our words had "taken on wings," so to speak. We have become so abstract, so metatheoretical, that we were in danger of ignoring the daily realities of and struggles over the actual policies and practices of curriculum, teaching, and evaluation in schools. For that reason, I devoted a good deal of my efforts to analyzing what counts as the curriculum in schools in many nations throughout the world—the textbook—and on the socio/cultural conditions of its production as a commodity for use in educational institutions. In that book, and in chapters three and four here, I set out to answer why and how the text becomes available as the dominant, officially sanctioned form of legitimate knowledge, and why and how the material and ideological relations within the publishing industry, the state, and schools themselves create the conditions that lead texts to have the form, content, and power that they do in times of rightist resurgence.[3]

Yet, the textbook is not the only "text" in schools that is given an official imprimatur. Of increasing importance in a time in which we are told that students are simply ignorant of the world around them and are incapable of fulfilling their duties as "citizens and workers," are the other ways schools—in an alliance among fractions of capital, the State, and many educators and community members—now want to inform students about the world. In the United States, one "reform" that is of major import is the acceptance of schools as sites of competition for profit. A new version of the "text" plays a crucial role here in transforming what schooling is about.

In this chapter, I return to the present. I analyze what I take to be a new generation of these kinds of transformations. Accompanying the recent growth of plans for privatization, for corporate control and funding for schools, for industry/school "cooperation," is something that may be less well known but it is a harbinger of things to come. I am referring to a specific kind of "text," a phenomenon known as Channel One. It is a commercially produced television news program that is now broadcast to thousands of schools in the United States. A description of it is overtly simple: ten minutes of international and national news and two minutes of commercials produced very slickly by Whittle Communications, one of the largest publishers of material for "captive audiences" in the United States. While the description is easy, the implications are more profound.

Of course, twelve minutes of "the news" will not transform education. It will not automatically make students into "better informed citizens," able to take their respective places as more enlightened participants in the supposedly pluralistic democracy that is given such rhetorical weight in current discussions about the need for a more knowledgeable (and more disciplined and more competitive) citizenry. Yet, it is what Channel One signifies—the *officially sponsored* opening up of school content to commercial sponsorship and organization—that is the sea change here. In order to understand this, we need to place Channel One in its economic, political, and ideological context.

TAXES AND TELEVISION

We have entered a period of reaction in education. Our educational institutions are seen as failures. High drop-out rates, a decline in "functional literacy,"[4] a loss of standards and discipline, the failure to teach "real knowledge," poor scores on standardized tests, and more—all of these are charges levelled at schools. And all of these, we are told, have led to declining economic productivity, unemployment, poverty, a loss of international competitiveness, and so on. Return to a "common culture," make schools more efficient, more competitive, more open to private initiative ("Mammon"); this will solve our problems.[5]

As I showed earlier, behind this is an attack on egalitarian norms and values. Though hidden in the rhetorical flourishes of the critics, in essence "too much democracy"—culturally and politically—is seen as one of the major causes of "our" declining economy and culture.[6]

As you know all too well, the conservative restoration is not only occurring in the United States. In Britain, Australia, and many other nations, similar tendencies are quite visible. The extent of the reaction is captured by the former British Secretary of Education and Science in the Thatcher government, Kenneth Baker, who evaluated nearly a decade of rightist governmental efforts by saying in 1988 that "the age of egalitarianism is over."[7] He was speaking positively, not negatively.

The threat to egalitarian ideas that this represents is never made explicit since it is always couched in the discourse of improving standards and quality in an educational system that is seen as in decline if not in crisis.[8] This is especially the case with Whittle Communication's entire package of "reforms," from Channel One to Whittle's recent proposal to establish a national chain of private schools.

Channel One needs to be seen in the context of this conservative reaction. Its status as a "reform" and its acceptance in many schools can only be fully understood as a partial embodiment of a larger conservative movement that has had a considerable effect not only on education but on all aspects of the society.[9] One of the effects has been to transform our collective sense of the roles schools play in this society. This has meant that equalizing the opportunities and outcomes of schooling has been seen increasingly not as a public right but as a tax drain. As we saw, public schooling—unless it is defined as meeting the more conservative goals now in ascendancy—is too expensive economically and ideologically,[10] a condition that may continue during Democratic leadership given the economic disasters of the Reagan/Bush years.

In the United States, among the major effects of this changing perception of schooling is that a large number of states have had to make "Draconian cuts" in education because of sharply diminished tax revenues and a loss of public support for schools. This has created a situation in which federal and state aid to local school districts—never totally sufficient in many poor school districts—has been less and less able to keep up with mandated programs such as classes for children with special needs or who speak languages other than English. It has meant that for many schools it will be nearly impossible for them to comply with, say, health and desegregation programs mandated by the state and federal governments, to say nothing of other needs.[11]

Part of the situation has been caused by the intensely competitive economic conditions faced by business and industry. Their own perceived imperative to cut costs and reduce budgets (often no matter what the social consequences) has led many companies to exert considerable pressure on states and local communities to give them sizable tax breaks, thereby "cutting off money needed to finance public education."[12] Such tax exemptions are not new by any means. However, in the increasingly competitive situation in which companies find themselves and in a context governed by capital flight in which states and communities are justifiably fearful that businesses will simply go elsewhere, such breaks have "drastically grown."[13]

State, city, and county governments "assemble packages that include the elimination or reduction of sales or property taxes or both, exemptions on new equipment, tax breaks for training new employees and reductions on taxes for school improvements." In some states, the rewards go further. In Florida, for example, companies even get tax breaks for fuel consumption.[14]

This has become a highly politicized area. Teachers on strike in the state of Washington included a specific demand to eliminate corporate tax breaks in their list of grievances. In Cleveland, the school system is facing a $34 million-a-year deficit. The school district has filed a complaint with the courts that maintains that it has been repeatedly damaged by the tax breaks that the city has given to business in "the name of economic development."[15]

The issues surrounding such breaks and outright exemptions are made even more powerful when compared to the withering criticism that the business community has levelled at the schools. This is coupled with the fact that business and industry have engaged in highly publicized programs of gift-giving to specific schools and programs.[16] Such gifts may increase the legitimacy of the business community in the eyes of some members of the public. Yet, it is clear that the amount of money involved in these public displays is considerably less than the taxes that would have been paid. The results are often all too visible in the classrooms of America.

For many chronically poor school districts, the fiscal crisis is so severe that textbooks are used until they literally fall apart. Basements, closets, gymnasiums, and any "available" spaces are used for instruction. Teachers are being laid off, as are counselors and support staff, including school nurses. Art and foreign language programs are being dropped. Extracurricular activities—from athletics to those more socially and academically oriented—are being severely cut back. In some towns and cities, the economic problems are such that it will be impossible for schools to remain open for the full academic year.[17]

The superintendent of schools of one east-coast district puts the situation bluntly: "I think it stinks." Facing even more reductions in essential programs, he concludes: "Nobody seems to care. They just say, 'Cut the Budget'." In the words of Harold Raynolds, Jr., the commissioner of the Massachusetts Department of Education, "We really are in a kind of catastrophic situation."[18]

In the context of such a financial crisis—one that is spreading even to more economically advantaged districts—even those school systems that know that corporate gifts almost never equal the amount that is lost in "tax bargaining" will by necessity look for whatever assistance they can get. A contract with Whittle Communications can seem quite attractive here.

The contract that is signed calls for schools to receive "free" equipment—a satellite dish, two central VCRs, and what amounts to approximately one color television receiver for each classroom—that will enable them to receive the broadcasts. At the same time, schools must guarantee that ninety percent of the pupils will be watching ninety percent of the time.[19] The ten minutes of "news" and two minutes of commercials must be watched every school day for three to five years as part of the contractual agreement.[20]

Always controversial, Channel One has a growing list of strong supporters. Thus, Texas has over 700 schools that are committed to Whittle. One California school voted to reinstate Channel One even in the face of a warning by the state education authorities that they would cut off state funding to schools that were integrated into the network.[21]

The combination of "free" equipment and a content that most educators, community members, and the business community believe is important (the "news") makes it difficult to resist. When combined with Whittle's aggressive advertising campaign, which portrayed Channel One as a crucial ingredient in the transformation of a stagnant and overly bureaucratic educational system that left its students unprepared for the "real world," school officials can be convinced that allowing their students to be something of a "captive audience"[22] is not a bad bargain. Whittle's partial success in this strategy can be seen in the fact that, while states such as New York, California, Rhode Island, and North Carolina have prohibited, regulated, or limited its use, as of June 1991, nearly nine thousand middle schools and high schools had agreed to broadcast Channel One's version of the "news" everyday.[23] At the time of this writing,

Whittle Communications reports that it has more than 11,500 schools under contract.

Economic crisis, a sense of public schooling being in serious trouble, a feeling that students are not being taught the knowledge that they need in order to be competitive, all of this creates conditions in which Channel One becomes acceptable, especially given the increasing success of the Right's hegemonic project of radically altering our discourse about education and all things public that I showed earlier. It can be seen by some educators, then, not only as a warranted trade-off among equipment, "news," and an audience for commercials, but also as a legitimate reform that shows the way for how business and education can cooperate. Indeed, William Rukeyser, executive editor of Channel One and a former managing editor of *Fortune* and *Money* magazines, puts the case this way. Channel One is a "test case for the viability of 'vigorous partnership' between business and education."[24]

CREATING THE CAPTIVE AUDIENCE

We shall miss much that is happening here if we keep our focus only on internal educational issues. Rather, we need to keep in the forefront of our analysis a simple fact. Television such as what we are considering here is first and foremost a business.[25]

Chris Whittle founded Whittle Communications in 1970. Its primary targets have always been what I have called captive audiences such as patients in doctor's offices. In a manner that presaged Channel One, Whittle provided reading material free of charge for patient use, if physicians would guarantee that no other magazines would be made available in the waiting area. Similar things were done with wall posters on health related issues, the assumption being that people with "time on their hands" would naturally read anything available, including material on a wall. Of course, advertisements were a key part of all the material.

In 1976, Whittle had revenues of $3 million. By 1989, its revenues topped $152 million at the beginning of the pilot project for Channel One. After its inception, revenues jumped to $210 million by June 1991.[26]

After completing the pilot program for Channel One, Whittle was more than a little optimistic, and deservedly so. Its field representatives aggressively recruited school systems throughout the country. The goal was to contract 1,000 schools by March 1990, and 8,000 schools by 1992. Contracts exceeded that goal considerably by 1991.[27]

According to Whittle spokespersons, this represented an initial
outlay of approximately $200 million; to earn a profit, the enterprise

would have to earn $85-to-$100 million each year. By October, 1989, Whittle had sold more than $149 million worth of commercials in three and four year contracts, with $51 million for 1990—over half the launch revenue projections. To put these figures in perspective, the ESPN television network [a popular sports-only network] sold only $10 million worth of commercials in its first year, and . . . [the] CNN network only $24 million.[28]

Channel One's rapid rise is truly phenomenal. After two years of development, it was launched nationally in March 1990. By June of 1991, it had involved 8,700 schools in forty-seven states, plus the District of Columbia. It had a viewing audience of 5.4 million students. Even then, this was fully one-third of the population of thirteen to eighteen year olds in the entire nation,[29] and as I noted, its growth is continuing.

Whittle Communication's recognition of the realities of the fiscal crisis and how it can be used rhetorically is clear. Declaring the uniqueness of Channel One in comparison to other attempts at producing news for classrooms, a spokesperson for Whittle put it succinctly. What sets Channel One apart from any of the others is one word: "equipment." No one else "provides schools with the equipment to receive and use their programming in the classrooms. [Other] services provide quality programming but it is like having a lot of gasoline and no automobile. Both have to be available to get anywhere."[30]

Yet, this is more complicated than it seems at first glance. The idea of a captive audience is given added meaning in that not only are students sold as commodities to advertisers, but the satellite antennae themselves are *fixed* to the Channel One station and cannot be used to receive other programs. In essence, after the pilot program—which did offer "free hardware"—Whittle's representatives offered only free installation and the use, not the ownership, of a satellite dish and a number of television monitors.[31] The equipment itself would be lost if the contract was not continued.

Employing the discourse of the fiscal crisis as a rhetoric of justification has proven to be very effective, even given the fact that the "gift" of equipment is not quite as it seems. Yet, this discursive strategy doesn't fully encompass how Whittle works ideologically on the fears of many groups of people.

In order to accomplish its economic goals, Whittle became even more subtle in its attempts to link its concerns to the ideological tensions and conflicts being produced in the current "educational crisis." Whittle's own advertising strategy capitalized on a particular construction of the literacy crisis. Students simply do not know enough about the world around them to participate effectively in a democratic society. Thus, one advertisement gives the example of a student who thought that Jesse Jackson was a baseball player and that silicon chips were a type of snack food.[32]

Whittle continually plays on this feeling that students are horribly misinformed about the world, given the texts and teaching now found in schools. In other material promoting Channel One, it is seen as a workable solution to the problems generated by the fact that many secondary schools students identified "the District of Columbia as a Central American country and Chernobyl as Cher's full name."[33] Hence, at the same time, both business and education would form a partnership "in which each party receives direct and immediate benefits."[34]

This strategy of combining the overt urge to provide educational assistance with the aggressive search for profit has not been lost on the business community. Advertising agencies have also been quick to recognize the linkage between "ignorance of the world" and product advantage. As a number of advertising directors put it, as a "media vehicle" Channel One "is a very interesting medium for reaching an audience that's hard to reach." "It's an age when [students have] got to take tests on American and world geography and have no idea not only what the capitol of their state is, or who their senators are, but think that Calcutta is a team on the National Football League. If this helps teach, and get facts across in an interesting and meaningful way, I don't see why educators wouldn't endorse it." With all this said, however, the primary reason advertisers have looked so positively on Channel One is stated rather starkly by one advertising executive. "Channel One provides an excellent targeting opportunity."[35]

That this is a *profitable* strategy is documented by the fact that a thirty-second commercial spot on Channel One was selling for approximately $120,000 in mid–1991. This should rise as more schools accept the program. To place this in context, it is a figure that is at least double that of the top-rated, prime-time news program. That this is a profitable *strategy* is evident in Whittle's own words. "Underneath everything we do . . . is the concept of targeted, high-impact, proprietary media systems. . . . Home-based media has dramatically declined as an environment for sending advertising messages. Place-based helps you target."[36]

Surrounding this, though, is still the public justification of providing content and material to schools who can ill afford it. Thus, Whittle points out that expenditures for "defense" are ten-times larger than those spent on education, at the very same time that in many states the amount of money spent on textbooks annually is as low as $20 per student. As one spokesperson put it, "Somebody has to pay the bill for education, and commercials are the most direct way to pay."[37]

Notice what is happening here. At the same time that capital is involved in intense struggles to reduce the amount of taxes it pays and is engaged in concerted political, economic, and ideological attacks on schools,[38] Whittle and its supporters are able to sell their own package of reforms by pointing out that business—through payments for commercials—will be paying for an enhanced education in citizenship for American students. The contradictions here are remarkable.

In the process, not only are schools increasingly incorporated into the market governed by the "laws" of supply and demand and by the "ethic" of capital accumulation, but students themselves become commodities. They too are bought and sold as "targets of marketing opportunity" to large corporations. Of course, schools have always been subject to pressure—often intense—by economically powerful groups. At the level of curriculum, as well, as I showed in chapter four, conglomerate publishers of textbooks have always seen schools and their pupils as sites for the generation of profit. Yet there is an immense qualitative difference between wanting the educational system to do a better job at the "production of human capital" or at buying textbooks and material for classroom use and the actual selling of students as potential consumers.

CULTURAL POLITICS

In the previous section, I have provided part of the picture of the political economy of Channel One. I have situated the discursive strategies employed within the crisis in the economy, in ideology, and in authority relations, and have shown why many schools have literally jumped at the chance to "sign on the dotted line" with Whittle Communications. Yet, the fact that these schools are now officially open to advertising's purview does not exhaust what should concern us. There is a cultural politics involved concerning the content and form of what gets broadcast to classrooms and what students and teachers do with it. The economics of the fiscal crisis and the struggle over it point to the material conditions surrounding Channel One's growth. These conditions are but one aspect of what Richard Johnson has called the circuit of cultural production, that of the production of the commodity itself.[39] Other aspects of production—the production of and struggle over *meaning* itself—are essential elements in the process. This very issue leads us to a difficult kind of analysis of Channel One.

Here, the terrain on which we need to operate seeks to offer insights into the ways that meanings are made and circulated. It focuses on the roles both these meanings and their organization play in the structure of society and in the structure of the consciousness and unconsciousness of the subjects of these societies. Thus, this kind of cultural study is about the "incessant play of meanings that relate the subject to the social system" and that underpin and maintain, and sometimes subvert, that system.[40]

Television inside or outside of schools is involved in the *struggle for meaning*. Like textbooks, it is not simply a transparent medium that reflects or conveys "information" about the "real world" into classrooms and living rooms.[41] In general, in order to understand this, we need to investigate a number of dimensions of television discourse. Combining all four dimensions enables a richer sense of how the discourse and meaning of television have a political dimension in which the ways of making sense and the sense that is made are related to a culture's dominant ways of producing, circulating, and maintaining power.[42]

First, we need to analyze "how television constructs a picture of the world, and how it makes sense of the real." This will enable us to show "how it hides its sense-making processes so that the viewer's attention is kept on *what* is shown, and not *how* it is shown." Second, we need to take the next step of "theorizing the work these meanings perform in and on the viewing subject." In essence, this step asks us to examine the media's ideological work in helping to construct subjectivity and consciousness.[43]

Third, we must then relate this ideological work to the discursive form and mode of address of the television discourse. That is, we connect "those television forms and subject positions to the way that power is distributed and exercised in our social system."[44]

Fourth, as I argued in chapter three, we need to examine closely the negotiated and oppositional "readings" of television, thereby moving away from the idea of television or any "text" as closed, as a site where dominant meanings automatically exert considerable or total influence over its reader.[45] Where are the gaps and spaces that open up television to meanings and reading strategies that may not be the preferred ones?[46] The question is not the "effects" of television, but rather "how a particular television work, seen as a polysemic potential of meanings, connects with the social life of the viewer or group of viewers." How is a "television text" created by the active reading of an audience? How does the process of common-sense making operate?[47]

In a chapter of this size, I cannot complete all of these analyses. However, I can suggest what they mean for a more complex cultural understanding of Channel One in the context of the conservative restoration. I shall begin with how "the news" in general constructs a picture of the world.

DOING THE NEWS

It is now all but a truism to say that cultural practices are not simply derived from or mirror an already existing social order, but are themselves major elements in the constitution of that social order. Thus, "reality" is brought into existence, is built, through the "construction, apprehension and utilization of symbolic forms."[48] While it would be foolish to infer effects simply from the ways these symbolic forms are themselves made available to the public, it would be equally foolish to ignore how the interpretive patterns that dominate symbolic productions like the news "cultivate particular assumptions, images and associations among readers and viewers."[49]

Meaning in the media is both variable and patterned. It is variable because real people actively intervene, interrupt, and create meanings in interaction with the media. It is patterned by the social, economic, and political conventions that set limits on what can and cannot be said or shown, and on who can say and show it.[50]

Many people have raised questions about Channel One's inclusion of commercials. It is evident from my arguments that I too am deeply concerned. Yet, also at issue is *the news itself.* What will be "reported"? Whose news? Under what ideological umbrella? What do we know about what counts as news in general that should make us very cautious of Channel One's continuation of these tendencies, a continuation that becomes even more obvious the more Channel One is seen?

As in previous analyses of the importance of the curriculum form on ideological practices in school,[51] so too is the form around which television news is organized essential to a more complete understanding of what "the news" does. As Jamieson and Campbell put it:

> Stories are stories. News reports, particularly televised news reports, are likely to be shaped into a narrative-dramatic structure. This kind of structure not only gives coherence to various bits of data, but is the natural structure for emphasizing action, drama, and conflict. Even within the conventional structure of the print story—moving from more important to less important facts—a news item is likely to begin with an action identified as a problem, develop through a narrative of increasing tension and conflict . . . and close with a suggested or predicted resolution. This structure dominates coverage in television news. It is ideally suited to reporting single, dramatic events, to presenting characters (spokespersons who are quoted), to focusing on action, and to covering novel exciting events. Conversely, it is ill suited to coverage of an idea, concept, or process.[52]

The form, then, that the news takes is critical. Equally important, however, is the content itself since both the content *and* the ways it interacts with the narrative form of news stories are crucial elements in constructing an "understandable reality." In my analysis, we have to examine both to see how they work.

How we think about something makes a difference. Let me give an example. We are now quite accustomed to seeing pictures of disasters in which thousands of people lose their lives due to storms, drought, and so forth. We are told to think of these as "natural" disasters. But is this the appropriate way of understanding the situation, or is it really a form of category error?

Take the massive mudslides that occurred in parts of South America in which large numbers of people were killed as torrential rains washed their houses down the mountainsides. A closer examination of this case reveals nothing natural about this at all. Every year there are rains, and every year some people die. This particular year an entire side of a mountain gave way. "Only" the thousands of people living on it lost their lives. No one in the valleys—the safe and fertile land—died. Poor families are forced to live on the dangerous hillsides. This is the only land they can find in which to eke out an existence that is barely survivable. They crowd onto this land not because they want to, but because of poverty and because of the land-ownership patterns that are historically and grossly unequal.

Hence, the problem is not the yearly rains—a "natural" occurrence—but the economic structures that allow only a small minority of individuals to control the very lives of the bulk of the people of that region. Notice that this altered understanding of the problem would require a different practice. Not only would we send immediate aid to help the "victims" of the rains, we would need to engage in a large-scale program of land redistribution to make it much more equal.

The ability to understand this, to deconstruct and reconstruct what counts as "the news," is of great importance to teachers and students given the way "news" is constructed on television. News is constructed usually as what disrupts the normal. Life is seen as "ordinarily smoothrunning, rule- and law-abiding, and harmonious."[53] If it is not, it ought to be. Such a set of norms is not descriptive. Rather these norms are inherently prescriptive.[54] They embody the values and beliefs of dominant groups by representing "a sense of what our social life ought to be not what it is."[55] The effects of this on our vision of people in other nations can be profound.

In his analysis of the ways the news presents Third World nations, John Fiske makes exactly this point.

The unstated, ideological norms which make this conceptual strategy possible are those of *our* society. Negative events in another part of the world do not bear the same relationship to these norms and are therefore read differently. Third World countries are, for example, conventionally represented in western news as places of famines and natural disasters, of social revolution, and of political corruption. These events are not seen as disrupting *their* social norms, but as confirming ours, confirming our dominant sense that western democracies provide the basics for life for everyone, are stable, and fairly and honestly governed. When deviations from those norms occur in our own countries they are represented as precisely that, deviations from the norm; in Third World countries, however, such occurrences are represented as *their* norms which differ markedly from ours. For the western news media, the Third World is a place of natural and political disasters.[56]

What students and teachers are getting in "the news" then is quite important. It does not lessen the incorporation of commercialism into the schools, but compliments it. The news is often "bad." "Good news is added to counterpoise it, to set it up as a deviation from the norm, how this society is organized today." The fact that this normative assumption is unspoken, is part of what we might call the hidden curriculum of the news the students will see, makes it even more powerful.[57]

The "natural" disaster example I employed was not accidental. T.V. news usually focuses on crimes, scandals, and disasters.[58] How it does this and who defines what counts as a crime, scandal, and disaster is significant. Let us begin with whose voices are heard and how they are organized, for as we shall see, the "voices" of television are more than a little selective.

For example, production-line and government workers historically have been nearly invisible on network and local news coverage. Corporate views have been much more likely to be shown than the views of workers on crucial issues.[59] This points to the utter importance of understanding not only what is there, but what is *not there*, the absent presences of television news.

If we take just one example—how unemployment is dealt with—we can see this clearly. While the people most frequently appearing on camera for those reports are unemployed persons, in essence they have no voice. They are a visual backdrop which authenticates the "reality" of the story against which "authoritative sources" speak. These "primary definers" are usually the president and members of his administration or other government officials.[60]

In a recent analysis of news accounts of unemployment, most of the stories dealt with industrial labor, not the service sector, both in their verbal and visual (closed factories, idle smokestacks, etc.) forms. There were very few accounts of unemployed service workers, secretaries, information processors, and government workers, even though their ranks are swelling. Added to this was the fact that even fewer (less than five percent) dealt with black unemployment or the lack of paid employment for women (less than one percent).[61]

Only a relatively small proportion of the stories contained any explanation for unemployment. Part of this is because television news is almost always drawn to consequences, not to causes. Also, a direct explanation (misguided policies, conscious attempts by capital to discipline workers, etc.) would open the broadcast to charges of bias.

Yet, even without overt explanations, there were a number of fragmentary themes that underlay the treatment. The dominant theme is "times are tough." Individuals or groups are portrayed as under duress, unable to find work; the situation is in essence causeless. No human actors, no groups, stand behind this situation or carry any responsibility for it. Individuals and groups are victims of the current situations. But, times can change. The crisis will pass. All will be better soon. These pessimistic and optimistic currents—both of which are present—are the "natural" progression of events that reside outside of our control.[62]

Yet, even here, there is enough diversity in the way this theme is handled in the news broadcasts to enable multiple interpretations. Society was viewed as both caring and uncaring, fair and unfair, technologically advanced or entering a period of steep decline.[63] Dominant readings *were* advanced, though in a manner that was less consistent than those might expect who hold to the idea that there is only one dominant ideology "reflected" by the medium. However, the combination of many explanations and themes organized around primary definers' views clearly limits one's sense of political efficacy.[64] Yes, "times are tough," but the reasons and the answers are out of our hands. Ideological contradictions are recognized, but they are solved on a terrain that favors dominant groups.

So much for the domestic scenes "represented" on the news in ways which—after having watched an extensive sampling of it—are closely followed by Channel One. Behind Channel One, however, is a criticism that students not only do not understand national events of importance, but they cannot be "world citizens" in an intensely competitive international economy unless they also "know the world" as well. How the world is known then is more than a little important. While this is a complex issue both conceptually and geographically, by focusing on three areas— Africa, Latin America, and Eastern Europe (in this case, Poland)—we can see what meanings are made available by newscasts in general upon which Channel One patterns itself.

CONSTRUCTING THE OTHER

As Jo Ellen Fair reminds us, "minority" groups and "minority" cultures have consistently been neglected in the media except for activities that are considered violent or confrontational.[65] In essence, in the absence of alternative portrayals of, say, Africans and African-Americans, the news seems to indicate that violence is "endemic to black culture" (remember my son and the fight on the playground) and is somehow a "natural" occurrence.[66] Blacks *are* mentioned, but what counts as "black" is incorporated into hegemonic discourse, just as in the textbooks I discussed earlier.

It is the discourse of "tribalism" that seems to dominate news accounts. Thus, in treatments of Africa, conflict "appears as seemingly incomprehensible self-destruction. It is irrational and primitive—in a word, "tribal." This is not limited to the treatment of conflict in, say, South Africa. A similar repertoire of visual and linguistic codes have often been employed to represent black youth actions in Britain and the United States.[67]

Rather than addressing violence as part of South Africa's political struggle, it is reduced to the discourse of political and cultural underdevelopment. It is the black population that is irrational, not yet ready for democracy. The dominant white South African government is the "rational peace keeper,"[68] the group that is engaged in serious compromises in the face of an uncertain, yet surely violent, future. In essence, it is the white capitalist West—ultimately rational and willing to be fair—that is the "keeper of the flame" against the persistent crisis caused by irrational native people. Yet, if this is the case for Africa, it is not only the case for Africa.

For instance, research on the content of "foreign" news reporting documents the correctness of the persistent claims by Third World nations that Western news media overplays crisis in these nations. Thus, in general the news "tends to emphasize single events which occur in the present or the immediate past and that 'the political affairs of foreign lands appear as spasmodic convulsions of a more or less violent turn.' "[69]

Where the news is from and how it is dealt with intermix in this situation. Recent investigations have demonstrated that over the last decade, Latin America and Africa receive considerably less coverage than, say, Europe and the Middle East. But it is not only the raw data on coverage that is important here. What specific *kinds* of coverage, from what specific *sources,* is crucial. A large proportion of coverage about Latin America, for example, was not done by on-the-spot correspondents. Rather, it was based on reporting from domestic sources. As the authors of an analysis of how United States networks report events in Latin America put it:

> As a region, Latin America led the world in the proportion of network reporting in the domestic video format, the "official Washington" story. While perhaps not surprising for the region which is a hemispheric neighbor over which the U.S. has historically exercised a degree of hegemony, [this] deserves careful scrutiny.[70]

Here again form and content intermix in important ways, constructing interpretations that limit alternative and oppositional readings of events and tendencies.

MAKING THE OTHER FAMILIAR

Foreign news tends to focus on personalities rather than social forces or social processes. Such news is ordered around "the primacy of the individual." It is the "personal subject" who is the engine of history.[71] The dominance of Lech Walesa in reports about Solidarity in Poland provides a clear example. While Walesa was important, by repeatedly focusing on him the broadcast news reduced social movements to "the great man" and, in essence, masked the origin and evolution of social movements and their importance in collective action.[72] In the process, the often radical demands by the movement's rank and file—full employment, the elimination of wage and social inequalities between enterprises, an income policy that guaranteed favorable treatment to the poorer segments of society, and similar positions—were deemphasized or not mentioned at all.[73] Egalitarianism was not on the agenda. The "simple worker" against the repressive state was.

The idea of *bits of data* is important here. Television news can be thought of as "one thing after another," sometimes randomly so. The "bits of news" in the stories presented about Solidarity continually stressed the culturally familiar: charismatic leadership, religious impulses for change, demands for political democracy, Poland's relations to the superpowers, and economic problems. The televised news "narrowed the ideological disharmony between the Polish workers' rebellion and contemporary American politics." It ignored Solidarity's relationship to the politics of worker control and egalitarian "welfare" policies. In the process, the news broadcasts "avoided concerns divorced from and antagonistic to the

American political mainstream. That the network news failed to even raise these concerns illuminates the ideological dimensions of news judgments and story selection."[74] That this was reinforced by the routine reliance on interpretations of what the story "actually was" given out by the State Department and Pentagon officials is worthy to note.[75]

In sum, American news media—and this is clear on Channel One as well as on newscasts in general—consistently define international events and especially foreign social movements in ways that confirm the dominant political meanings and values of American society.[76] These definitions have their contradictions, of course. They are not simply unalloyed expressions of dominance. Yet, what counts as news, who has the power to speak about it, and what the discourse over it actually does, all of this creates the conditions of existence for limiting the possible readings of the news to dominant ones. Alternative and oppositional readings *are* possible, something I point out later; but they are clearly made more difficult to accomplish.

STILL TO BE DONE

An examination of what counts as national and international news on Channel One documents a similar pattern of construction, though there are differences. There are more "human interest" stories and more stories geared to teenagers. Further, in one series of reports, Russian and American teenagers talked directly to each other via Channel One's satellite hook up, thereby enhancing Channel One's claim to help students become "world citizens." Also, the people presenting the news—the "talking heads"—are different than what one might find on regular broadcast news. The newscasters are less formal, more youthlike in their appearance. Finally, the news and commercials blend together in an almost seamless way.[77] These similarities and differences are worthy of further investigation, as are a number of others I now note.

It has long been noted that the media not only "reflect" the changing conditions of a society, but they actively *produce* interpretations of events and people. As I just showed, this is done in fact by selecting and emphasizing certain "stories" over others. It is accomplished as well by the visual and linguistic codes that structure the presentation of the news.

I have not spoken of the visual imagery and format used, how the codes of television news (e.g., the ways interviews framed by crowds can suggest the potential irrationality of collective action) all act to connote specific preferred readings of power relations and interpretations both of what counts as "the news" and who has the right to report it.[78] Nor have I talked about the way internal power relations and production values enter into this (e.g., the fact that actors, action, and objects *that can be filmed* are the foundation of television news).[79]

Nor have I taken up the concept of "planned flow." For example, Raymond Williams reminds us of the need to understand television not as a string of discrete units—news, programs, commercials, etc.—but as a flow. News, programs, and commercials merge together into an unbroken flow. The ideological efficacy is found as much here as in the "message embodied" in the units themselves.[80] This may be crucial in analyzing Channel One, since a number of its commercials, though certainly not all, take the form of "public service messages" (stay in school; don't use drugs) that make them difficult to distinguish from "the news." And, as I noted above, news and commercials flow together, creating a partial mixing of the standard codes of television.[81]

Finally, in order to go further we need to engage in the labor-intensive task of what Stuart Hall called the "long preliminary soak," examining the stabilities and transformations of what counts as news and the codes of its presentation over time on Channel One, constantly comparing it to other newscasts. Who are the "primary definers" of the news? Who speaks authoritatively and who does not? What are the recurring patterns, emphases, and images that constitute the discourse?[82] How does the news change as the fortunes of rightist movements themselves change? And, of course, how is all this "read" by teachers and students *in classrooms?* It is to this that I now turn.

CONTRADICTION INSIDE THE CLASSROOM?

Channel One, of course, is aimed at someone. But is the "message sent" the "message received"? Is it possible that Whittle's Channel One serves the interests of the dominant and subordinated at one and the same time? Can it be read oppositionally or subversively? What do the vast range of students—defined by the contradictory dynamics of race, class, gender, sexuality, religion, region, and so on—actually *do* with Channel One?

It is possible to claim that the realm of meaning "is as much a site of struggle as is economics or party politics." Television programs including "the news" attempt, but often fail, to control meaning "in the same way that social authority attempts (but fails) to stifle voices and strategies of opposition."[83] John Fiske, at his usual sardonic best, puts it this way. The consumers of television "are not cultural dupes lapping up any pap that is produced for them."[84]

As we know, there is usually an "excess of meaning" in television. Even when dominant interests are served by the television news itself, there are levels of potential meaning that spill over the banks of dominant control and that are available for different readings by subordinate groups.[85]

While this can be taken too far, behind this is a recognition that subjectivity is constructed both socially and discursively. Meanings are polysemic. There can be and are multiple meanings in any situation. And those as well can be more than a little contradictory. They are constructed around one's experience in social institutions such as gender, class, race, nation, region, religion, and so on.[86]

> Society [then] is not a collection of individuals, each bearing the same and equal relationship to the whole, but rather a complex network of categories of people, each related to others via differential relations of power and control; any individual is a member of different categories. These categories must necessarily imply different and potentially contradictory relationships to each other. Subjectivity, therefore, is neither unified nor coherent, but a mass of contradictions.[87]

These very contradictions allow for multiple readings, readings of the news that may not cohere with dominant interpretations even when Channel One and the other broadcast news try to limit possible readings to those largely acceptable within the hegemonic accord of a particular period.

Thus, what counts as "the news" may be actively deconstructed by students. Just as Willis demonstrates in *Common Culture*,[88] where youth construct and reconstruct aesthetic and political meanings that may be very different from those that are officially sponsored or made available to them by the market in cultural commodities, so too may youth in school do similar things with Channel One's version of the news.

As a number of people remind us, students are engaged in constant attempts to make sense out of their social experience. Television plays no small part in that sense-making struggle.[89] Thus, students seeing television dramas about prisons often exploit the potential for multiple meanings by actively comparing their own experiences of powerlessness in schools with those of prisoners. Aboriginal children in Australia when "reading" television shows that portray African-Americans and Native American's as being defeated or misunderstood, actively construct a category which includes blacks, Indians, and themselves in opposition to dominant meanings. "Reading television in this way provided them with a means of articulating their own powerlessness in a white dominated society."[90] If the "ability to articulate one's experience is a necessary pre-requisite for developing the will to change it," then the active reading strat-egies of these children is evidence that students have at least some of the resources to do this.[91] The same is undoubtedly true not only for televi-sion dramas, but for the news as well.

There can be another more hidden curricular impact of Channel One, however. The news that is broadcast is seen by students at a special time each day. Thus, "the news" is set aside. It is walled in and set apart from "real knowledge." In Bernstein's terms, it is strongly classified and strongly framed.[92] Yet, by admitting that the world outside the school, outside of academic knowledge, is essential and now has an officially sanctioned and recontextualized place in school's daily life, it enables the conflicts and tensions of society to enter into the school. It creates a space for the very semiotic surplus of meaning that could enable further interrogation of the routine curriculum to go on. If "reality" is like this, why isn't the rest of the curriculum? Could this create subtle pressures upon what now counts as more legitimate knowledge? Is a situation of intertextuality cre-ated in which academic content is seen *in relation to* what is excluded—the more exciting news of the "real world"? This is worth thinking more about in terms of the possibility of different, more critical, readings of the official curriculum by students and teachers. The impact on how students might "read" the textbooks I discussed earlier might be more than a little interesting.

In fact, there is some evidence that the subject content of regular classes is being partly transformed to bring it more closely into line with the content of Channel One's news.[93] Whether this will lead to partial de-constructions of what counts as legitimate knowledge or to further incor-poration of students into the ideological categories that I showed now organize the news remains to be seen.

Yet, even if students do not always engage in such deconstruction, even if they may not create alternative or oppositional rather than dominant readings of Channel One's version of the news or of the official curricu-lum, students in general are active in other ways that are more than a little interesting. For instance, ongoing research by my colleague Ann DeVaney indicates that students often ignore the news content of Channel One. They often talk to each other while it is on, do homework, etc. *What they do watch is the commercials.*[94]

In many instances, the news was unimportant. Students and teachers used Channel One for different purposes. In a discussion with me of what teachers and students did with Channel One, teachers often pointed to the benefits at the same time as they described what students did. As one teacher from Texas put it, "The best thing about it is the VCR. The kids and I basically ignore the news. But we can use the VCR in a lot of other areas." The idea of schools *using Whittle* to get what they can't usually afford documents the strategic moves going on from below and this is important. The VCR allows very different definitions of official knowledge, given the wide array of material now available on videotape. However, and this is crucial to my argument, this is leavened by the fact that this same teacher continued, saying that "It was the commercials that got to the kids. My seventh and eighth grade students would try to guess which commercials would be on and would sing along with the jingles."

Here, we need to understand what *pleasure* students get from commercials in the classroom as opposed to the normal routine of school life, even when this normal routine may deal with similar kinds of "news." There is a complicated politics of pleasure at work here. Commercials provide an opportunity for "play," for collective enjoyment. The commercials are sometimes even parodied in a manner not unlike Bakhtin's discussion of how carnival is employed to subvert authority.[95]

This possible subversion is contradictory, of course. One *pays attention* to commercials. Even with the joy, one is at the same time addressed as a consumer, positioned as a purchaser. While postmodern theory asks us to pay particular attention to the politics of consumption as a site of possible emancipatory actions, we still need to remember that here the students cannot collectively employ such subversions in any lasting collective ways.

Thus, as in other instances of potential resistance I have pointed to throughout this book, we need to be very careful about being romantic here. Channel One is seen by students and teachers inside classrooms, and the structures of classroom life as well as the political economy of teachers' time and labor may make it very difficult for either teachers or students to engage in a *disciplined* deconstruction of Channel One that would lead to a more organized critical sense of the politics of the news or of the carnivalesque nature of commercials.

Hence, where television is viewed is essential. The experiences of viewing it at home are very different than in a classroom.[96] Television here does not stand alone. It is situated into the daily flow of classroom events. It is both respite from and continuation of the formal curriculum and the formal patterns of classroom interaction. Analysis of its "effects" must understand that.

Of course, as I noted, neither students nor teachers will be passive "consumers" of what Channel One broadcasts. They will actively construct and reconstruct the meanings of what is reported while watching and listening to it. Nor will all of these constructions of meanings be the same. They will be a contradictory assemblage of responses based on the class, gender, race, religion, region, sexuality, and age relations in which people are formed.[97]

Yet, as I demonstrate in much greater detail in the next chapter, this may be difficult, especially for teachers, given the *intensification* of their work. Teachers' work is becoming considerably more time consuming. Almost never is anything dropped from the curriculum. Instead, time and again, more is added. And given the steady growth of accountability measures and tests, the amount of paperwork for which teachers are responsible is often overwhelming. Channel One enters this situation as one more addition. It is more than a little romantic to assume that teachers will always be able to spend already scarce time on deconstructing the news or "playing" with the commercials.

Thus, as teachers' work becomes increasingly intensified, there may be almost no time to counteract the way the news is portrayed. Here, I am not only discussing what time pressures will be like in classrooms, though that will be of considerable moment. We also need to focus on the lack of time outside the classroom as well. As I argued in *Teachers and Texts*[98] and as I show in the next chapter, many teachers have very little time even to simply keep up with their respective fields, more and more having to rely on outside "experts" and prepackaged curricular material and standardized texts given the immense pressures placed on them to do and teach more in their classrooms.

This pressure-cooker atmosphere spills over into one's time at home as well. As Andrew Gitlin[99] documents, the amount of paperwork that needs to be done by teachers has now often reached such extreme levels that many teachers come in early in the morning and stay late after school, as well as face up to two more hours at home each night, simply to keep up with the daily record keeping, grading, and so on. This situation has been exacerbated considerably by the current accountability movement where one gets the impression that administrators, legislators, neo-conservatives, and economically powerful groups have tacitly said that, in classrooms, if it moves it must be measured.

I do not wish to be "cute" here. In such an intensified situation—where there is always more to do and less time to do it for students as well as teachers—it is unrealistic in the extreme to assume that most teachers will easily find the time and resources to expand and/or reconstruct what Whittle Communications has determined is "the news." Whose "news," guided by what norms and values, taking what vision of society for granted, are questions of immense interest here. Commercials act as a "relief" in this situation, even while offering the theoretical possibility of something more interesting politically.[100]

With this said, however, it is clear that the process through which students and teachers produce their own meanings about "the news" is complex. The social situation and material conditions in which it is watched may limit what meanings are created, but both students and teachers will not simply internalize "the message sent." The polysemic quality of the medium, the surplus of meanings available, the play allowed by the commercials, the lack of focus by students on the news itself, and the different readings that different students will make of all this, should make us sensitive to the complicated realities of cultural politics here. And all of this *does* offer possibilities for sensitive and committed teachers. But, once again, being sensitive and being naive about how students are positioned as consumers and sold as commodities, about whose perspectives *are* being presented, are not the same thing. We still need to face up to what is happening as honestly as possible.

CONCLUSION

In my previous analysis of the politics of textbooks, I demonstrated how the economic, ideological, and cultural pressures from above and below created the context in which textbooks came to dominate the curriculum in many nations, and often provided the rightist coalition with important mechanisms of influence.[101] In the process, I argued against imposition theories. Rather, educational policy and practice are the result of compromises at many levels with dominant groups attempting to shift the terms of the compromise onto their own terrain. The example of Channel One demonstrates how a depressed economy, the discourse of crisis, and the concrete needs of schools create the conditions of existence for the creation of students as a captive audience. A business/ school partnership is formed in which business gets profits and legitimacy while schools get equipment and students get to be "informed citizens."

Yet, inside the classroom, Channel One is partly recontextualized.[102] While the content and form of the news largely conforms to dominant interpretations of the world, students and teachers partly mediate and transform it. These mediations and transformations are limited by daily classroom life, but they do exist.

However, Channel One as a phenomenon also signifies something well beyond what happens to students and teachers in classrooms. It is a paradigm case of the social transformation of our ideas about public and private, and about schooling itself.

It is not just at the level of social goals or curriculum and teaching that the "industrialization" of education has proceeded. Channel One stands at the intersection of other tendencies as well. As I showed earlier, the Right has attempted to alter our very perception of schooling itself, turning it away from the idea of a common ground in which democracy is hammered out (an intensely *political* idea involving interactive notions of citizenship in a polity). Instead, the common ground of the school becomes no longer based on a set of democratic political commitments (no matter how weak before); rather, it is replaced by the idea of a competitive marketplace. The citizen as a political being with reciprocal rights and duties is lost. In its place is the self as *consumer.* Schooling (and students) becomes a "retail product."[103] Freedom in a democracy is no longer defined as participating in building the common good, but as living in an unfettered commercial market, with the educational system now being seen as needing to be integrated into the mechanisms of such a market.[104]

I have discussed the inherent weaknesses of these proposals—such as voucher and choice plans and the like—elsewhere.[105] The important point is to see the ideological reconstruction that is going on, to understand that in the process of making the school (or in the case of Channel One, the students as a "captive audience") into a product to be bought and sold, we are radically altering our definitions of what it means to participate in our institutions. Participation has been reduced to the commercialization of all important public social interaction.[106] The unattached individual, one whose only rights and duties are determined by the marketplace, becomes ascendant. While we don't want to be overly economistic in our analyses, the ideological imprint of our economy is hard to miss here. There may be few examples more powerful or symbolic of this than Channel One.[107]

Convincing the public at large to see education as a product to be evaluated for its economic utility and as a commodity to be bought and sold like anything else in the "free market" has required a good deal of hard ideological work on the part of the Right. This has meant that the citizenry must be convinced that what is public is bad and what is private is good.

Hugh Stetton evokes the tenor of these claims when he says that

> the commonest trick is this: of people's individual spending, mention *only the prices they pay.* When they buy a private car and a public road to drive it on, present the car as a benefit and the road as a tax or a cost. Tell how the private sector is the productive sector which gives us food, clothing, houses, cars, holidays and all good things, while the public sector gives us nothing but red tape and tax demands.[108]

While the convictions of a majority of the American people may not have been totally swayed by such conservative ideological tendencies, it is clear that the processes of redefinition are part of the larger strategies involved in the conservative restoration. As recent polls have shown, in fact, there has been clear movement toward acceptance of some of the positions embodied by the Right by groups within the larger society.[109]

The fact that Channel One is growing so rapidly indicates that it is not only at the level of ideology that such acceptance can be found. The internal dynamics of curriculum and teaching inside our classrooms—and our very children themselves—are now subject to major transformations. Like all "citizens," students will now be known as consumers. But, for our children we will now go further. They will be bought and sold, consumed, as well. And all this is happening with a more "moderate" administration in Washington.

Channel One, then, is a symbol of the results of the transformations we are experiencing every day. Its roots lie in the conservative restoration and in the "opportunities" this restoration has given to business to slowly transform the educational system into one more site for the generation of profit. In everyday life, there is good news and bad news and news in between. Channel One is bad news.

Channel One does exist though. And it is growing in importance. Even given the intensified situation faced by many teachers, Channel One offers critically oriented teachers an opportunity to do some very interesting educational work with students in middle schools and high schools. It provides the context for a serious deconstruction—*with students*—of its content and form, of its ethics of selling students as audiences, and of its interests. It does offer technology that students themselves can "play" with, using the VCR and the monitors to broadcast their own productions and meanings,[110] and to make parodies of and reconstruct "the news." As Paul Willis reminds us, our cultural lives are continually structured by location and situation. However, as he goes on to say, locations and situations are not only to be understood as determinations. They are also, and profoundly, "relations and resources to be discovered, explored, and experienced." They are lived and experimented with. This is so even if only by pushing up against the oppressive limits of established order and power.[111] While I argued earlier against an overly romantic position on this situation, it is still crucial that we understand the *critical* possibilities that something like Channel One offers. Good teachers have always somehow managed, with students, to challenge the limits of accepted bureaucratic and ideological structures. Channel One provides not only a way of making this harder to do, but an opportunity to once again show what can be done.

6 Whose Curriculum Is this Anyway? (with Susan Jungck)

INTRODUCTION

Channel One, with its economic and ideological agendas and its growing acceptance, is a powerful example of the effects of the conservative restoration. Yet in some ways, because it is such an overt attempt at transforming schools into sites for the generation of profit, we may miss equally significant effects if we focus only on such overt programs and policies. To see this, we need to go inside some classrooms where the changing politics of official knowledge has had a significant impact on the lives of students and especially teachers because of other aspects of the rightist reconstruction. These aspects are concerned with creating the conditions for linking schools to the paid labor needs of our economy. In this instance, class and gender relations will play a very significant part, with racial dynamics being present by virtue of their absence because of economic and residential segregation in housing patterns in the United States. (The absence of people of color, thus, often is just as important as their presence in a racially structured society such as this.)

TEACHING IN CRISIS

With all of the rhetoric about teaching and professionalism, about enhancing teachers' power and about raising pay and respect, the reality of many teachers' lives bears little resemblance to the rhetoric during this period of conservative triumphalism. Rather than moving in the direction of increased autonomy, in all too many instances the daily lives of teachers in classrooms in many nations are becoming ever more controlled, ever more subject to administrative logics that seek to tighten the reins on the processes of teaching and curriculum. Teacher development, cooperation, and "empowerment" may be the talk, but centralization, standardization, and rationalization may be the strongest tendencies, even with the increasing media focus on privatization, marketization, and decentralization. In Britain and the United States—to take but two examples—reductive accountability, teacher evaluation schemes, and increasing centralization have become so commonplace that in a few more years we may have lost from our collective memory the very possibility of difference. Indeed, there are areas in the United States where it has been mandated that teachers must teach *only* that material which is in the approved textbook. Going beyond the "approved" material risks administrative sanctions.

As I showed in chapter two, an odd combination of forces has led to this situation. Economic modernizers, educational efficiency experts, neo-conservatives, segments of the New Right, many working and lower-middle-class parents who believe that their children's futures are threatened by a school system that does not guarantee jobs, and members of parts of the new middle class whose own mobility is dependent on technical and administratively oriented knowledge have formed a tense and contradictory alliance to return us to "the basics," to "appropriate" values and dispositions, to "efficiency and accountability," and to a close connection between schools and an economy in crisis.[1]

While we need to be cautious of being overly economistic (and indeed have argued at great length against such tendencies in other places[2]), it is still the case that educators have witnessed a massive attempt—one that has been more than a little successful—at exporting the crisis in the economy and in authority relations *from* the practices and policies of dominant groups *onto* the schools. If schools and their teachers and curricula were more tightly controlled, more closely linked to the needs of business and industry, more technically oriented, with more stress on traditional values and workplace norms and dispositions, then the problems of achievement, of unemployment, of international economic competitiveness, of the disintegration of the inner city, and so on, would supposedly largely disappear.

In the United States, a multitude of reports told us that because of the inefficiency of our educational system and the poor quality of our teachers and curricula our nation was at risk. In Britain, a similar argument was heard. Teachers were seen as holding on to a curriculum that was "ill-suited to modern technological and industrial needs and as generally fostering an anti-industrial ethos among their students. In all respects, schools and teachers were portrayed as failing the nation." Industry was turned into a "dirty word," a fact that supposedly contributed greatly to the nation's industrial decline.[3]

As I argued earlier, there is currently immense pressure not only to re-define the manner in which education is carried out, but what education is actually for. This has not remained outside the classroom but is now rather rapidly proceeding to enter into classroom life and alter our defini-tions of what counts as good teaching. As we shall see in the second, more empirical part of this chapter in our analysis of what happens in computer literacy classes—one of the newly formed high-status areas of curriculum and teaching during the "educational crisis"—this can have a serious impact on the reality of teaching.

Among the major effects of these pressures is what is happening to teaching as an occupation and as a set of skilled and self-reflective ac-tions. Important transformations are occurring that will have significant impacts on *how* we do our jobs and on *who* will decide whether we are successfully carrying them out. Seeing what is happening will require that we recapitulate a set of arguments about the relationship among teach-ing, the complicated processes involved in how one's work is controlled (what has been called "proletarianization"), and the struggles over what counts as and who has skills,[4] since the politics of official knowledge involves the power to define both what important skills are and who has the right to label them as such.

TEACHING AS A LABOR PROCESS

In order to understand this argument, we need to think about teaching in a particular way, to think of it as what might be called a complicated *labor process*. It is a labor process that is significantly different from that of working on an assembly line, in the home, or in an office. But, even given these differences, the same pressures that are currently affecting jobs in general are now increasingly being felt in teaching. In the general sociological literature, the label affixed to what is happening is the "deg-radation of labor."[5] This degradation is a "gift" our dominant economic and ideological arrangements have given us.

In the larger society, there has been an exceptionally long history of rationalizing and standardizing people's jobs. In industry, a familiar ex-ample of this was management's use of Taylorism and time-and-motion studies in their continual search for higher profits and greater control over their employees. Here, complicated jobs were rigorously examined by management experts. Each element that went into doing the job was broken down into its simplest components. Less-skilled and lower-paid workers were hired to do these simpler activities. All planning was to be done by management, not workers. The consequences of this have been profound, but two of them are especially important for our discussion.[6]

The first is what we shall call the *separation of conception from execution*. When complicated jobs are broken down into atomistic elements, the person doing the job loses sight of the whole process and loses control over her or his own labor since someone outside the immediate situation now has greater control over both the planning and what is actually to go on. The second consequence is related, but adds a further debilitating characteristic. This is known as *deskilling*. As employees lose control over their own labor, the skills that they have developed over the years atrophy. They are slowly lost, thereby making it even easier for management to control even more of one's job because the skills of planning and controlling it yourself are no longer available.[7] A general principle emerges here: in one's labor, lack of use leads to loss. This has been particularly the case for women's labor. Women have been particularly subject to the deskilling and depowering tendencies of management.[8] These tendencies are quite visible in a multitude of workplaces throughout the country, from factories and clerical and other office work to stores, restaurants, and government jobs, and now even teaching. More and more of these seem to be subject to such "degradation."

How is this process now working through the job of teaching? At the outset, it is important to realize that it has taken teachers decades to gain the skills and power they now have. Even though in many school systems teachers in reality have only a limited right actually to choose the texts and other curricular materials they use, these conditions are still a good deal better than in earlier periods of our educational history, when text and curricular selection was an administrative responsibility, or as we saw in chapter four, the product of state textbook adoption policies. The gains that teachers have made did not come easily. It took thousands of teachers in hundreds of districts throughout the country constantly reaffirming their right to determine what would happen in their classrooms to take each small step away from total administrative control of the curriculum. This was even more the case at the elementary school level, where the overwhelming majority of teachers historically have been women. Women teachers have had to struggle even harder to gain recognition of their skills and worth.[9] (And if you are a woman of color who is also a teacher, the situation has even been worse.)

Yet while curriculum planning and determination are now more *formally* democratic in most areas of the curriculum, there are forces now acting on the school that may make such choices nearly meaningless. At the local, state, and national levels, movements for strict accountability systems, competency-based education and testing, management by objectives, a truncated vision of the "basics," mandated curricular content and goals, and so on are clear and growing. Increasingly, teaching methods, texts, tests, and outcomes are being taken out of the hands of the people who must put them into practice. Instead, they are being legislated by national or state departments of education or in state legislatures, and are either being supported or stimulated by many of the national reports, such as *A Nation At Risk* and many later documents, which are often simplistic assessments of, and responses to, problems in education,[10] ones which demonstrate the increasing power of conservative ideologies in our public discourse.

For example, at the time of writing, in the United States nearly forty states have established some form of statewide competency testing. Many of these systems are very reductive and more than a little unreflective. While this is ostensibly to guarantee some form of "quality control," one of the major effects of such state intervention has been considerable pressure on teachers to teach simply for the tests.[11] It is part of a growing process of state intervention into teaching and the curriculum and signifies another instance in the long history of state intervention into the work of a largely women's labor force.[12]

As has been demonstrated at considerable length in *Teachers and Texts,* much of the attempt by state legislatures, departments of education, and "educational managers" to rationalize and standardize the process and products of teaching, to mandate very specific content and teaching, to define all teaching as a collection of measurable "competencies," and so on, is related to a longer history of attempts to control the labor of occupations that historically have been seen as women's paid work. That is, we do not think it is possible to understand why teachers are subject to greater control and to greater governmental intervention, *and what the effects of such mandates are,* unless we step back and ask a particular kind of question. By and large, *who* is doing the teaching?

In most Western industrialized nations, approximately two-thirds of the teaching force are women, a figure that is much higher the lower one goes in the educational system. Administrators are overwhelmingly male, a figure that increases significantly the higher one goes in the educational system. Thus, both statistically and in terms of its effects, it would be a mistake of considerable proportions to ignore the gendered composition of teaching when we discuss the rationalizing ethos increasingly surrounding it.[13]

These rationalizing forces are quite consequential and need to be analyzed structurally to see the lasting impact they may be having on teaching. In much the same way as in other jobs, we are seeing the *deskilling* of our teachers.[14] As we noted, when individuals cease to plan and control a large portion of their own work, the skills essential to doing these tasks self-reflectively and well atrophy and are forgotten. The skills that teachers have built up over decades of hard work—setting relevant curricular goals, establishing content, designing lessons and instructional strategies, "community building" in the classroom, individualizing instruction based on an intimate knowledge of students' varied cultures, desires, and needs, and so on—are lost. In many ways, given the centralization of authority and control, they are simply no longer "needed." In the process, however, the very things that make teaching a professional activity— the control of one's expertise and time—are also dissipated. There is no better formula for alienation and burn-out than loss of control of one's labor (though it is quite unfortunate that terms such as "burn-out" have such currency since they make the problem into a psychological one rather than a truly structural one concerning the control of teachers' labor).

Hence, the tendency for the curriculum to become increasingly planned, systematized, and standardized at a central level, totally focused on competencies measured by standardized tests (and largely dependent on predesigned commercial materials and texts written specifically for those states that have the tightest centralized control and, thus, the largest guaranteed markets)[15] may have consequences exactly the opposite of what many authorities intend. Instead of professional teachers who care greatly about what they do and why they do it, we may have alienated executors of someone else's plans. In fact, the literature on the paid labor process in general, as well as that specifically related to women's paid work, is replete with instances documenting the negative effects of tight systems of management and control and the accompanying loss of skill, autonomy, craft, and pride that results.[16] As is too often the case, educational bureaucrats borrow the ideology and techniques of industrial management without recognizing what can and has happened to the majority of employees in the service sector and industry itself.[17]

These kinds of interventionist movements will not only have consequences for teachers' ability to control their own work. It is also becoming very clear that they are having some very problematic results in terms of the kind of content that is being stressed in the curriculum.

A simple way of thinking about this is to divide the kinds of knowledge that we want students to learn into three types: knowledge "that," "how," and "to." Knowledge "that" is factual information, such as knowing that Madison is the capitol of Wisconsin or Baton Rouge is the capitol of Louisiana. Knowledge "how" is skills, such as knowing how to use the library or how to inquire into the histories of, say, women or unions in the United States. Knowledge "to" is dispositional knowledge. That is, it includes those norms, values, and propensities that guide our future conduct. Examples include knowing to be honest, to have pride in one's racial heritage, to want to learn more after one's formal schooling is over, to be intellectually open-minded, or to see oneself as part of a democratic community and to act cooperatively. Each of these is important; but if we were to place them in some sort of hierarchy, most of us would agree that knowing an assortment of facts is probably less important than higher-order and critical skills of inquiry. And these in turn are made less significant than they should be if the person is not disposed to use them in educationally and socially important ways. The combination is what I earlier called critical literacy.

With control over content, teaching, and evaluation shifting outside the classroom, the focus is more and more only on those elements of social studies, reading, science, and so forth that can be easily measured on standardized tests, no matter what the current rhetoric about portfolios and performance tests idealizes. Knowledge "that" and occasionally low-level knowledge "how" are the primary foci. Anything else is increasingly considered inconsequential. This is bad enough, of course, but in the process even the knowledge "that" that is taught is made "safer," less controversial, less critical. Not only is it a formula for deskilling, it is also a contraction of the universe of possible social knowledge into largely that which continues the disenfranchisement of the knowledge of women, and of people of color and labor, knowledge that is increasingly important given the levels of exploitation and domination that exist not only within our nations but between them as well.[18]

So far we have discussed at a very general level certain of the social dynamics that threaten to transform curricula and teaching. This discussion cannot be complete unless we add one other significant concept, the idea of *intensification*.[19]

Intensification is one of the most tangible ways in which the working conditions of teachers have eroded. It has many symptoms, from the trivial to the more complex, ranging from having no time at all to go to the bathroom, have a cup of coffee, or relax, to having a total absence of time to keep up with one's field. We can see it most visibly in the chronic sense of work overload that has escalated over time. More and more has to be done; less and less time is available to do it. This has led to a multitude of results.

Intensification leads people to "cut corners" so that only what is "essential" to the task immediately at hand is accomplished. It forces people increasingly to rely on "experts" to tell them what to do and to begin to mistrust the expertise they may have developed over the years. In the process, quality is sacrificed for quantity. Getting done is substituted for work well done. And, as time itself becomes a scarce "commodity," the risk of isolation grows, thereby both reducing the chances that interaction among participants will enable critiques and limiting the possibility that rethinking and peer teaching will naturally evolve. Collective skills are lost as "management skills" are gained. Often the primary task is, to quote one teacher, to "find a way to get through the day." And finally, pride itself is jeopardized as the work becomes dominated by someone else's conception of what should be done.

As we noted, with the growth of interventionist styles of management and a focus on reductive accountability schemes in many nations, more and more curricula and the act of teaching itself are dominated by pre-specified sequential lists of behaviorally defined competencies, "outcomes," and objectives, pretests and post-tests to measure "readiness" and skill levels, and a dominance of standardized textual and often worksheet material. The amount of paperwork necessary for evaluation and record keeping is often phenomenal under these conditions.[20]

This is exacerbated by the fact that, given the pressures now being placed on schools, what has actually happened is that not only are curricula and teaching more tightly controlled but more, not less, has to be accomplished. As I noted in chapter three, nothing has been removed from the curriculum. Instead, elements have been added on. One of the best examples has been the addition of "computer literacy" programs in many school systems. In most districts, nothing indeed has been dropped from the already immensely crowded curriculum and teachers are faced with the predicament of finding the time and physical and emotional resources to integrate such programs into the school day. This may have even greater implications for women teachers, as we point out in the following section.

It is important to say here, however, that—as with other labor processes—one of the effects of these processes of deskilling and intensification is the threat they pose to the conception of teaching as an "integrated whole activity." Concerns of care, connectedness, nurturance, and fostering "growth"—concerns that historically have been linked to skills and dispositions surrounding the paid and unpaid labor of women—are devalued. In essence, they are no longer given credit for being skills at all, as the very definition of what counts as a skill is further altered to include only that which is technical and based on a process "which places emphasis on performance, monitoring and subject-centered instruction."[21] As we shall see, such transformations can occur all too easily.

Concepts such as deskilling, the separation of conception from execution, and intensification can remain abstractions unless we can see how they represent processes that have a real and material existence in day-to-day school life. Many teachers are experiencing these dynamics as very real alterations in their lives inside and outside the classroom. In the next section of this chapter, we shall situate these processes within the activities of a group of teachers in one particular school that was the subject of a long-term and comprehensive ethnographic study of the growth and effects of a mandate to make all students "computer literate." The introduction of such a new curriculum emphasis was officially there to help students and teachers become more technically literate. Yet, it had a number of unforeseen effects that often led to the opposite. The new curriculum mandate to develop computer literacy was a response by this particular school system to the calls from a variety of groups for a more technically oriented curriculum that would teach the skills needed for access and mobility later on. It occurred in an educational, economic, and political context in which the state department of education, business and industry, and many middle-class parents were placing considerable pressure on schools to immediately develop programs that guaranteed not only a computer-literate school population, but to make such "literacy" a requirement for graduation from secondary school and to establish closer links between educational and economic goals.[22] In a time of a redefined accord, these goals had become "common-sense." Yet, as Stuart Hall reminds us, things are "obvious" or "commonsensical" only when we have lost parts of our collective memory. Indeed, this very obviousness "is itself a sign that ideas do [participate in] particular ideological configurations—they are 'obvious' only because their historical and philosophical roots and conditions have somehow been forgotten or suppressed."[23]

As we shall see, *gender relations,* the changing conditions of the labor of teachers, and as with Channel One, the organizational and material realities brought about by the fiscal crisis of the state directly impinged on the construction of classroom life. In this site, the intensification of the teachers' workload, the lack of availability of sufficient resources, the organizational structure of the school as it had evolved over time, and the complicated reality of gendered labor, all combined to create a situation in which few teachers were fully satisfied with the outcomes.

INSIDE THE CLASSROOM

Lakeside-Maple Glen school district has decided, in the face of national trends and considerable pressure, to make its curricula more responsive to recent and rapid social and technological change.[24] A mostly middle-class and overwhelmingly white district, it wants to ensure that its curricula are more responsive to the "needs of the economy" and the perceived future labor market. Computers are one of the keys in the school district's strategies for accomplishing this, something that is much less often the case in financially crisis-ridden urban schools serving children of color and the poor and working class. Yet, because of a local accord and the power of parents from the new middle class who often favored a more participatory approach for both teachers and students, this district has also taken the stance that such curriculum programs should not be imposed from above, even given the considerable pressure being placed on it. Rather, teachers themselves must be deeply involved in the curriculum development process.

This latter point about giving more responsibility to teachers is important. All too often, the critical literature has assumed that pressures toward deskilling, the separation of conception from execution, and intensification must be imposed continually from the outside through administrative mandates, centralized curriculum determination, or externally produced and controlled evaluation plans. This is not always the case and in fact may ignore the complexity of decision making on the ground, so to speak. Because teachers have always sought ways to retain their day-to-day control over classroom reality, and are not passive receivers of top-down strategies, complexity must be recognized.[25] In fact, as we document in this section, these external conditions do not totally determine the reality of curriculum and teaching. Teachers may indeed still have space to maneuver. However, these pressures also may actually create a context that makes it seem unrealistic and not in their *immediate* interest for many teachers to do other than participate in parts of the business agenda and, thus, in recreating conditions that foster continued difficulties in their own labor. To a large extent, this is exactly what happened here.

One of the first curriculum programs to be developed and implemented under the district's new Computer Literacy Project was the ten-day Computer Literacy Unit (CLU). It was to be added in every middle school seventh-grade math class.

Mr. Nelson, a middle school math teacher and the district's computer "expert," and Mr. Miller, another middle school math teacher, were given summer curriculum compensation to develop the seventh-grade unit which they and three other seventh-grade math teachers were expected to implement in the fall. Although Mr. Nelson and Mr. Miller had conceptualized the unit before fall, they had not specifically planned each daily lesson or assembled the necessary materials to be used. They began in the fall with most of what became their unit outline completed:

Day 1   History of and parts of a computer
Day 2   Operation of a computer and computer vocabulary

Day 3   Interaction with a computer (lab)

Day 4   Input to a computer

Day 5   Output from a computer

Day 6   Flowcharting

Day 7   Introduction to programming in BASIC

Day 8   Writing a program in BASIC (lab)

Day 9   Group activity—a computer simulation (lab)

Day 10   Test and effects of computers upon society

Mr. Nelson and Mr. Miller met frequently during the first six weeks of school to work on the unit, a comprehensive task which consisted of preparing daily lesson plans, procuring worksheets, filmstrips, tape recordings, audiovisual equipment and rescheduling the computer lab. The unit was developed with a number of "givens" in mind, givens that bear on our earlier arguments.

One given that Mr. Nelson and Mr. Miller considered was that the school's seven computers were being used in the computer lab for the eighth-grade computer elective courses, and were not available when several of the seventh-grade math classes met. Therefore, they recognized that most of the unit would have to be taught without the use of computers, a major obstacle because they believed that hands-on computer experiences were very important. Through elaborate planning, the teachers were able to schedule three of the ten days in the computer lab, not very much considering that there would be about twenty-five students sharing seven computers on those lab days.

Minimal computer access, a problem of considerable moment in many budget-conscious school systems, affected the curriculum and the teaching because skills and concepts most effectively developed through using a computer had to be taught in more vicarious ways, such as observations and lectures, or eliminated altogether. (Here the economic situation partly mirrors the rationale seen behind the acceptance of Channel One: the cost of equipment.) For example, too few computers and too little time in the computer lab meant that most students were never able to write a program in BASIC even though it was a specific objective and represented the generally active, hands-on experiences that were consistent with the district goals.

A second given which influenced how the unit was developed was stated by Mr. Miller this way. "You have to remember that we have faculty in this department who don't know much about computers. We needed a program that everyone could teach." Mr. Nelson explained that a crucial factor in developing the unit was that teachers who know nothing about computers would be able to teach it. He said, "You see we really needed to develop a canned unit." The three other math teachers, all women, were uninvolved in developing the unit and didn't even find out about it until the fall. One woman, Ms. Wilson, a recent graduate who was newly hired on a part-time basis, had no computer experience and was quite apprehensive about having to teach a Computer Literacy Unit. Another woman, Ms. Linder, had some computer experience but was returning from a year's leave of absence. The third teacher, Ms. Kane, was experienced in the department but had no experience with computers. Thus, the unit was "canned" so that these or any future teachers would be able to teach it.

A third given resulted from the organization of the math department. It was a regular practice in the department to test all seventh graders after the first ten weeks of school and transfer those with "superior ability" to an eighth-grade math class. Selection by "talent," with all of its stratifying implications, was not an invisible process at work here, especially because of the fact that the pressure to identify such "talent" is rapidly increasing in schools given the sense of the importance of mathematical and scientific knowledge in international economic competition.[26] This schedule therefore determined that the unit would have to be completed in all seventh-grade math classes before the tenth week of school. In order to be able to share the computers and other equipment and schedule the computer lab, half of the math classes had to implement the unit during weeks seven and eight and the other half had the unit during the ninth and tenth weeks of school. This schedule placed tremendous time pressures on Mr. Nelson and Mr. Miller to complete the unit quickly.

Given these time pressures and the intensification of their own work, Mr. Nelson and Mr. Miller had to assemble the materials rapidly and communication with the other math teachers about the unit was minimal. What they did was to examine some commercially prepared computer literacy curriculum materials that were available.

The foundation of the unit that they planned consisted of two filmstrips and a prepackaged commercial curriculum consisting of tape-recorded lessons and coordinated worksheets. The topical outline that had been partially completed was finalized on the basis of some of these materials. The unit became very structured, detailing the objectives, the equipment needed, and the lesson plan for each day. The plan specified that six days were to be spent in the classroom, mostly listening to the commercial tape recordings and completing the worksheets. Three days were to be spent in the computer lab: two for interacting with instructional software and one for writing a computer program. A unit test was planned for the last day, and after the test a film about the social implications of computers would complete the unit. Due to the bulk of all the worksheets and equipment, the curriculum was usually rolled around from room to room on a cart.

In many ways, the "curriculum on a cart" may be viewed as an efficient, practical, and sensible solution to the several "givens" within the school and given the outside pressure on the school from various groups with somewhat different but overlapping agendas. What occurred inside the classrooms, however, documents how the realities of teachers' lives inside and outside of the school and what is happening to the job of teaching in a time of increasing conservatism carries with it contradictions that are very serious.

A CURRICULUM ON A CART

Students and teachers expressed enthusiasm about the two-week computer unit because it represented something new and popular. There were five teachers teaching a total of eleven heterogeneously grouped seventh-grade math classes and, as we noted, due to the time pressures, the unit was not prepared and ready to go until the time to begin teaching the unit. The women teachers had little or no time to preview the unit. In essence, they experienced it as they taught it.

In all classes the unit began with some enthusiasm *and* two filmstrips and two worksheets. Students were shown a filmstrip which focused on the history and development of computers and were given a time-line of events for note taking. The content emphasized dates of events such as the invention of the transistor and computer terminology. There was little class discussion because the filmstrips took the whole period. Homework consisted of a word search worksheet with hidden names of computer parts.

To give a sense of daily activity, let us focus on day five. The daily routine that occurred on day five was representative of all days in which worksheets and tape recordings were predominant. Day five is distinct, however, in that it represents a mid-point in the unit and events on this day illustrate how the routine use of tape recordings and worksheets were beginning to have an impact on the teachers' and students' initial enthusiasm for the unit, on the teachers' sense of skill, and on the intensification of their work.

DAY FIVE

As the students came into class, one boy shouted out, "Are we going to the lab today?" The teacher answered, "We've got those sheets again and the tapes . . ." Invariably, when hearing that it was a worksheet day, students would start to grumble, "that man's dejected," "I hate this, this is boring," "Do we have to do this all the time?" "I can't stand this class," "This isn't computer class, this is worksheets . . . what do we learn, nothing . . . how to push a button" (referring to the tape recorder). One student turned to one of us (Susan) and, referring to the worksheets, complained, "We know this stuff already, maybe not these fancy words . . . but we know this stuff." Although the students complained about the tapes and the worksheets, they did not disrupt the class routine. The opportunities for what was called the politics of pleasure in the discussion of what students did with Channel One were much less available here, at least at first. The students came into class, made a number of inquiries and remarks, took their seats, and cooperated with the teachers. Their attitudes were for the most part ignored or made light of by the teachers, who appeared to regard a certain amount of negativism and complaining as typical adolescent behavior in school.

The first daily procedure in every class was the distribution of worksheets, which took about ten minutes because there were so many of them. Teachers usually passed around a stapler and this became the occasion for individual entertainment as students dawdled with it, withheld it from the next student, slid it on the floor, and generally used it to attract attention and delay beginning the worksheets.

The teachers began the lesson by turning on the first tape-recorded lesson for the students. A man's voice read the captioned information on the worksheets and students were to follow along. He then explained how to complete the worksheet and said "now turn off the tape and complete the worksheet." Teachers who, given the immense load of paperwork that the quest for administrative information and control had thrust upon them, used this time to do independent work at their desks, frequently missed this directive and the students would shout, "Turn off the tape." After a few minutes, the teacher turned the recorder back on and the narrator read the answers while students were supposed to correct their worksheets. As the unit progressed, many students would just wait for the answers to be read and would fill in their papers at that time. After a worksheet was completed, the narrator would then say, "If you want to continue . . ." which was an invitation to go on to the next worksheet. This invitation invariably met with responses such as, "But we don't!" One teacher in a sing-song voice said, "Oh we do, we do." (After one of the first classes, this teacher said "I don't think this was a good day, the kids didn't really get much out of this." This was a surprising remark at first because the students had been very attentive, completed the worksheets, and the day had progressed according to the lesson plan. It expressed, however, the teacher's intuitive sense that this material, as conveyed through the tapes, was not very effective.)

As the tape recorder droned on, students found many quiet and unobtrusive diversions. Students would comb their hair, clean dirt from their sneakers, daydream, doodle, and chip pencils. One girl worked all period getting a piece of candy that was wrapped in crinkly paper out of her pocket, unwrapped, and into her mouth all unnoticed. These activities were generally quiet and private and students in all classes during this unit were outwardly very orderly. These diversions were rarely disruptive. Most of the students, however, were very quiet and completed their worksheets. There were material reasons for this.

Mr. Miller said that the math department had the reputation of being quite strict and the seventh-graders, still new to the school, might be a little intimidated by it. The students were also repeatedly told that (a) after this unit the teachers were going to determine which students would be transferred to an eighth-grade math class, and (b) they should complete and keep their worksheets because they would be able to use them during the unit test. For many, the possibility of being advanced to the eighth-grade math class—determined by their behavior, their accumulated grades including their test score on this unit, and a math achievement test—contributed to their good behavior during this unit.

Teachers passed the time during the tape-recorded lessons in various ways. Some would correct papers from other classes and catch up on the seemingly endless backlog of routine paperwork. At first these taped lessons seemed to be more tolerated, probably because they gave teachers some extra preparation time, which in this school was limited to only forty-five minutes a day. (In some schools, because of the fiscal crisis accompanying the conservative restoration, even forty-five minutes of planning time a day seems like a luxury, since any "extra" time is being lost as a cost-savings device.) But by day five, it appeared that even the opportunity to catch up on other work was not totally absorbing. One teacher paced around the room, stared at a poster for five minutes, stared out the window, and finally stopped near one of us (Susan) and said, "I'm so sick of these tapes!" One teacher dozed during a tape. On day five, as most days, the teacher's main role was to distribute the worksheets and manage the tape recorder. If all the daily tapes and worksheets were used and completed as specified on the lesson plan, then there was little or no time for questions or discussions. In all classes, other than supervising the use and distribution of the instructional materials, the teachers had little to do as the tapes and worksheets established the content and form of the lesson.

However, teachers did not always sit passively by and watch; they intervened into the planned lessons. Mr. Miller turned off the tape one day to explain a concept. He later told one of us, "We have to discuss and clarify some, smooth the rough edges of these worksheets." However, because of this interruption, he never did get back on schedule and did not complete the entire taped lesson. Ms. Wilson lost a day due to a school assembly and tried to consolidate two days by "talking through" some of the lessons herself. "We have to catch up today, so we can go to lab tomorrow." They couldn't catch up, however, and ended up skipping some tapes. Ms. Linder stopped a lesson to clarify a mathematical formula, the inclusion of which irritated her because, as she later said, "If I had seen the lesson first . . . I would have taken that out; seventh graders don't know that, it shouldn't be in there." On day six she modified the flow chart assignment by requesting her students to write a flow chart on a topic of their choice which she later explained to one of us would be "more interesting for the students."

Mr. Nelson explained that computers are "dumb" because they perform on the basis of how they are programmed and cannot reason or use common-sense. He gave several examples of the kinds of errors that have been made by computers such as astronomical billing errors that most humans would immediately recognize as erroneous but which, of course, a computer could not. Mr. Nelson frequently supplemented the lessons in order to increase student interest and understanding. While he also strove to maintain the schedule, he was sufficiently knowledgeable to supplement and enrich the daily lessons.

Mr. Miller took time one day to illustrate the difference between thirteen- and sixteen-sector disks. The computer program selected for use in the lab was on a thirteen-sector disk. Therefore, the students would have to go through some extra procedures in the lab the next day and he wanted them to understand why. The point was not that this explanation about sectors was important, but that Mr. Miller's explanation represented an attempt to demystify the computer, to help the students understand why the computer responded the way it did. In fact, it was the "mystical" aura of the computer that the general goals of the CLU was attempting to avoid. Teachers unfamiliar with computers of course could not explain these kinds of things. In the other classes, the sector incompatibility was not explained and the students were just told to "first use this disk, then use the program disk."

The male teachers did more explaining in class than did the other teachers, primarily because they were familiar with the unit and were more knowledgeable about computers, for reasons we shall see later. However, they too were committed to following the lesson plans, and their diversions to "smooth out the rough edges" invariably lost them time. Completing daily lesson plans was important to all the teachers because (a) the daily lessons were too long to make up the next day, (b) the schedule for the computer lab and the completion of the unit were fixed, (c) some lessons were sequential in nature, and (d) the final unit test was correlated to the information on the tapes and filmstrips. Therefore, the time that it would take teachers to explain the "whys" of computers was inevitably brief or not taken at all. To take the time would jeopardize the completion of the two-week unit.

Two points are important here. One is that while the teachers, in varying degrees, did stop the tapes and clarify, explain, or enrich the lessons, none attempted to (a) eliminate a lesson, (b) change the nature of the lessons, or (c) change the unit. The second point is that, in the context of a pressured and crowded curriculum and an intensified labor process, when teachers did interject discussions they invariably fell behind schedule. This made the pace of the unit even faster as they later tried to catch up. Thus, teachers felt that they had to maintain the schedule because the unit was a requirement for which they and the students were responsible. Therefore, the completion of the CLU became highly dependent on following the unit plans, and this instrumental goal usually took precedence over teacher- or student-originated activities, even when teachers became more than a little uncomfortable. Knowledge that, and low-level knowledge how, dominated almost "naturally" in this situation. So much for critical literacy.

COMPUTER LAB DAYS: HANDS ON?

The three days in which the students met in the computer lab were quite a contrast to the classroom days because the students were using the computers. On day three the students were to select and use programs from a specially prepared demonstration disk. The general enthusiasm was dampened only by the fact that the students had to work in groups of three or four to a computer, and in the forty-five minute class period, each individual got little hands-on computer time.

On days three and nine, the plan was to have half the class work with the teacher at one computer using a simulation program, while the rest of the class shared the six remaining computers and were to complete a lab worksheet and write their own programs, mainly because the teachers did not have time to give them individual help, given their workload. Ms. Linder recognized this and later said that she did not like this lesson plan because, by working with the large group on the simulation game, she was not able to circulate and help those students who were trying to write programs.

The computer lab days were by far the most favored by students and were planned to provide hands-on experiences. Yet, since there were only seven computers to be shared, students had to work in groups of two, or on day three, in groups of three and four. Because periods were forty-five minutes long, most students spent more time observing computer use than actually using a computer. Many educators claim that it is preferable to have students work in pairs rather than individually at a computer because it promotes peer interaction and learning. We do not wish to reject that claim. However, when groups became larger than two they usually became dysfunctional because individual interest waned as students were unable to sit and observe comfortably around the small computers. Invariably, some students sat and engaged in unrelated conversations while waiting for "their turn" which some never got. Therefore, actual hands-on computer time was very limited.

Even with this, however, students were in the lab and were generally enthusiastic about being there. If their computer use was more vicarious than actual, they were at least observing computers. The computer lab days were active and exploratory in nature and this provided a major contrast to the classroom days.

THE FINAL UNIT TEST

The CLU final test on the tenth day was a short-answer summary of the worksheets, tapes, and filmstrips. The students could use their notes and worksheets to complete the test which was composed of matching, listing, and fill-in-the-blank short-answer items such as the following:

> Name 3 ways of putting information on printouts_____
> The first computer was built in Philadelphia and was named _____
> Put the outcome of each program on the output line.

Reflecting on the relatively reductive nature of the test, Mr. Nelson said that he questioned whether the test really measured what was most important. Ms. Linder, who did not really like the test, said, "I felt that the final test could be better; some of the items were ambiguous and all the vocabulary stressed at the beginning was too technical." Ms. Kane felt that there should have been a review sheet of the "really important things" rather than having the students study and use all their notes during the test. Ms. Wilson said that the students "did well" on the test and the other teachers referred to the test scores as acceptable. In general, the teachers did not seem to place much emphasis on the test or its results, although the students, who had been repeatedly warned that "this unit will be tested and your score will count in your quarter grade," did seem to take it seriously and worked carefully on the test.

Yet, it is crucial here to remember the fact that the material on the effects of computers on society was dealt with *after* the end of unit test. Thus, pressures to teach the "facts" about computers—defined as technically oriented knowledge and skills—did indeed make any more critically oriented knowledge less important. The politics of official knowledge during an age of conservatism in practice meant that low-status knowledge became that which situates technology into the larger society. Conservative definitions of technology, as asocial sets of technical skills and neutral machinery, became the norm. This did not require a conspiracy by dominant groups. It occurred as common-sense.

TEACHERS' RECONSTRUCTIONS

In later interviews and a departmental meeting, teachers talked about how they felt about the unit. Mr. Nelson, one of the developers, said "I felt hamstrung. I would probably do things differently, but I felt that I had to pilot it." Since Mr. Nelson had computer expertise, he was not as dependent on the unit, and he, more than most, expanded the daily lesson plans.

Interestingly, use of the prepared CLU was not felt by all the teachers to be a required or even likely practice in the next years. Mr. Nelson did not feel further pressure to use the unit in the future and he explained that it now exists as a "resource for those who want it" and that as long as the objectives are "covered," it didn't have to be done in the same way in every class. This is consistent with everyday practice in the math department, where all the teachers use the same standard textbook and cover the same objectives, so, as Mr. Miller said, "you know that each student has been exposed to the same things."

However, it is important to state that many of the teachers may indeed still choose to *continue* to use the "curriculum on a cart" in its current form, even though they recognize that it is minimizing their ability to affect the curriculum and that they are relatively "hamstrung." As noted earlier, the unit provided some "extra" time that teachers could and did use to catch up on routine paperwork and planning. For instance, when Ms. Kane was asked how she felt about the use of the tapes, she said:

> Well, it was good. . . . I mean, naturally it got boring and monoto-
> nous, but I would just tune out during those times. I used that time to
> work on a new unit, or on [some school committee work], and I'd do
> other things during those tapes. I'd try not to show boredom to the
> kids, but I really didn't mind it; after all it was only for two weeks. And
> during that time I didn't have to prepare, everything was prepared . . .
> and I didn't have papers to correct during that two weeks . . . If I'd
> change things next year, I'd lecture more but I'd still use a lot of those
> tapes; maybe not all, but a lot of them.

We cannot understand this response unless we situate it into the reality of teachers' workloads, workloads that are increasing in many areas, especially as there is a growth in class size and a downturn in teacher hiring (and many layoffs) in a considerable number of school districts throughout the country. Ms. Kane taught five seventh-grade math classes in a row and, while she acknowledged that these tapes were boring for her, she essentially took advantage of these two weeks to gain time and relieve the pressures of keeping up with the planning and grading for five math classes. She was aware of the fact that the unit marginalized her own curriculum autonomy, but she did not overtly resist her designated role in it. Instead, she interpreted and used the unit to compensate for her otherwise intense routine. She recognized the unit for what it was; she used the "extra" time that it gave her and she was not negative in assessing her role in the unit.

Her colleague, Ms. Linder, also referred to the intensity of work and said that she didn't like the daily teaching schedule because "There are no breaks in the day, not time to correct papers, plan. . . . You don't get to know the students as individuals . . . I have a seating chart." Therefore, the unit that was all prepackaged, ready to go, and included few assignments to be corrected, provided some benefits to teachers whose normal routine is far more labor intensive, a situation that is worsening in many schools throughout the country.

For some teachers, then, a curriculum that separated conception from execution can sometimes seem to be a benefit, not a loss, a result of the contradictory realities teachers face and the contradictions in their own consciousness. In addition to providing some time for teachers, the unit also was seen to provide the pedagogical support and information about computers that Ms. Wilson, a first-year teacher who was unfamiliar with computers, interpreted as helpful. Ms. Wilson said that the tapes helped her because she learned about computers along with the students and anticipated using the same lessons again, although she would "branch out" as she became more computer literate. Teaching a unit for which she was unprepared was intimidating, and she welcomed the prepared unit in which she could turn on the tape recorder and use worksheets. When asked about how she viewed the content on the unit, she said, "I think it covered the important things . . . but I really don't know much about computers, you know."[27] Ms. Wilson, in general, was positive in her assessment of the unit.

Even though all the teachers had equally intensive schedules, they did not all interpret the form of the CLU in terms of benefits. For example, Ms. Linder was more than a little distressed by the form of the unit as well as some of the content. Her main objection was that she preferred to plan her own curriculum. She said.

> You didn't have to be a teacher to teach this unit. Just turn on and off tapes . . . I would have done things a little different. I have enough computer background to have done some things differently if I had had time to prepare it . . . I was dependent on their plan, tapes, and worksheets. . . . I kept asking to see the unit, but it wasn't done and I was told, "Don't worry, there isn't much to do, just tapes." But I didn't like those two weeks at all. I knew when I was out those days, the sub would be able to do it, she just had to turn on the tape recorder."

These comments are echoed in other places and by other teachers, though perhaps not as strongly. To varying degrees, most felt something was being lost by relying too heavily on "the curriculum on a cart." Yet by and large, the teachers accepted these two weeks as they were originally planned and did not markedly alter the standardized curriculum. How can we understand this?

GENDER AND THE INTENSIFICATION OF TEACHING

The rhetoric of computer literacy often turns out to be largely that—rhetoric. Even given the meritorious aims of the staff and the school district and even given the extensive amount of work put in by teachers, the curriculum is reduced once again to worksheets, an impersonal prepackaged style, and fact-based tests.

A good deal of this can only be fully understood if we place these attempts at curriculum reform back into what has been evident throughout this volume, the fiscal crisis of the state. School systems are often caught between two competing goals: that of accumulation and legitimation. They must both support an economy, especially when it is in crisis, and at the same time maintain their legitimacy with a wide range of different groups. The fiscal crisis makes is nearly impossible for schools to have sufficient resources to meet all of the goals they say they will meet; yet not to at least try to meet a multitude of varied goals means that an educational system will lose its legitimacy in the eyes of the "public" even further, something the Right has been masterful at accomplishing. Given this, many goals will simply be symbolic. They will serve as political rhetoric to communicate to the public that schools are in fact doing what concerned groups want them to do.

Yet they will not be totally rhetorical. Many teachers will be *committed* to the goals, believing that they are worth meeting and worth spending the exceptional amounts of additional time trying to take them seriously. These teachers will exploit themselves, working even harder in underfunded and intensified conditions to overcome the contradictory pressures they will be under. At the same time, however, the additional workload will create a situation in which fully meeting these goals will be impossible.

This school developed a Computer Literacy Unit under the same conditions and with the same intentions that many schools are currently developing similar curricula. Computer knowledgeable teachers, ample computers, and adequate time, and scheduling flexibility are more like wishes than realities in most school districts. Mr. Nelson and Mr. Miller worked intensively for over a month to develop a curriculum that would provide introductory experiences for all the seventh graders. The CLU they developed was significant because it exemplified how the process of transforming a very general goal like computer literacy into a specific curriculum was mediated by the "given" organizational factors and resources—both human and material—typifying the school, and by the gender divisions that organized it, a point to which we return in a moment.

It was apparent that the structure of the unit and its implementation schedule, as well as the heavy load of teaching and paperwork that these teachers had, made it difficult for the teachers to contribute more than brief and occasional additions and clarifications to its content. A "canned" or prepackaged curriculum did emerge. Yet, it was valued by some teachers as a practical and sensible solution to the problem of curriculum time, resources, and "skills."

Certainly the major condition here was that of curriculum planning time, both in the immediate and long-term sense. In this school, only the two men teachers were technically prepared to teach the unit. Because the unit had to be completed within the first ten weeks of school, the other teachers did not have time to prepare themselves to develop the new curriculum for their classes. Paying two teachers to develop the unit for the department was the district's way of compensating individual teachers for their lack of curriculum preparation time. However, lack of comprehensive curriculum planning time is characteristic of the structure of most schools, even more so as schools come under increasing attack. Thus, the "curriculum on a cart" solution tends to be a generalized response to the demands of new curriculum projects in many schools, especially since other responses would require more money, something we cannot expect in times of the fiscal crisis of the state.

This practice compensates teachers for their lack of time by providing them with prepackaged curricula rather than changing the basic conditions under which inadequate preparation time exists. In the immediate context, some teachers may interpret this as helpful and appreciate it as a resource. But in the broader context, it deprives teachers of a vital component of the curriculum process. Over time, these short-term compensatory practices function as deprivations because they limit the intellectual and emotional scope of teachers' work. This deprivation was specifically recognized and articulated by Ms. Linder in her quote at the end of the previous section. As an experienced teacher who was very anxious to resume her full responsibilities, she expressed her feelings of alienation and unimportance when she said, "You don't have to be a teacher to teach the unit," and went on to say that she wasn't worried when she was absent and a substitute had to teach her seventh-grade class during the unit. Her skills and her curriculum responsibilities had been usurped and this angered her. Thus, while in the immediate context the availability of the "curriculum on a cart" was interpreted positively by some teachers, in the long term this form of curriculum functions to compensate for and not to alleviate the problem for which it was viewed as a solution, that of time and "expertise."

While we do not wish to be essentialist, it is still important to state that the condition of time must be examined in *gender* terms here. It was the women teachers, not the men, in the math department who were seen as less prepared to teach about computers and they were the ones most dependent on the availability of the unit. Typically, the source of computer literacy for in-service teachers is either through college and university courses, school district courses, or independent study, all options that take considerable time outside of school. Both Mr. Miller and Mr. Nelson had taken a substantial number of university courses on computers in education. Given the gendered specificities of domestic labor so beloved by the New Right, many women, such as those with child-care and household responsibilities like Ms. Linder, or women who are single parents, may have considerably less out-of-school time to take additional coursework and prepare new curricula. Therefore, when a new curriculum such as computer literacy is required, many women teachers may be more dependent on using the ready-made curriculum materials than most men teachers. Intensification here does lead to an increasing reliance on "outside experts." An understanding of the larger structuring of patriarchal relations, then, is essential if we are to fully comprehend both why the curriculum was produced the way it was and what its effects actually were.

It is absolutely crucial to say, however, that at the same time, the commitments to environments that embody an ethic of caring and connectedness—commitments that are often so much a part of women's daily experiences and are so critical in an education worthy of its name—may actually provide the resources for countering such rationalized curricular models.[28] The sense of loss, of an absence of community, the struggle to personalize and reduce anonymity, all of this enables one to restore the collective memory of difference. The women teachers here may have some of the most important resources for resistance in the long run.

These points about the gendered realities of the women teachers are significant in another way. It would be all too easy to blame the women teachers in this setting for basically following the "curriculum on a cart" and, hence, ultimately partly participating in the degradation of their own labor and a reductive "that"-based curriculum. This, we believe, would be a major error.

As a number of commentators have suggested, the real lives of many women teachers, when seen close up, are complicated by the fact that one often returns home exhausted after being in the intensified setting of the classroom only to then face the emotional and physical demands of housework, cooking, child care, and so on. Since many women teachers are *already* doing two jobs, their caution and "lack of enthusiasm" toward additional work is anything but a simplistic response to "innovation." Rather it is a realistic strategy for dealing with the complications in the objective reality they daily face.[29]

We need to remember that doing nothing is a form of action itself. Though it is not always the result of a set of conscious decisions, it can have serious consequences.[30] Women teachers, like all workers, may overtly resist intensification and the loss of their autonomy and skills. At other times, from the outside it may seem as if they are "passively" accepting a separation of conception from execution or the deskilling of their jobs. However, as we know from an immense amount of research, most individuals on their jobs will attempt to take even the most alienating experiences and turn them to their own advantage, if only to maintain control over their own labor to simply keep from being alienated and bored,[31] or as in this case, to solve other equally real problems brought about by the conditions of fiscal scarcity, overwork, bureaucratic realities, and external pressures and constraints.

Teachers are never dupes, never simply the passive puppets that structural models would have us believe. Their agency, their actions in concrete situations such as these, may have contradictory results. They may have elements of "good sense" and "bad sense" in tension as they construct their responses to a crisis in the economy, in authority relations, and in education. Yet, the fact that they *do construct* these responses once again shows the very possibility of difference. In a time when the Right would like to commodity education[32] and to once again turn our schools into factories or into mechanisms of social stratification based on the cultural capital of elite groups even more, that possibility is of no small importance. These constructions are *not* preordained. They can be reconstructed in ways that will allow us to join with teachers to challenge the redefinitions of skills and power that are currently going on. As the section on "progressive possibilities" in chapter two showed, this is not only a conceptual possibility, but is going on in the daily lives of many schools. Connecting the teachers like the ones described here with those who are engaged in more overt work against the rightist reconstruction of the practice of education is an essential task, something being accomplished now as Rethinking Schools and groups such as the National Coalition of Education Activists grow. Thus, once again there are possibilities, not only limits, in the politics of official knowledge. These possibilities may perhaps be able to be expanded now that strongly rightist elements are somewhat less powerful at the national level in the current administration.

The struggles to increase these possibilities, with all of their own difficulties and contradictions, are not "only" there for the teachers described here, however. The struggles and possibilities also exist in the lives of people who write books such as this one. It's time now to turn our attention not to "others," but to our own activities. What are some of the actions I (we?) do in a time of rightist resurgence? The stories I tell in the next two chapters—stories of joy and sorrow—are set in the context of my own work and in the larger context of the continuing attempt to counter—even in "small" and "limited" (*local* is a better word) ways—the transformation in education so many of us are experiencing. They aren't grandiose and they do not totally encompass all of the political and cultural work I do with unions, activist groups, dissidents, cultural workers, and others both here and abroad. However, I tell these stories to return us to where we began, so that, as I mentioned in chapter one, a dialogue internal to you and between you and me can begin. As with all texts, these stories can produce different kinds of readings. My own readings don't have "a lock on reality."

7

"Hey Man, I'm Good": The Art and Politics of Creating New Knowledge in Schools

INTRODUCTION

The last chapter's account stressed how technology of a specific kind is employed in ways that were not the most democratic, given the pressures that conservative groups, business, and the new middle class have placed upon schools to make certain that students are "technically literate" to meet the needs of the economy. Yet there are alternatives to such usage, alternatives that enable a different kind of knowledge production to evolve. I want to describe how these can operate in real settings, with real students. I center this on my own personal experiences. The story I tell highlights not only the very possibility of a more critical pedagogy and curriculum; it also stresses the tensions and conflicts involved in the attempt to do something different.

As I noted early on in this book, the stories I tell in this chapter and the next are meant to be suggestive. They tell of temporary "solutions," not final ones. They sometimes raise as many critical questions as they answer. But, then again, if there is no one grand narrative, no one political (and educational) act that is always guaranteed to be "progressive" in every way and along every social dynamic, then we should expect that all of our "solutions" will contain contradictions. Because I talk of local activities and struggles here, however, this should *not* be interpreted as having given up at all on more structural issues. Rather, I want to situate the range of "larger" and "smaller" issues within its local context. After all, this is where we act.

Those of you who are familiar with my other work and from the previous chapters in this book know that I approach educational issues in a

143

way that is different from many other educators.[1] Rather than seeing our
task as finding efficient ways of getting students to learn the knowledge
already selected for the curriculum, I have urged us to ask *whose* knowledge it is in the first place. That is, I have asked us to take very seriously
the intricate connections between what we teach in classrooms and the
unequal relations of power in the larger society. Power, of course, is both
social and personal. It not only signifies one group's attempt to dominate
another; as I argued in chapter three, it also refers to a person's or a
group's ability to help *create* the social conditions and meanings that
make life more fulfilling.

These are not only abstract issues. They influence nearly everything I
do as an educator, especially in the courses on curriculum development
that I teach. Here I try to deal practically with questions of power and the
production of personal meaning.

I do not approach the issue of curriculum design as a technical problem to be solved by the application of rationalized models. Rather, following a long line of educators from Dewey to Huebner, I conceive of curriculum as a complicated and continual process of environmental design.
Thus, do not think of curriculum as a "thing," as a syllabus or a course of
study. Instead, think of it as a symbolic, material, and human environment
that is ongoingly reconstructed. This process of design involves not only
the technical, but the aesthetic, ethical, and political if it is to be fully
responsive at both the social and personal levels.[2]

I want to stress these elements in this chapter. They are so necessary
that I cannot conceive of curriculum design going on without integrat-
ing their concerns into the very heart of the process. Here I refer to activities that connect aesthetic concerns for personal meaning (in a nonessentialist way) with a clear ethical and political commitment.

If curriculum is in fact a *design* problem, then by its very nature it is an
aesthetic act. In many ways, it is more like painting a picture than building a bridge. Because of this, and because of the fact that most educators
have themselves been "trained" to use cost/benefit and behaviorally oriented technical models in approaching curriculum problems, an orientation that is now common-sense in an era of business models in schools,
it is essential that we recapture the aesthetic sensitivity that has been so-
cialized out of all too many teachers and administrators. Oddly enough, it
is in one of the most technically oriented parts of designing environments—the use of technology itself—that I believe the aesthetic, the ethical, and the political nature of curriculum design can be illuminated.
What I do in a course entitled *Elementary School Curriculum* can serve as
a case in point. Here I stress not the usual ways technology is used in
classrooms, but its personal, political, and aesthetic possibilities to do

different things in schools. The focus is on filmmaking. This involves a vision and uses of technology that are significantly different from the captive audience of Channel One and the very limited vision of "computer literacy" in chapter six, and goes well beyond the conservative agenda about what counts as important knowledge.

Elementary Curriculum is filled with an entire range of people—teachers, administrators, social workers, librarians, full-time undergraduate and graduate students inside and outside of education, many of whom are from other countries. Almost none have had any "formal" experience with the relationship among politics, aesthetics, technology, and curriculum. By the time the semester is over, nearly three-quarters will have engaged in filmmaking.

We tend to think of technology in education as something of a "better mousetrap." Given a process/product curriculum model that says that education is good if it gets us from point A to point B efficiently and cheaply, technology simply becomes one more means to get prechosen knowledge into the heads of students. Films are seen as better than dry text material or a lecture. Goals don't change. Only the means do. Film, in essence, becomes one more "delivery system" of official knowledge. The teacher sends; the student receives. "Banking" education goes on.

If we think of film not as a "delivery system" of prechosen messages, but as a form of aesthetic, political, and personal *production,* our entire orientation changes. If we think of it as a way that people help produce their own critical forms of visual literacy, this too forces major shifts in our perspective on the politics of official knowledge as well.

Just as written literacy has its own "grammar" and its own politics,[3] so too do forms of visual literacy. And just as the exploration of writing as a creative act leads to self-production, so too can the exploration of the possibilities inherent in each aspect of visual production lead to the uncovering of alternate ways of making meaning both individually and collectively.

I choose working with film and video for a number of partly overlapping reasons. One is to engage students in "my" *Elementary School Curriculum* class as soon as possible in a process that demonstrates, in action, the connections among symbolic, material, and human resources in an environment. At its most practical level, making films requires reflections on this. Second, and again on a very practical level, I want to demonstrate how curricular areas in the elementary school can be integrated together through, say, film projects. Art, music, mathematics, science, language arts and reading, and so on can be made sensitive to each other as each is brought to bear on making the film. The linkages here to the "project method" are self-conscious. Third, I want to illuminate how technology is not simply one more way to get from point A to point B in classrooms, but *inherently* offers more ethical, aesthetic, and political possibilities that can go well beyond what now exists in so many classrooms. It enables us to do very different things that can expand the range of literacies and their grammars that teachers and students are able to work with. Finally, as I mentioned earlier, one of my aims is to reawaken that very sense of aesthetic possibility with teachers, to enable them and me not to be "connoisseurs" of the "art" of teaching but to engage in aesthetic (and political) production itself by actually making films singly or collectively. These all become aspects in the development of critical literacy.

Two kinds of film work tend to dominate. The first involves using 16 mm film, but not at all in the way we usually employ it. What I am decidedly not interested in is "instructional film"—you know, the content-laden and often oh-so-deadly presentations on the agriculture of X put out by commercial firms and publishing houses. Instead, the focus is on student aesthetic and often political production. Here, 16 mm film is not seen as "containing" already decided content, but as something of a moving canvas through which students themselves create meanings. This is done by either bleaching old 16 mm film (literally unrolling it and dropping it in a bucket of household bleach to remove all of the previous images, thereby leaving transparent film as a result) or buying white film leader which usually comes in boxes of one-hundred-foot lengths. These blank or white lengths of film are then drawn upon. One can create relatively intricate animations by drawing pictures frame by frame on the film; or Jackson Pollock-like effects of color, line, and shape can be created by simply using magic markers to go down the film relatively randomly. When put to different kinds of music, (usually simply by playing a tape during the showing of the film, but sometimes with more elaborate attempts at synchronization), the effects can be quite startling.

The second style of film work involves the use of 8 mm film (or videotape). Given its size, this film is not written upon, but instead is used in the camera itself to create animations, political statements (examples include a film made by middle school students against the stringent dress code of their school, antipollution statements, and feminist images), or simply interesting visual effects by exploring what one can do with slow and fast motion, single-frame release cables, zoom lenses, and so on. Once again, the focus is not on creating Hollywood-like artifacts, but on playing (in the richest sense of that concept) with the medium to explore its grammar. The fact that this is usually done cooperatively, with small groups of students in my class or with groups of elementary and secondary students in schools working with people who are taking *Elementary*

School Curriculum, creates a collective experience that is important in and of itself.

I want to take one concrete instance of film work that grew out of the class, one in which two students who had taken the class and I decided to work together to see if filmmaking as an integrative and personal form could make as much of a difference in real children's lives as we thought it could. We believed the best way to test this out was to go into an environment that was "difficult." The three of us had all taught in inner-city schools and two of us had experience in working with some of the hardest-to-reach kids, those involved in the corrections system. We asked if we could come in to one of the state-run juvenile corrections institutions, a school for "girls" that had a reputation of being a tough place but where we had enough contacts and support from a teacher there to make access possible.

We walked into the most difficult cottage on the grounds. Twenty-two young women aged fourteen through seventeen, many of them girls of color, confronted us. They were there for a multitude of reasons: running away, prostitution, drugs, theft, and so on; all those labels the juvenile justice system affixes to the troubled children of the poor, disenfranchised, or oppressed. This is a growing population, since the Right is creating a discourse and a common-sense that increasingly makes it legitimate to solve our social problems by jailing large numbers of people of color and the poor and disenfranchised. One thing was very clear immediately. This was a group of tough kids. Both words are important here: toughness and kids. There was no doubt that these adolescents *were* angry, difficult to reach, and mistrustful (sometimes for very good reason). Yet the toughness covered up their fragility. These were often children inside, wrapped up in bodies that belied, had to belie, the fear and confusion and feelings of lack of self-worth inside. Many of them had undoubtedly had experiences strikingly similar to those of my son early on in their lives, as well.

Having worked with kids like this when I was a teacher and youth worker in the inner-city schools of Paterson, New Jersey, I already had some understanding of what these kids felt and an unromantic appraisal of what they were capable of doing to themselves and others. We began by showing two films by Norman McLaren, the noted Canadian filmmaker who had, in essence, pioneered many of the cinematographic techniques that had influenced me. We explained to the girls the kinds of things that could be done with film and spent some time discussing and demonstrating how this could be done by showing other films that students such as themselves had made. Since most of these films were accompanied by music that the kids liked, the atmosphere began to loosen up. Combining the joking yet still serious manner that we each had developed in working with kids, we answered their questions and then handed out lengths of film and brightly colored magic markers, making it clear that they could easily get more material if they needed it.

Of the total group, eleven began working. The theme they chose was simple, yet so evocative: school. What started out as an activity that was seen by them as an excuse not to do "school stuff," shortly became totally engrossing as the girls got into the project.

Soon everyone, *everyone*, was deeply involved. Magic markers were shared. Comments and criticisms that were meant to help, not to cut down someone, were given by the kids to each other. Jokes and laughter, sighs and grimaces, calls for assistance, words of satisfaction and frustration also filled the air. It was at times noisy, at times remarkably quiet. It was the controlled chaos that organizes and reorganizes itself when kids are deeply involved in doing something that is playful and yet utterly serious to them.

At the end of the day all the segments of film—some of which were now quite long—were collected and spliced together. Each girl took a turn at splicing her section into the larger film. And then we watched it. It was funny, immensely creative in places, and often brutally honest about their perceptions of schooling. Because of this, it may also have been threatening to some of the people on the staff.

The film had to be shown multiple times, as each girl had to see and resee her part of it and as each cottage had to be brought in to see it as well. The excitement was visceral. The sheer sense of competence, of having done something that was lasting and that proved to the world that "I am worth something 'cause *I did this*," was palpable. There were cooperative discussions among the girls about how to improve each other's sections. Plans were made about what to do next time, plans that were sometimes too elaborate, but showed a personal and collective spark that had been missing throughout all the prior school experiences these kids had been involved in. Many of the girls grabbed the books I brought in about animation, video, making "write on" films, etc., and after reading them passed them on to others in preparation for the next film we would do together. We were excited and so were the girls. They were *ready* to go further. They *wanted* to read and discuss. This was one of those occasions when the "teachable moment" had expanded to such an extent that so much more could be integrated into it. Their pride in themselves, enthusiasm, and their growing sense that they, who had been labeled stupid for so long, had real yet untapped resources and talents, provided ideal conditions to go on and do even more serious things.

And then it died.

We were informed that, while this was interesting and "seemed to involve the girls and to keep them out of trouble," it was in essence a frill. They had to get back to official knowledge, to their remedial reading and "life-skills" classes, ones the students tolerated at best and often dismissed as irrelevant, boring, or, and I quote, "bullshit." We then had to face the kids, to tell them it was over, to face their disbelief and their anger and the return of the cynical expressions that we had seen before we started the film work.

A group of youth who had been so beaten down in classrooms, had learned to hate school, had learned not to trust a system that seemed to have little to offer them, and hence had built impenetrable walls between their intimate feelings, hopes, and dreams and the institutions in which they lived, had removed large chunks of that wall. They let their defenses down and trusted some white teachers. Doors into themselves were opened. Talents were uncovered. Joys and possibilities were made visible, only to be once again denied.

There is a scene in Herb Kohl's book, *36 Children*,[4] in which one of his students, a boy named Robert, comes back to see Kohl. Robert had been told he was stupid. Yet in the course of a year, he had been transformed in Kohl's classroom, had learned to trust himself, had learned that he was talented in that sixth-grade classroom. The next year he went on to another school, another teacher, and was shattered. Nothing had really changed. It was boring, alienating, and repressive, perhaps worse for Robert now that he had experienced the very possibility of difference. He was angry at Kohl. How could Kohl have done this to him? How could Kohl have allowed him to drop his defenses, defenses that had enabled Robert to survive the numbing experiences of a schooling process that daily denied his very being as an individual and as an African-American? Wouldn't it have been better just to leave him alone? In essence, it was like allowing a nearly starving person to sit at a food-laden table for one night and then locking her or him out on the other side of the door from then on. Wasn't this simply unethical?

Many issues could and should be raised about this experience in filmmaking in hindsight. Were we too naive? Should we have involved the administrators and educational staff more directly from the beginning? Did we think through all of the possible effects and contingencies? Add to this the multitudinous issues surrounding the usual questions of the micropolitics of the institution, of bureaucracy and educational reform and we could spend many hours detailing what went wrong and the "should have dones" that arise from this episode. But through it all, one question remains. It haunts me. It provides the concluding story I tell each and every time we complete the weeks on ethics, politics, technology, aesthetics, and curriculum in *Elementary School Curriculum*. The question is so simple to state, yet so damnedly torturous to resolve. Should we have done what we did? Should we have opened these young women up to the sense of what they could do, to reawaken hopes and a sense of self-worth, only to have the door slammed shut again before we and they could go further and build upon these initial awakenings?

Yet, there was this Christmas card that came in the mail five years later. It was from one of the girls of that cottage, Ramona. She had been one of those who was most excited by the experience of making the film. She had nearly cried when she saw her portion of it, a lengthy section in which she had painstakingly drawn a school burning down, a group of children playing basketball, and a segment in which multicolored rods and dots seemed to dance around each other. She had been positively glowing. This was *hers*. As she had put it, "Hey man, I'm *good!*"

Ramona was now working as a commercial artist and wanted to write to let me know. "You probably won't remember me. I did that film stuff at [the cottage] with you. I hope you like this card. I designed it."

I am still tortured by the experience of making films with those girls. In that one week, we did succeed, often well beyond what we had expected. We *had* challenged the politics of official knowledge. We had used technology in ways that were strikingly different than the "talking heads" of Channel One or the test-based, deskilling, and boring attempts at computer literacy documented earlier. Yet, hadn't we also failed? Hadn't we reawakened hopes and senses of self-worth that, of necessity, had to be partly repressed by the girls in that cottage, only to fail them again? Did we go far enough in linking their emerging senses to a "critical literacy," to the Freirian idea of "concienticization?"[5] With enough time, I think we could and would have gone significantly further. But then there's Ramona. Would she have been successful without the experience we helped create? Don't we have an ethical and political duty as educators, even when we can't change the entire range of one's school experiences, to struggle to make each single experience as personally meaningful and politically powerful as we can especially in a time of a powerful conservative agenda and a return to elite knowledge? Ramona's letter helps, but still I wonder. I'll leave it up to you to decide.

8 The Politics of Pedagogy and the Building of Community

INTRODUCTION

In this period of what I have called throughout this volume the conservative restoration, it is difficult to keep progressive visions alive and to not slide slowly into cynicism. Just as difficult is the struggle to keep the critically oriented tradition in education from becoming so overly esoteric, so hermetic, that it is totally cut off from the real politics of real people in real institutions.[1] These are complex issues, ones that are as much collective as they are individual. Because of this, they require a collective response. Yet, this in itself necessitates the building of a community in which such responses can be articulated, shared, challenged, and rebuilt. I want to focus here not on the realities of elementary and secondary schools that I have discussed in the prior three chapters, but even more than in chapter seven on my own activity at the university in working with students who have chosen to study with (not under) me. I think we may have much to learn from reflecting on the dilemmas and tensions here as well as those we experience when thinking about the case of Ramona.

In this book, as in all of my previous ones, I give a special acknowledgement to a particular set of people—the Friday Seminar. For the past twenty years, every Friday afternoon has been set aside as a special time when my doctoral students, visiting scholars from other institutions, activists, and I meet to read each others' work, to support each others' research, to help plan political and cultural action, simply to find respite in personal and political conversation about the realities of our and others' lives, and so on. I want to focus on what happens in the Friday Seminar, not because I believe it is so totally unique—many of you may have similar experiences—but because I think it can tell us something about the realities and the politics of our discourses and practices in educational institutions and can say something as well about a nonessentialist politics of education that recognizes and works through differences,[2] especially in institutions that may be under intense pressure over both the knowledge they teach and the connections they do (or don't) have to the economic programs of the Right.

What I have to say may be deceptively simple. It is a story of the conscious attempt by one limited group of people to maintain a sense of community, one both grounded in an ethic of caring and connectedness and at the same time one meant to challenge the existing politics of official knowledge and each others' thinking about it, in a kind of institution where this is difficult to maintain. I want briefly to tell a story about tensions, conflicts, moments of exhilaration, and the struggles to keep a small-scale "community" functioning even in the face of material and ideological conditions that make it even more difficult for this to go on. This requires that I situate this story within those conditions.

KNOWLEDGE, POLITICS, AND COMMUNITY

It is important at the outset to state something about the participants in the Friday Seminar. *All* are or have been politically active. *All* come from a background of having engaged in concrete action to change prevailing economic, political, and cultural inequalities or to defend gains that have been made. For many this continues, unabated. For others, especially those from other countries with oppressive governments that are unfortunately backed by the United States, to engage in overt action while they are here would mean possible deportation and jailing. Even with this, however, the flavor is openly political. These overt similarities mask important distinctions, distinctions that make the continual rebuilding of a sense of community essential.

There are on the surface two groups of people in the seminar and, while the differences should *not* be overstated, they do signify somewhat different orientations. One group, usually the larger one, studies in the Department of Curriculum and Instruction. By and large, these are individuals with a background in teaching and curriculum development either here in the United States or elsewhere. Their affiliations, while no less political, center around rigorous analysis of and action on the politics and practices of classrooms, teaching, and curriculum. Another group works with me in Educational Policy Studies, specifically in the

Sociology of Education. Again, this is a very political group. Yet, their concerns are often slightly more distanced from the political dynamics of actual school settings and involve, say, the politics of technology, of popular cultural forms, the role of the state and class dynamics in struggles over educational policy, and theories of ideology and subjectivity, among others. Both groups, however, are theoretically sophisticated. Members of both have a history of struggles for democratic possibilities. Both are equally committed to continuing those struggles and to make a difference in education, broadly conceived.

It is important to understand the geographic differences of the people involved in the larger group, however. A simple listing of the countries is not sufficient to convey the utter importance of this, but it is indicative of not only widely divergent educational experiences but distinct cultural, political, and economic histories as well. For example, over the years members have come from Japan, Korea, Thailand, India, Burma, Taiwan, Nigeria, Puerto Rico, Costa Rica, Colombia, Canada, England, Ireland, Israel, Barbados, Dominica, Granada, Australia, New Zealand, and various parts of the United States. Visitors for shorter periods of time make it look like the general assembly of the United Nations.

The experiences of the individuals involved are wide-ranging as well and are often crosscutting. They include presidents and organizers of teachers unions, faculty members of colleges and universities, members of feminist movements, cultural and educational leaders in newly emerging democratic socialist governments or in other democratic nations, members of dissident groups in nations with repressive regimes, researchers from institutes of social and educational research, educational and community activists, environmental and animal rights activists, elementary and secondary school teachers, and so on.

Race, class, and gender have all played a significant part in constructing different experiences as well. At any one time the group is usually, though not always, divided equally between men and women. There is always a significant presence of African-American, Afro-Caribbean, Asian, and/or Latino/Latina members. Class differences are often registered as well in the institutions out of which people arose, from elite institutions to small teachers' colleges. They are signified as well by those who come from somewhat advantaged backgrounds (actually very few) to those—like myself—whose class trajectories are grounded in working-class economic instabilities and poverty and who went to undergraduate school at night. Finally, issues of sexuality have surfaced and gay and lesbian politics and experiences have provided distinctions[3] (and as well have provided points around which solidarity is formed among all the participants).

These relations are never stationary. People complete their degrees; they leave to do research or to return to jobs or feel compelled to leave to continue more pressing political struggles in the countries and institutions from which they come. New members arrive each year. They too bring their political/educational agendas. And since all who arrive *are already* politically engaged, they too wish to be heard.

The material conditions in this group then—differences in biography, political experiences, agendas, and priorities—have meant that community has had to be built along particular kinds of lines. And, just as importantly, that it has to be continually rebuilt, cared for, consciously nurtured.

All this has of course led to tensions, ones I certainly feel. What is *my* role in all this? Am I a "leader," "only" one among many participants? Can community be sustained with so many seemingly contradictory political commitments, with some participants still believing in the predominance of class while others are just as committed to feminist and/or antiracist forms? Can the socialization that all of us have experienced to a certain degree as professors and graduate students—competitiveness, point scoring, aggressively pursuing arguments even when the style may interfere with the formation of collectivity, leading as opposed to listening, etc.—be overcome? Does a masculine style pervade our discourse too often? Does theory always count more than personal experience? Are we sometimes in danger of losing a sense of the realities of the everyday lives of teachers.[4]

The theoretic debates and the arguments about political-educational priorities and practices are often grounded in these collective and biographical experiences. The decentering of the Marxist problematic in which all things are explained in class terms has *had* to occur. The relevance of feminist analyses and of theories of racial formation have *had* to take center stage. This has occurred not "only" because of the compelling case that has been made for the irreducibility of gender and race in our theories and actions,[5] but just as crucially because of the lived experiences of the people involved. Theory, politics, and autobiography merge here.

Because of all this, the idea of difference plays itself out in particular ways, forcing a *decentered* unity upon the Friday Seminar. This decentered unity involves both the theoretical/political level and the level of everyday interaction in the group itself. Let me initially focus on the issue of theory.

In political and conceptual terms, what has happened is that we have had to acknowledge that the commonly accepted privileged points of view from which action and analysis were supposed to come from—and these again usually centered upon class dynamics—have ceased to take *the* center stage.[6] As Laclau and Mouffe put it in their argument about the dominance of class analysis in most radical work, "The problem of power . . . cannot be posed in terms of the search for *the* class or *the* dominant sector which constitutes the centre of a hegemonic formation."[7] Such a center in fact will always elude us. Rather than one central logic of power, there are multiple "centers," with class, gender, sexuality, race, and nationalism among the most important. As they go on to say, "All of them are contingent social logics which . . . acquire their meaning in precise conjunctural and relational contexts, where they will always be limited by other—frequently contradictory—logics."[8]

These are of course rather heavily laden abstractions, but by depriviliging, decentering, the traditional emphasis on class relations and power (while still appreciating its importance) and placing it on a more parallel plane with these other dynamics—and then recognizing the contradictions within as well as among all of them—we are able to come much closer to an analysis of the social dynamics and possibilities of progressive action in education.[9] This also enables a more intense focus on the politics of social movements which, as Wexler has argued so well, may be the most important harbingers of social change in education.[10]

In political terms, this has also meant that our focus on radical democratization should not exclude a priori any possible sphere of political action. "Juridical institutions, the educational system, labour relations, the discourses of the resistance of marginal populations construct original and irreducible forms of social protest, and thereby contribute [to] the . . . complexity and richness on which a program of radical democracy should be founded."[11]

An explicit focus, then, on relations of power—with a conscious attempt to live out a theory and practice that does not necessarily privilege any one relation as primary—has had to be built. The debates continue: they are never settled once and for all. The tensions over this continue as well and these are never only theoretical but are deeply related to our individual and collective biographies as classed, raced, and gendered subjects. However, in the very recognition of the tensions and in their tentative resolution in plurality, a community based on this recognition is somehow still basically maintained.

Historically, other things have bound the community together as well. Among the most important was the shared experience of working with student teachers. Because of the downturn in fellowships and scholarships, a large proportion of the members of the Friday Seminar—at times fully three-quarters of its members—were employed as supervisors in the teacher certification program at the university. They officially worked twenty hours a week, although real hours were often much more than that, given their commitments to their students and given their structural position as the "buffer" between schools and teachers on the one side and the university and student teachers on the other. Each of the members of the Friday Seminar who was a supervisor also taught a seminar for the ten to twelve student teachers in her or his care. These seminars were often attempts to repoliticize the experiences the students were engaging in and to explore more democratic and critical pedagogical and curriculum practices.

The shared experience of supervising and teaching created a bond not only of joint discussions over how the seminars should be organized, what should be taught, and how they should mirror the democratic commitments the supervisors avowed, but also a bond of joint exploitation. As the fiscal crisis of the state deepened and the university's budget became tighter, student loads increased for supervisors, hours were cut back, and the labor itself became increasingly intensified. While this did create pressures, it also acted to cement social relationships in personal and political ways among many members of the Friday group.

The fiscal crises did not ease and in fact worsened. Working conditions had become nearly intolerable for many of the supervisors and it became clearer that the primary reason for their being at the university—the rich political/educational environment of their graduate education—began to suffer. Choices between reading, collective action, and getting through the intensified schedule of a supervisor's week with all of its daily crises and time-consuming activity had to be made. And often the personal goal of graduate study had to take a back seat to the equally ethically compelling goals of simply earning enough money to live on and pay for tuition and books and doing one's best in assisting students to become reflective and politically sensitive teachers.

These conditions had a multitude of effects. Many members of the Friday Seminar fled supervision. They looked for positions as research and project assistants on the various large federally funded or foundation-supported research projects housed in the Wisconsin Center for Educational Research or in individual departments. These too are increasingly intense in terms of time and emotional labor, in part because many of these positions required the graduate students often to be away from Madison for up to a week at a time to do fieldwork on national research projects. Others competed for lectureship positions in the program, positions that might have been even lower in pay at times but where the load was not so extreme and where more respect was given.

The intensified conditions also led to other problems. One of the things that historically bound the Friday group was a program of joint readings. On most weeks we read important material suggested by a group members. The schedule of such readings was democratically arrived at. The readings were often at the forefront of the debates in economy, culture, and politics and in gender, race, and class. Material on the debates within and about feminist epistemology, postmodernism, the state, analyses of class and race went on side by side with readings on national testing, democratic curriculum, and critical and feminist pedagogy. Yet, a slow but real change evolved. What often included entire books early on in the career of the Friday Seminar moved almost imperceptibly to shorter single articles. Where almost no one would miss the opportunity to read and discuss the material, increasingly the work load everyone was experiencing often forced members to only skim the reading or sometimes not to read it at all. Even those who did not have an opportunity to read the weekly material always felt free to come, to get a gist of an argument and participate and this sense of community did not change. However, the number of members who could not find the time to add even one more reading to this already nearly out of control schedule increased measurably. It was more than a little reminiscent of the teachers described in chapter six.

Yet only to talk about the material conditions of supervisors' and researchers' lives risks marginalizing the many "foreign students" in the Friday Seminar. Since most of them could not be supervisors—they had not taught in the United States and, hence, were harder to place in such positions no matter what their personal excellence—they usually had been employed on various research projects or on small stipends from their own nations. As the world economic crisis deepened, the effects were visceral on these people.

The altered economic conditions had a profound impact on participants from other nations. While it was always more difficult for students from Third World nations to find support or to generate enough money even to come here—given the exploitative economic relations between the United States and the Third World and the rightist nativism that dominates much of the public discussion in education and economic policy—it now became significantly more threatening. The sacrifices foreign students often had been called upon to make to engage in graduate study, especially for those students who were dissidents in their own nations and therefore were never high on the list for government assistance, were always extreme. Now an exceptional amount of time and physical and emotional energy had to be spent finding employment at the university. This was simply draining. The effects could even be seen on such simple matters as schedules. Whereas before, schedules could almost always be organized so that the time for the Friday Seminar could be kept sacred, for many of the foreign students the positions they were able to get left them with little flexibility. Not only were they sometimes exploited in terms of hours of work, but the time itself was not always easily arranged so that Fridays were set aside. This could and did lead to tensions, not usually in the Friday Seminar but in terms of the students having constantly to negotiate hours so that there was indeed time to participate on Fridays. And they too found it harder and harder to keep up with the reading.

Community is best developed out of shared experiences. With the loss of the shared supervisory experiences, and the increasing difficulties of finding support for foreign students, something of importance was missing, something that indeed had bound most people together. When this was coupled with the tensions that did, *and should,* evolve over political, educational, and theoretical agendas, one could begin to feel, in an almost bodily way, the partial splintering of some of the solidarity that had been so painstakingly built over the years. This was itself made even more problematic by a large turnover in the group in which three people completed their Ph.D.s and six new members arrived to study with me all in the space of one year. Thus, not only was the group now appreciably larger but in many ways it was now a new group. (I don't mean to point to this as only a "problem." But it does signify that caring communities are fully contingent and historical. They are grounded in people's lives. Both the people and the lives can and do change.)

This required a conscious attempt to come to grips with the tensions in the group itself. Nearly a month was spent specifically focusing on the dynamics, on the contradictory agendas people bring, on what could be done. At times it was emotionally laden and could have been damaging not just to the group but to specific individuals as issues were raised that could easily have become personalized—the dominance of men, of those whose first language was English, of those who were "more advanced" theoretically or who were "more apt to speak first." Sometimes, genuine anger surfaced.

Yet, through it all, the ethic of listening and of caring that had been part of the history of the seminar seemed to provide the ultimate backdrop. As issue after issue was raised, more people talked. Members self-consciously held their own, sometimes very strongly held, positions in check as they listened to those who often spoke less. The sense of the special quality of the interactions, of the special space Friday afternoons still created, and of its possible fragility in the current conservative restoration not only in education in general but at universities as well, somehow maintained itself. "Somehow" is not quite the appropriate word, of course. It took hard work for it to be maintained. It took people taking personal risks. And it took people sacrificing individual agendas and reaching down inside themselves to rebuild the norms of collectivity for the preservation of the space.

Concrete action at the university helped reestablish these bonds as well. The politics of pedagogy does not simply involve how or what one is teaching, but the rights of others who are "being taught" to jointly participate in creating the pedagogical environment. As Giroux and others would put it, it involves the politics of student voice. Yet, the formal graduate programs in which all of the members of the Friday Seminar are involved has little place for students' voices. By focusing the groups' agenda on ways to stop the marginalization of such voices and on ways to reintegrate issues of gender, race, class, and sexuality as organizing frameworks into the pedagogy and curriculum at the university, a decentered unity—one that allowed for multiple political voices, but one that was still a *unity*—again began to come to the fore. Actions have been and are being taken now and are beginning to have some effects on the processes of priorities in hiring, on what courses should be offered, on the politics of official knowledge within existing and new courses, on possible student representation on *all* important committees, and so on.

Another focus was on the exploitative relations of employment of those members who were still supervisors and on those who had become research assistants. Here too all members seemed to rally around an issue of lived experience and sought to elaborate steps—perhaps demands is better—that the institution itself could take in reducing the intensification of the supervisors' work and giving them more autonomy and control. Issues of pay and excessive demands of time (demands that sometimes go well beyond the twenty or so hours a week supervisors and researchers are hired for) have been important foci. Here too gains have begun to be evident.

Finally, much more time is now spent on discussing each others' political and intellectual agendas. Less reading of other people's books and articles is done (though this is still a substantial commitment of the seminar). Rather, discussions and collective assistance on thinking through one's research, papers, pedagogy, political actions, and so on—and the ethical, educational, and political tensions and implications of all this—are more central. This has enabled a more open space for all of us to devote attention to what is happening in the other nations represented by the participants. Leadership can now be exercised more often by all members of the group. Thus, for example, the ways we could support the attempt by Korean teachers to form an independent teachers' union and to bring the Korean government's repression of it to everyone's attention played a major role in our discussions and actions.

I do not want to romanticize what I have said here. Tensions still exist. The decentered unity that we are trying to construct is exactly that, a construction. Like all social constructions that strive to be democratic, it is a fragile construction, especially in times when so many of the economic and ideological conditions that are certainly not missing in the life of an educational institution can work against it.

This story is not necessarily generalizable of course. But some lessons may be useful. A community, no matter how carefully nurtured and no matter how politically astute and committed its members, does not sit isolated from the contradictory economic, political, and cultural dynamics of the institutions in which it resides. Nor does it sit isolated from the race, gender, class, and other dynamics of the larger society. No matter how strong the political commitments toward democracy and against relations of oppression in education and elsewhere—perhaps *because* of them—it will be difficult to maintain the bonds among people in times of fiscal and ideological attacks on the things we hold dear.

Yet, caring and connectedness, a sense of mutuality, trust and respect, and a freedom to challenge others, as well as a commitment to challenge the existing politics of official knowledge whenever and wherever it is repressive, can be rebuilt and maintained. This seems to require a recognition of the *plurality* of possible political interests within a broad, shared, progressive framework. Of course, we know all this at the theoretical level, especially those of us who have written or read extensively on the necessity of moving beyond the class and economic reductionism that was so prevalent within the critical tradition. Knowing something theoretically and knowing it bodily are two different things, however. This is why it also requires constant attention to the politics of whose voices are heard within the group. It requires patience, a willingness to live through difficult times when internal dynamics seem to threaten group unity. Finally, and of considerable importance as well, is the focus on concrete action.

In this case, a community of people that is split in so many interesting ways, but unified in so many others, is based on one over-arching commitment: to alter the dominant politics of culture and the ways pedagogy and curriculum are now carried on. These politics are not only somewhere "out there," in the supposedly "real world." As I have argued earlier, they occur "right here" in the day-to-day lives of all of us who work at universities. Our best analyses can be usefully refocused on our own daily experiences and on acting collectively to alter the conditions that often make these experiences less compelling and rich than they should be. Such collective action will not be easy. It will not always be successful. But in the process, the community that is built will enable the political knowledge that people like the members of the Friday Seminar *already have* and are gaining to come into practice in our daily lives. Reflection and action combined to solve real political/cultural problems—isn't this what praxis is all about?

I have discussed one kind of community, in reality only a limited one since its boundaries usually but not always extend only as far as the walls of the university. As many of you know, those boundaries need to be extended well beyond that institution, to the politically committed teachers, community organizers, feminist, gay and lesbian, antiracist, differently abled, and labor and environmental groups, and to others who will provide the context for larger social movements. It is these social movements that will enable us to move toward a society based not on exploitation and domination in all of its forms but on a society organized around seeing all of us as "coresponsible subjects" on that "journey of hope." As a political activist and as a former teachers' union president, I am constantly reminded of how important it is that we participate in those larger struggles as well.[12] Not only might we teach, but perhaps more importantly we might allow ourselves to learn even more important lessons about constructing the decentered unities we call communities of struggle.

WHOSE STORY IS THIS?

I have told a seemingly simple story here. Yet my account needs to be deconstructed, for there is another politics working here. This story is told from and through one voice: my own. However, my role in the group remains largely invisible in this account. Who am I representing? Have I exploited the group for "academic" reasons? Does the very act of presenting a public account of a group that has been so important in my own development, as well as in all of its many participants' development over the years, do more than commodify these experiences? The "professor," perhaps unconsciously acting out the role of a member of the unattached intelligentsia, puts her or his name on a chapter based on a community's experiences. The community is displayed at that ultimate marketplace in which cultural capital and personal status provide the cash: the world of educational publishing and research. Whatever benefits accrue from the public display, the sale, of this commodity come to me.[13]

When I presented a draft of this chapter at the Friday Seminar, the discussion was intense. Had I gotten the story "right"? Who had I marginalized in the categorizations of difference I pointed to? Wouldn't it have been better to stress the similarities, including the fact that everyone there had come to study with me and that was the most crucial bond?

Haven't I underplayed the crucial positive moments, the very real reasons that the Friday Seminar is worth talking about in the first place, the utter importance of the seminar's role in fostering the *continuing* political and educational growth of all its members? People come in partly formed by their past political and educational experiences and are reconstructed in significant ways by the internal politics and pedagogy of a group that is always in formation yet always somehow "there" to enable them to question and go further. Aren't feminists radicalized over racial issues in the group? Aren't those so deeply committed to class analysis transformed by the feminist impulses that provide such a strong focus in the seminar? Isn't all of this what gives the seminar a good deal of its meaning?

Other questions and issues emerged as well, ones that were equally political and *needed* to be raised. By decentering myself, had I presented an accurate picture? And, finally, shouldn't a chapter such as this be collective?

The discussion *was* intense, but never was it rancorous, never was there a question of a lack of trust or caring. (But, of course, here I go again—*my* voice, *my* construction.) It was agreed that I should present the "story"—corrected, added to, made more complicated. It is clear that a "complete story" (yet, as we know, there can be no such thing) would have to be collective. It would have to enable the voices of all participants in the Friday Seminar, past and present, to speak, to deconstruct and reconstruct their individual and collective stories, to be authors of their own lives.[14] (Yet, isn't this what *all* education should be about? Isn't it what the educational programs I described in chapter two begin to accomplish, a new politics of official knowledge?)

So what started out with a simple aim—to tell about the experience of building and rebuilding a space where progressive people could come together to support and build upon each other—is not so simple after all. The seminar has a politics. So does the telling. And in telling, and struggling with the power relations involved as the teller, new political questions again should and did emerge. The act of keeping the Friday group alive is, as the members reminded each other during our discussion, a political act in and of itself. The political questions I have raised here emerged from that collective experience, once again proving to this "voice" how much he owes to that collectivity. But, then again, knowing is itself a collective project of naming the world, being appreciative of multiple namings. Through my analyses and stories in this book, I have named parts of the world. What stories, what names, what struggles, do you wish to add to enable a more democratic education to be built? The Right may not want to hear them, but there are many people throughout the world who do.

Appendix: Education, Power, and Personal Biography: An Interview

INTRODUCTION

What follows is a lightly edited interview with me originally published in 1990. It was conducted by two scholars and activists for whom I have the highest respect: Carlos Torres, then of the University of Alberta and now at the University of California, Los Angeles, and Raymond Morrow, of the University of Alberta. As I mentioned in my introductory chapter, I believe that it is important that we situate our theories within lived experiences and, especially, that an author try to lay out the grounds—both political and personal—for the claims that she/he makes and for the stories that she/he tells about what is happening in this society.

There are many forms through which this can be done. I tried a number of them when I was writing this book. I ultimately decided that an interview, partly in the form of a conversation, would be best. First, it returns us to the personal, something I have done in the previous two chapters. It's hard to hide behind a linguistic wall when you make yourself, as a person, present. Second, a dialogue with someone else forces you to try to make better sense, to communicate actively with another person in ways that are more mutual, more sensitive. Third, while it can lead to the reduction of complex issues into simplicities (and this is a real danger), it does enable one (me) to move among different "levels." Practice, politics, biography, and theory can all be blended together.

Pierre Bourdieu points to some of these benefits when he says that "the logic of the interview . . . has the effect of removing one of the main forms of censorship which belonging to a scientific field [sic] can impose, one that may be so deeply internalized that its presence is not even suspected:

that which prevents you from answering, in writing itself, questions which, from the professional's point of view, can only appear trivial or unacceptable."[1] It also enables you "to state quite fundamental propositions [openly] that the elliptical style of academic dignity or the properties of scientific etiquette lead you to conceal."[2]

Now, I've never been one who is overly in love with "scientific etiquette" and "academic dignity," though I have contributed more than my share of weighty prose to critical research on the relationship between culture and power in education. The model of "science" that is usually appropriated by educators in fact seems not only wrong but more than a little masculinist and acritical to me.[3] While Bourdieu may wish to uphold a model of social science that is still a little too "sciency" for me, he does locate one connection between power and knowledge. Dominant academic styles may position both author and reader in such a way that what is "unacceptable" to say is concealed.

Of course, much is still concealed in interviews. Thus, one always tries to put one's best foot forward. No person completely understands either the meanings and causes of her or his actions or the underlying and often unconscious (and perhaps less laudatory) reasons certain paths are taken and not others. I'm certain I have no special talent that differentiates me from any of you in figuring out any of this. So what follows is yet another story, my own reconstructions and reflections, that will undoubtedly be recontextualized and reconstructed by you.

I started this volume with a story of my son, Paul. I end with a personal statement, this interview. Both are grounded in a recognition of the structures of domination and subordination that encompass and are encompassed by real lives of real people. That is where the politics of official knowledge—and our ethical and educational responsibilities in altering it—begins and ends and begins again.

INTERVIEW

Raymond: One of our objectives today is to give a sense of the political culture of education in relation to American society and particularly to contextualize that a bit for Canadian students, for we have a somewhat different situation. I think the key thing to understand is that Michael Apple is one of the leading representatives of a new current in educational scholarship in the United States which goes under many different names (radical, critical, etc.), but I think one of the key distinctions is to see it in terms of its origins as a critique of American liberalism, whereas in Canada we have a very different situation with the preexisting social democratic tradition with liberalism already an object of criticism which goes way back. So I think the first question I would like to address is the origins of Michael Apple's work in education and the phase of development his work entails out of the critique of liberalism and the particular contradictions of American society in relation to education.

Michael: This has to be in part autobiographical, as you would imagine. I have an odd history. I did my undergraduate work at night while I was working as a union printer and truck driver for a number of years. I come from a family that would have been pleased to be called working class and we were very poor. Because of this, there was a question about whether there was any money for me to go on to higher education. Given the fact that money simply wasn't there, I supported myself. I went to two small state teachers' colleges at night while I was working in the print shop during the day until I had to go into the army. While I was not overjoyed about this, to say the least, I went in the army. It seemed wiser to do that than to go to jail at the time. The army made me a teacher. I taught compass reading and first aid. After being discharged, I had one year of college credits. Urban schools in New Jersey were facing a massive teacher shortage, especially in schools serving "minority" children. I had taught in the army and could say ¿como esta?" which unfortunately was all you needed to be able to say, it seemed, in Paterson, New Jersey, to be put in front of the classroom. I began teaching at the age of nineteen as what was called a "floater"; a full-time substitute as you would call it. Every morning at 6:45 I was told what school I would be in. I was almost always assigned to schools that were populated by children who were of color, partly because I was very active in the African-American and Hispanic communities in Paterson. I was one of the founding members of the Paterson chapter of CORE (Congress of Racial Equality) and had already done a good deal of activity involving literacy work and desegregation of the United States. There were areas where they closed black schools or resegregated them in other ways rather than have black children and white children go to the same school. Groups of people like me would go down there on buses (some of which were burned) and many of us were jailed. I went there to protest and to help reopen literacy classes for African-American children. Thus, I was politicized at a time in which you had to act on it, politicized as an educator. I was someone who, even though I was not really trained yet as a teacher, was deeply involved in political, cultural, and educational struggles in the U.S. Because of this, I was formed by racial conflicts over the politics of literacy, the politics of access, etc. This is important, I think, to understand why I move in certain directions. By situating what I do in these fairly young experiences in political engagements, it's possible to see why the politics and struggles in education have always formed me in significant ways.

Raymond: These events would have been in the early to mid '60s?

Michael: The late '50s, early '60s. I got out of the army in 1962.

Raymond: You were really on the ground floor of a whole series of very powerful movements and confrontations.

Michael: Yes, this was even before the "end the war" movement. While I was teaching in New Jersey, it became quite clear to me that the kinds of struggles I was engaged in needed to be broadened. Much of this was because of Paterson itself. Paterson is one of the worse-off cities of its size in the United States. It now has a large portion of the population on some form of assistance and 80 percent "minority" (in quotes) population with almost no right to a decent economic life. I say "minority" because people of color are the majority in the world, and the word minority is definitely an ideological construction.

Again it was politicization that led me to begin teaching in a particular way. I was very angry about what I was seeing around me. The schools were largely failing. The knowledge was filtered through ideologically laden curricula. And the rich cultures of working-class and "minority" life and history were totally absent. Thus, the politics of knowledge and the politics of teaching had to be transformed with my own actions in classrooms. Having to put this stuff into practice every time you walked into the classroom meant that the reading and political work I was doing was translated immediately into what I had to do when I faced the forty-six children in my classroom everyday. I was still deeply involved in racial politics and class politics at the level of practice in Paterson and the educational practice inside schools and political practice in the larger community together continued to form me.

From there I got deeply involved in teacher politics. I was president of a teachers' union for a while. Again, I was disheartened by what I saw, and disheartened by the promises that were never kept—all of which I think led me to certain readings as well as actions, especially to a critique of liberal policies. Paterson was a "machine" city politically. It was controlled as well by what in the United States was called a "Democratic party machine," people who were of the mainstream Kennedy or Johnson liberal type who promised to wage a war on poverty. Yet no matter how much I and other people in education and political work would kill ourselves trying to make a difference in classrooms and elsewhere, all too many of the children still would wind up in jail, on drugs, with no jobs, in poverty, were discriminated against, and often brutalized by the system.

Raymond: You were sitting on the front lines, while the bureaucrats are sitting in their plush offices thinking of solving the problems?

Michael: Yes, although in Paterson there weren't a heck of a lot of plush offices. But that is exactly the point. That led to a good deal of anger and partly to the search for my political roots. I am what is called a "red or pink diaper baby," a joke which in the United States refers to someone with deeply involved leftist parents. This involved finding myself politically, not just as an activist in racial politics, but by situating myself in this long family tradition, which is more important. These autobiographical points are important for social theory as well, since critical theory often has its roots in senses of lived oppression as the feminist and antiracist movements have so clearly shown. From there I went on to graduate school at Columbia at a time when campuses in the United States were deeply polarized and politicized about the Vietnam War, racism, and so forth. This experience studying at Columbia enabled me to link my own educational and political history with an entire range of radical literature and to ground myself within it intellectually as well.

Raymond: Were you there in 1968?

Michael: Yes. And then moved from there to Wisconsin—a story that people may enjoy and that again may explain why I am in Madison as opposed to other institutions, especially given my politics and my penchant for not keeping an exclusive interest in writing, but in wanting to do something about it. When I was interviewed for a position here in Madison in 1970, there were literally tanks rolling down the streets in response to the strong antiwar movement on campus. This was a very liberal community in the best of that sense in those times. I knew when I was interviewed (and during the interviews the building was tear-gassed), well I knew that this was the place I wanted to be. So this is a personal story and also a political history. Finally, there are other things I think that contributed to my politicization. Speaking very personally, I am the father of an African-American child. This means that not only again must I work at the level of thinking these things through, but must live as someone who faces having the child come home from school every day angry, hurt, or scared because of racial polarizations, utter insensitivity on the part of the school, etc. This too increases my sense that I have to struggle everyday. The phenomenology of children, and here my *own* children, adds something crucial.

Raymond: Let's shift to the specific content of your research strategy. In some of your retrospective reflections and introductions you've noted certain shifts in perspective, particularly the general movement from correspondence theory through a broader conception of the possibility of resistance. If you could briefly comment on how that has affected the direction of your work.

Michael: That makes it seem as if these shifts occurred primarily because of a shift in tradition of the theoretical literature. (We are going to have to think about this somewhat more dialectically I think.) Of course I was influenced by emerging debates within the various critical traditions. But, political action also causes different kinds of thinking. I tend to be fairly materialist about this; circumstances changed for me, and then things changed within me as well. Much of the work that I engaged in originally was something like politicized phenomenology. It tended to blend together some of the traditions of social phenomenology, Habermas, and critical theory (before these last two were changed into something safe). Furthermore, the person I had worked with at Columbia (Dwayne Huebner) also taught courses in liberation theology and phenomenology at Union Theological Seminary there. Much of the work that I engaged in originally was an attempt to blend together a nonstructuralist Marxist position with phenomenology because those were the two fields I was trying to pull together in some way. As these two traditions merged in my mind (and of course created tensions as well), part of the work that I began to engage in was an attempt to see how that merger could help us understand the politics of class in the actual curriculum, the way we think about class and education, and our own structural position as educators. Now what that meant was that I had to support the antiliberal positions of people like Bowles and Gintis in *Schooling in Capitalist America*—what has been called correspondence theory. For them, if you understand the hidden curriculum, you understand schooling, and the only way to understand it is to actually compare children by class trajectories. While I was a bit uncomfortable with this because of its "teacher bashing," its unsubtle sense of culture, of the complexities of human experience, I wanted to support it because it seemed to me that it was at least an attempt at politicizing a tradition and destabilizing the more conservative and reformist liberal tradition. On the other hand, I wanted to show and highlight the notion of culture as having some autonomy. The result was *Ideology and Curriculum*, a book, I trust, that helped to establish that culture has materiality, that it was influenced by but wasn't a total reflection of economic structure.

Raymond: So your kind of structuralism was motivated by incorporating culture as a theme whereby you actually became sensitized to it in the practical side of politics.

Michael: That's right.

Carlos: In looking at the intellectual tradition of Marxism outside the U.S., there are two serious traditions that try in a way to fight against determinism and the authoritarianism of Stalinism: Althusserian structuralism and Gramsci's approach. The structuralist overtones are much more related to the French origins of Althusser than with the reading of Marxism. Althusser's is a particular reading of Gramsci. Whether one agrees or not with the reading is not the question here. The drawing board of Althusser is Gramsci. How would you escape drawing the same conclusions as Althusser did when you were reading Gramsci at that time?

Michael: As I have argued in many places, a good deal of the Marxist tradition needed to be seriously challenged and reconstructed. Perhaps because of this, I was taken by Althusser's structuralism, in part because of its emphasis on contradictory moments at a number of levels. It was in fact not necessarily only the prison house for many people as it is made out to be. It was in fact a reading of that tradition that enabled us to think about structure and the specificities of culture, and the specificities of the political. Of course, it is a prison in some ways, as any structural analysis can be; but it enabled us to think about the way culture was partly separate, and how it was relatively autonomous. After all, isn't this what a theory of contradictory levels is all about? So I was very taken with the Althusserian position, but clearly what it didn't do was allow any room for the point you made before, for human agency, for resistance, for struggle, since it was in fact ultimately guided by a logic of reproduction. The next books I wrote began to push at that. *Education and Power* began to look at the contradictory and not necessarily only reproductive relationship between culture, economy, and the State. It also began to look at gender and race as well as class dynamics. *Ideology and Curriculum* is an analysis by and large of domination and exploitation. It does end on a note of hope—about human agency, the next theme—but it was still primarily in class terms.

After I had written *Ideology and Curriculum* and *Education and Power*, I began to talk about some of the material on deskilling teachers and changes in the class position of teachers that are embodied in them. (Remember, I had been a president of a teachers' union, and had worked very closely with teachers and cinematographers on film work with children and teachers—beautiful, loving material with no necessarily overtly political overtones, but which showed the very possibility of different ways of creating personal and political meaning in schools.) This meant I had a good deal of credibility with teachers. I was speaking with a group very similar to the Boston Women Teachers' Group in the United States, to part of the "feminist teachers' alliance" in Madison, and I was laying out the tradition of interpreting teachers' labor that I was attempting to build, and what that means in terms of their deskilling and loss of curricular control. After listening intently to me for quite a while, one teacher said, "Michael, did it ever dawn on you that you are speaking to thirty people who are sexed in particular ways?" And it was like a light bulb going off. It became crystal clear that class analysis itself, even with the focus on resistance and struggle that I had integrated into it, simply could not deal with the major fact that gender was the absent presence in most of our work. It was all too silent on the issue that teaching was an extension by and large of women's unpaid labor in the home. We cannot understand class without understanding gender. I was helped immensely here as well by my wife, Rima, who is a historian of medicine whose focus is on the struggles by women to control their bodies and knowledge.

I began to move from a focus by and large on the intricacies of class relations and nonreproductive forms to the immensely contradictory formations in education and elsewhere of class, race, and gender relations in politics, in economics, in culture. That required a radical reconstruction of Althusserian theory. It included a theory of human agency and just as importantly included a theory of overdetermination, where gender both helps produce class and contradicts it, and both are often produced by and contradict race. These are the *dynamics* that make up a social formation. They work their way out in the relatively autonomous spheres of culture, economy, and politics. This is an admittedly complicated theory. I've tried to lay it out clearly in the introductory chapter of *Ideology and Practice in Schooling* and in my work with Cameron McCarthy. (The fact that, as I now argue, there are contradictions *within,* not only among, each of these dynamics and spheres makes it even more complex, but since I am not in a church, I am not worried about heresy.)

Raymond: That's much closer to the original Gramsci without the Althusserian epistemology. In many ways your work was not merely reflecting the changes in the literature and the radical education position, so much as reconnecting elements in your own biography and work in developing a more synthetic position.

Carlos: That's right. In a way theory seems to be illuminating practice, which is a principle of a materialist perspective in culture. It is intriguing that a crucial aspect of your writings has not been reading, but by interacting with people and by being able to listen and be challenged.

Raymond: By that time the theory had gotten ahead of your practice, whereas before your practice was ahead of your theory?

Michael: Partly, but again an example is *Education and Power* which I think is actually a much more fluid book than the more structuralist reproductive readings in *Ideology and Curriculum*. Two political and personal, as well as scholarly, reasons account for this. As I just mentioned, I began to work with a dissident women's group; yet, I also began to work with a union group struggling to democratize in an automobile plant in Wisconsin. One of my students was a Vietnam veteran and a political activist. I'd been to rallies with him and we had done some political work together. He couldn't get a job as a teacher and worked on an assembly line in the plant. He was trying to work with others to form a dissident union group that would challenge both the union ideologies and structures and management strategies that were quite conservative in that plant. They asked me to come and to help them build material for political education. This is part of my training; I was originally educated at Columbia in the curriculum area. My training as a curriculum worker meant that I could offer some assistance in how you create material that was responsive and, I hoped, powerful.

As I began to work with this group, it was quite clear that the stuff I was doing in *Ideology and Curriculum* bore little resemblance to what was happening in the day-to-day life of these workers on the assembly line. They were dominated in some very interesting ways ideologically; the hegemonic form was visible, but it was also very contradictory and they were struggling with it every day. So again there was this constant dialectical process between the action I was doing in working with the union and having to rethink, massively, the positions I was taking that said, well, people by and large internalize these things and did so in an unmediated way. And again, while some of the workers were often sexist and often very racist (though to a much lesser extent within this group than some of the all-too-common stereotypes of working-class culture in the literature would allow), their situation actually looked closer to Paul Willis's work with its emphasis on class capacities and cultural production than it did to the more straightforward reproductive emphasis that I had partly slid into by the end of *Ideology and Curriculum*. So, yes, the theories were more advanced than practice, but the practice was quickly catching up and pushing the theory another way.

Raymond: Could we move up to the present? I think for those of us working in Canada, for example, we're quite impressed by the incredible, remarkable development in critical scholarship in the United States over the past ten to fifteen years. But the other side of that, of course, is the grim reality of American politics. The Bush administration continues the longer term of Republican hegemony, and there is also the public invisibility (perhaps except for Jesse Jackson) of the kind of concerns expressed in your work in the mass media and in the overt political agenda. What is your assessment of the possibilities for long-term transformation given the deadlock at this particular moment, and the invisibility of what you represent outside of fringe communities and the academy?

Michael: That is a very complicated question. By and large, it is the case that the Left is more marginal in the United States. The United States has a very populist nature, and populism can be transformed in a right-wing direction or a left-wing direction. Right now, with the fracturing of what I call in recent work "the social democratic accord"—the liberal accord— there is an alliance of the New Right, the fraction of the new middle class that gets its own mobility through accountability measures, management techniques and so on, neo-conservative academics, and economic modernizers. This alliance clearly is winning in important ways. I think your analysis of the situation is correct. Part of the tragedy of this at the level of people at universities, in labor unions, etc., has been their participation in making that happen.

Raymond: By the attack on liberalism?

Michael: Yes, in part. Let me explain the emerging situation. I think there has been a rapprochement with what is called liberal "person rights" by many people on the Left now. Earlier, we tended to see liberalism as simply an attempt by ruling-class interests to mystify certain things. More and more, however, it is quite clear that many of what used to be called "bourgeois rights" were the result of struggles. They were not simply ways of coopting dissent. Instead, they were compromises, accords. We began to realize that our attacks on liberalism in education and elsewhere— which were correct in many ways—came at a time when actually it would have been wiser to focus more on the real concerns of people in local communities. We too often forget how tenuous these "liberal" gains actually are in the long history of the particular kinds of struggles at the present time. Also—and this is where I think many of us created troubling results—I think that much of the discourse that we participated in was truly negative criticism. Negative work is important of course as a form of "bearing witness" to oppression, but often it did not give people a sense of possibility. It also was done at such a theorized level that it was unable to connect to the real-life experiences of people—and that is a tragedy. This partly enabled the creation of a situation in which the Right has been able to rebuild its hegemonic forms around peoples' real sense of anger. There are populist sentiments in the United States, for example, that are fundamentally opposed to big business, but somehow the Right has been able to recuperate those feelings. The Left and populist forces should be able to work with that, but we have been unable to do so because we have been too concerned with our elegant abstractions and have forgotten about the connections we have to make with real life. For too many of us, our only political work is writing for other theorists. I don't want to disparage this; such writing is crucial. But in the process, we have all too often given the political and educational field over to the Right and have let them define the public agenda.

Carlos: What would probably be the reason for that? My experience in the U.S. has been very brief, but while I was at Stanford, I had the sense that there was a kind of break between the Old Left and the New Left in the U.S. which affected the creation of a socialist tradition. Would that be one of the reasons why the focus of attack was misplaced in this new wave of criticism of schooling?

Michael: I don't think that the focus of criticism was totally misplaced, and I think that I am still largely opposed to the liberal tradition, as a tradition that is too isolated from the roots of oppressive conditions. But I do think that there were major gains within it, and they must be repoliticized. Our task, then, is in part to defend and extend these gains in more democratic directions in all of our institutions, both "public" and "private." This is a program of radical democracy. Parts of this program are already there if they can be reconstructed. For instance, the tradition of antiracist and democratic socialist work in the United States in education is very long. This is not new. For this reason, I object to being called a "reconceptualist." I am not reconceptualizing anything, but building upon and reconstructing a whole history of the relationship between cultural politics and democratic socialism in the United States. There were always alternatives and many of the same kinds of claims I am now making, other people were making in 1910 and 1920. If you want to talk about where the blame lies, the democratic socialist tradition and the populist tradition in the United States have been marginalized consciously and placed under attack, for decades. Remember, this is the country of the "Red" scares, the Palmer raids, etc. Add to this the murderous history of attacks on Latinos and Latinas, Asian-Americans, Indians, and African-American women and men, on gays and lesbians, and others. Thus, while there *were* serious problems with "Old Left" approaches, rather than blaming major parts of the critical tradition for its lack of connectedness or for some of its partly misplaced criticisms, we might want to remember the history of its forced marginalization.

Raymond: That was at the end of the first world war when the socialist parties became scapegoats for fears about the Bolshevik Revolution in Russia, and the socialist parties were destroyed by police professionals.

Michael: Yes, part of the results are seen in the fact that the union movement in the United States is still among the smallest in terms of the percentage of people in most Western industrialized nations. Unions have won major victories and have helped create the social-democratic accord, but they also have been weakened by the State through oppression, marginalizing, etc. So we want to be cautious about blaming the Left for fracturing itself, even though the joke about how many leftists it takes to go fishing is correct. The answer is one hundred—one to hold the pole and ninety-nine to argue about the correct line. We have been culpable about that. But again this is also part of a longer story. The United States has always been less able to build a large-scale democratic socialist tradition in part because the boats were often just as filled with immigrants going back as they were coming. Many people who were often the most politically active did not stay because either they didn't make it or they went back repeatedly to deal with pressing problems. As well, the vast openness of the nation and the fact that *political* liberties for white males were granted originally at the beginning of nationhood meant that, unlike in, say, England, they did not have to be struggled for as part of a class-based politics as much. It was in England where class politics and political struggles had to be joined. In the United States, there was a very different articualtion of that struggle. That means that it was very hard to organize around an avowedly socialist program in the United States. To make a difference it has to be populist. Although class relations do have a long history in the United States, they are given a peculiar flavor due to the specific political, cultural, racial, and religious history of the country.

Raymond: Can I ask you a related question? From the point of Canadian and European observers, one of the things that is most distinctive about American political culture is the predominance of single-issue politics which reflects the absence of this integrated framework which a socialist movement would provide, and which the liberal program did provide for a period of time. Do you see this still as an ongoing problem?

Michael: Yes; one of the things the Right has been markedly successful in doing is forming coalitions of single-issue groups around a particular agenda. An agenda in education of standardization, of a false "common culture," of a romanticized past of "choice," of guaranteeing a connection between school and paid work; this is the coalition that has been formed. The Right has been able to do this, to provide this hegemonic umbrella. In essence, it says, we will compromise. You want certain things (e.g., populist and middle-class forces that want mobility and opportunities). We will give you that provided you form this coalition under the umbrella of economic modernization (to compete with the Japanese, etc). The Right has blended together themes of nationalism and patriotism, "pro-family" issues, standards, sexuality, drugs, and so on under its own leadership and has used them for its purpose of taking an economic ideology of "free enterprise" and spreading it into every sector of society. Single issues have been in fact articulated together brilliantly by the Right in the U.S. But I think the prospects for that coalition being retained structurally are actually slim. In order for economic modernization to take place in this way, "capital" must be set loose. Now, the ideological forms of capital, and the way capitalism itself operates as an economic mode, means that commodification must subvert sacred traditions and visions of sacred knowledge. Thus, as a paid worker, I must not get meaning on my job (if I'm now lucky enough to have one), I have to wait until I am walking out of the factory, out of my office, going on my vacation, or buying a TV or a VCR or having a camper. Yet, in the process, discipline on the job is subverted. At the same time, to maintain legitimacy and create profits, our economy must act against the romanticized visions of the family, home, and school, of women's place being defined only by the domestic sphere. Thus, the New Right populists' ideology cannot combine with the "free-market" emphasis on making everything for sale.

Raymond: A Disney view of the world?

Michael: In part, yes, which is under threat. You cannot have industrialization and unleash these market forces and at the same time defend traditional positions on the family and sacred knowledge of the past. They are mutually exclusive. So my sense is that this coalition must fracture in the long run. All this means is that it provides us the objective possibility of forming coalitions between those of us who favor democratizing the school and the paid and unpaid workplace and these other disaffected groups. We can form a different coalition that articulates these people who are now being organized by the Right with more democratic positions.

Carlos: Hearing you previously discussing the role of informal education I was very pleased. You are not known as a nonformal educator, but as a school-based researcher. May this assumption that a right-wing coalition cannot hold indefinitely lead you to say, yes, there is a need to develop new forms of resistance in education as the eventual basis of a more "offensive" strategy? Is that a fair reading of your comments?

Michael: Yes, definitely. The hard part is to try to find out where the appropriate group is, and who the "we" is who does it. However, this makes it sound too strategic, unfortunately, and less organic than what I mean. I have moved to a position that might be called a position of "decentered unity." I do not believe that class is the fundamental engine that provides the only organizing force for social change. I articulated in *Teachers and*

Texts a parallelist position where there are multiple agents and multiple struggles. Social movements including, and often going well beyond, class dynamics are powerful agents here.

Raymond: So you have been influenced by poststructuralist debates but not taken in hook, line, and sinker in the way some might accuse, say, Philip Wexler?

Michael: Definitely. Philip is a dear friend of mine and we have written things together, and as you know, his volume on these issues appeared in the book series, *Critical Social Thought,* that I edit. I think that his intuitions are probably correct. That is, we have to decenter the notion that class is the only place where human agents are available (while still appreciating the power of class relations). That is made visible if we look at the issue of racial formation and of gender politics, with men as well as women. Perhaps not so oddly, this is actually a return to my previous politics where I was not only formed in part by working-class politics because of the political background of my family—a family union tradition, having been a printer myself, etc. As I mentioned earlier, I was also profoundly formed personally in racial politics. So it's a return to part of my biography. But some of the poststructuralist position worries me and I will be honest about this. I think that we can multiply forms of domination to such an extent that there are no meaningful organizations left to combat oppression. I think the position runs the risk of becoming an embodiment of the postmodern condition itself; that is, it mirrors our inability to see and to recognize what structures exist and how they actually work in relation to large-scale forms of domination and exploitation.

Let me give you an example. I must admit that when I am in Brazil, Thailand, and other countries doing educational and political work and participating with groups of people struggling to keep babies alive, to *find* enough food to eat, to even get a minimum of schooling for their children, when I work with others to build international movements to support these peoples' struggles, because of all that, I think the relations that make up what we can objectively call capitalism are much more oppressive than other kinds of relations *in many situations.* In our (largely meritorious, as feminist theories have brilliantly shown) attempts to move beyond class reductionism and recognize how domination in race, class, gender, sexuality, and other relations works, we have at times forgotten the massive structuring forces that *do* exist. And because of personal experience, perhaps because I grew up poor, I think that we must in fact begin to think through what are the dangers of a position that when taken too far rests totally on the notion that there are an infinite multiplicity of discourses of power. It can too easily support the notion that everything is an equal form of oppression, isn't it? For political reasons, I don't think we can say that. Of course, we must organize with people in their own felt sense of oppression. That's the phenomenological urge, that's cultural politics. However, I must admit that in my heart of hearts I don't think that all oppressions are equal, that I think there are vicious results arising out of the national and international movement to bring all of us the "benefits" of capitalist economies, cultures, and politics. And it is not only an image; these are real objective conditions. The politics of production has not totally been replaced by the politics of consumption. Talk about discourses *is* powerful and freeing indeed; but unless we recognize its limitations and its current overtheorization, we will also be in danger of our own kind of mystification while the world crumbles down around us and the lives and hopes of identifiable people are shattered. It is important, though, that I not be misunderstood here. I do *not* want to dismiss the utter power of race, gender, and sex oppressions, and of the tensions within them. The brutality of the oppression of women in what is called the "domestic sphere" is exactly that: brutal. My point, however, is to have us focus on *material* conditions, something we are forgetting in our rush to see everything in "discursive" terms. Thus, though discourse *does* have its own materiality, I think there are very real dangers, as well as benefits, of seeing the world as only a "text." I am not being a class essentialist or an economic reductionist here. However, living under capitalism means something, and I believe that this should never be forgotten.

Raymond: Let's change the focus a bit to the world system and particularly the relationship between metropolitan countries and dependent countries.

Carlos: It's clear from this conversation that the three of us are outside the mainstream traditions of [North] American society. But I am a double "outsider" coming from a Third World society. The question I have is the following: How can we discuss the creation of a transformative teacher who is part and parcel of a more comprehensive system of domination and control in a metropolitan society in the context of the world system?

Michael: I think one has to struggle where one is. I don't want to dismiss the issue of understanding the international context in which we exist at all. All of our actions need to be interpreted relationally. For instance, take the fact that to do this interview we walked into this room and turned on a light. We can interpret this act positivistically as an objective fact. We could simply say that Michael Apple walked into this room in which we were to videotape and I turned on a light. Yet this interpretation is not social enough. It doesn't recognize that not only did I turn on a light, but in the process I had an anonymous social relationship with the miners that have dug the coal, many of who have died or were badly injured, or suffered long-term illness in the process so that the electricity was produced to enable the light to go on. So I think we want to think about these things in terms of our concrete relations with other people. This obviously requires that we think in international terms; I agree with that. Yet there is also a theoretical and political issue about changing the minds of people in the center, people who now do not recognize how much their comforts rest on the work of people in poorer nations. To the extent that alterations within the imperialist center have an impact at the level of people's lives outside that political center, I think we have no choice but to engage in political education with teachers, children, adults, and others here to make it very clear how our everyday lives are in fact tied up in systems of domination. It is important for us to understand that to make the cultural, political, and economic conditions of Third World peoples less oppressive, changes must be made not simply in Haiti, Senegal, Mexico, Nicaragua, or elsewhere, they also must occur in the capitalist center, the belly of the beast, the U.S.A.

Now, I am constantly reminded of this because many of my students come from nations that have oppressive governments or that are newly democratized. I too spend a good deal of time in those nations myself, and in fact was arrested and ultimately sent home from one repressive nation in Asia because I spoke out against the government's antidemocratic policies in education and politics. This means that we as educators must take a stand against antidemocratic relationships wherever they are found. For whatever power education has, it can in fact make very clear to teachers what these relationships are. I am not saying that this will alter the universe of multiple oppressions on an international scope, but I think, to the extent that I call myself someone who is an educator, I have no choice but to act.

Yet "center/periphery" relations do not exhaust these issues. There is a Third World within the first world. I am not only talking about what goes on in Argentina or Chile or Brazil. I must talk about Third World peoples in the United States and that's part of the struggle that many people have to understand as well. We're not simply exporting the working class of the United States or Canada to Mexico, Malaysia, Haiti or elsewhere. We are exploiting Third World populations in the United States. We're destroying them at the same time through economic and educational policies and practices that are truly disabling. There are nations inside this nation, and again the educational practice that goes on surrounding that issue is critically important. That is the Gramscian part of me. You surround the imperial center not just outside the nation but inside it as well with alternate cultural and political forms. Thus, our task is also to surround the relations of cultural and economic domination and exploitation at home, and build possibilities as well here. This, of course, involves concrete work at the level of pedagogy and curriculum, to recapture our lost collective memories of successful struggles, and to continue the path that Raymond Williams to cogently called the long revolution.

Raymond: I would like to just suggest one final question without wanting to promote divisiveness within the tradition of radical and critical educational scholarship. How would you respond to the kind of strategy represented by Henry Giroux, in particular his emphasis on the language of possibility, etc., and his attempt to draw upon critical theory in the Frankfurt tradition, as well as his relation to Paulo Freire? How would you view that in relationship to the kinds of strategies that you represent?

Michael: Henry and I have been friends for a number of years. I was one of the first to reestablish the neo-Marxist cultural tradition in the early '70s in the United States, before Henry and others joined me. Being largely alone in 1970, it was a pleasure to welcome him in the middle of the decade. When Henry first began writing, he would send me all his material. In the process we both taught each other a good deal. He is clearly very smart and has an exceptional ability to integrate work together. We all stand on people's shoulders. For a number of years, Henry stood on mine, and there were times when I stood on his. There have been times when we have or will criticize each other both in print and elsewhere. Yet I think this has to be done in an immensely cooperative manner. There are times that we disagree. For example, there may be a danger with the level of overabstraction of his work at times. There are times when we must make clear connections with people's lives and sometimes that requires a level of specificity that Henry sometimes doesn't do. While I am less sanguine about the poststructuralist and postmodern traditions than he perhaps is, I am now even less enamored with the critical theory tradition than he is, in part perhaps because my training was initially Habermasian. I had left that for particular conceptual and political reasons, in part because I think that there are traditions (e.g., the neo-Gramscian and the radical democratic) that say it better and clearer and offer a different and more democratic kind of politics as well. On the other hand, I think the work he is doing with Aronowitz on issues such as building "a language of possibility," on the Bloom-Hirsch debate in the United States, and on antiracist and postcolonial theory is of critical importance to cultural politics. So again, by and large I will do nothing but support his work, though perhaps he, like many of us, could value criticism of our work more since he at times overreacts to committed progressive people who may disagree with some of his arguments. We must be both teacher and taught at the same time. However, I was chosen by the faculty there to be an outside evaluator in his tenure case at Boston University where he was brutally and unethically dealt with. I supported him as much as I could then.

I think our task is to criticize each other in the best sense of learning from each other; otherwise how will the tradition grow and learn from its mistakes? *Because* we are on the democratic Left we must model a kind of openness and democratic behavior in our own discourse. We must welcome criticism—when it is itself given in an open and honest fashion—if we are not to recapitulate the relations we are supposed to be fighting against.

Carlos: You have drawn a lot of material from Freire. What would be your main criticism of the Freirean approach? What would be the idea of Freire that impressed you most?

Michael: There are few people I am willing to sit at the feet of, and Freire is one of them. He is someone I am proud to say I know. But with all people there are times, there are certain things, we must criticize. We have a tendency to create gods. I know this is uncomfortable for Freire. When I was in Brazil, it became quite clear to me that there were many people who are progressive who also disagree with him, and one of the disservices I think we do in creating gods is that we forget that there are debates over their work in their own nation. So the first thing I would suggest that we do is to find out what the debates are over Freire's pedagogical theories where they were developed. In this way, we can make certain we do not import things that could be strengthened by linking them to those original multiple and often conflicting traditions. We could then better understand their strengths and weaknesses as opposed to seeing them just as political/pedagogical resources that can be used anywhere, with no necessary reconstructions and no thought given to their contradictions. To simply take these things in an unreconstructed way goes against the very notion of a Freirian pedagogy.

While I very much agree with the notion that one begins one's pedagogy in the lived experience of actors and that there are ways of stimulating that—and here Freire is unparalleled in the world—I am in other ways probably more Gramscian in that I think that we have given up too much on the question of content. I am distressed in part by an idea that some people have that says that when dealing with people in creating political literacy, which is a slow process, we assume that the knowledge that we too often call "bourgeois" is not essential for engaging that literacy. We assume that the necessary resources are always somehow already there in the community and "we" do not need to bring it to them. I think that all of this knowledge, even in the traditional disciplines, was built off the labor of these people. And it is theirs and it deserves to be theirs. I would go further—though I think that the pedagogy might be the same—and would take much more seriously the issue of content. I also think that we are in danger of appropriating, and making politically safer, brilliant material that was developed in the Third World and in practical kinds of struggle. In this way, we contribute to the loss of its critical commitment to liberation. As I said, I don't think it is easy to translate that into our classrooms and I don't think the conditions are necessarily exactly the same. So I think it has to reappropriated, rebuilt around the themes, the structures, of the lives of real people in industrialized nations. We need to be very careful not to simply create another bandwagon.

I think that, in fact, what we too often do is we take on Freire as an easy model, as simply a transportable technique, a technique to pull out of our pocket, forgetting that it is built in struggle and it must be reconnected and rebuilt with the people. Thus, there are a variety of dangers that I see. But on the other hand, Freire's approach is such an advance over the normal ways of how we think about nonformal education, about whose knowledge is appropriate, and how we can articulate that in a very critical way, that it would be an act of bad faith not to allow it to influence much of what we do.

Our work is a form of cultural politics. This involves all of us working for what Williams called the "journey of hope" toward "the long revolution." To do less, not to engage in such work, is to ignore the lives of millions of students and teachers throughout the world. Not to act is to let the powerful win. Can we afford to let this happen?

NOTES

CHAPTER 1: INTRODUCTION: THE POLITICS OF OFFICIAL KNOWLEDGE

1. Jonathan Kozol, *Savage Inequalities* (New York: Crown, 1991).

2. One of the best analyses of the racial structuring of this society is still Michael Omi and Howard Winant, *Racial Formation in the United States* (New York: Routledge, 1986).

3. Marcus Raskin, *The Common Good* (New York: Routledge, 1986), 8.

4. Ibid. See also the discussion of this in Landon Beyer and Michael W. Apple, eds., *The Curriculum: Problems, Politics and Possibilities* (Albany: State University of New York Press, 1988), especially chapter one.

5. Madeleine Arnot, "Schooling for Social Justice" (Paper presented at the Twelfth National Conference of the New Zealand Association for Research in Education, Auckland, New Zealand, 1990).

6. I discuss the contradictions between the neo-liberal and neo-conservative wings of the rightist movement in much greater detail in Michael W. Apple, "The Politics of Official Knowledge: Does a National Curriculum Make Sense?" (The John Dewey Lecture presented at the American Educational Research Association Annual Meeting, San Francisco, 1992). See also Roger Dale, *The State and Education Policy* (Philadelphia: Open University Press, 1989).

7. Bob Jessop, Kevin Bonnett, Simon Bromley, and Tom Ling, *Thatcherism* (New York: Polity Press, 1988), 39.

8. Ibid.

9. Ibid., 40. To characterize the growth of the New Right—with its uneasy alliance between neo-liberalism and neo-conservatism—is actually less easy than one might expect. It implies that we already know its character and its nature.

56

Yet, this movement has changed, in part because of resistance from others and in part because it has evolved under shifting economic, political, and ideological conditions. Since it has not as yet consolidated its position, and its hold on power is certainly not total, we need always to be open to the possibility that the characteristics I outline are subject to change. Ibid. 12. See also Education Group II, *Education Limited* (London: Unwin Hyman, 1991) and Geoff Whitty's continuing important work on this.

10. Education Group II, *Education Limited,* x.

11. Henry Louis Gates, Jr., "What Is Patriotism?" *The Nation* 253 (March 15–22, 1992): 91.

12. Michael B. Katz, *The Undeserving Poor* (New York: Pantheon, 1989), 7.

13. Adam Smith, *The Wealth of Nations* (Oxford: Clarendon, 1976), 709–10.

14. Michael R. Real, "Demythologizing Media," *Critical Studies in Mass Communications* 3 (December 1986): 467.

15. Graeme Turner, *British Cultural Studies* (Boston: Unwin Hyman, 1990), 5–6.

16. See Michael W. Apple, *Teachers and Texts: A Political Economy of Class and Gender Relations in Education* (New York and London: Routledge, 1988), especially chapter eight.

17. See Michael W. Apple, "Education, Culture, and Class Power," *Educational Theory* 42 (Spring 1992): 127–45. See also Bryan D. Palmer, *Descent into Discourse* (Philadelphia: Temple University Press, 1990); and Steven Best and Douglas Kellner, *Postmodern Theory* (London: Macmillan, 1991).

18. I defend parts of the agenda of class analysis—but *only* when reconstructed and done well—in Apple, "Education, Culture and Class Power." See also Basil Bernstein, *The Structuring of Pedagogic Discourse* (New York: Routledge 1990); and Stanley Aronowitz, *The Politics of Identity* (New York: Routledge, 1992).

19. For an articulate and insightful discussion of identity politics, see Hank Bromley, "Identity Politics and Critical Pedagogy," *Educational Theory* 39 (Summer 1989): 207–23.

20. For some support of this position as well as a number of interesting criticisms of it, see Best and Kellner, *Postmodern Theory.*

21. Nancy Fraser, *Unruly Practices* (Minneapolis: University of Minnesota Press, 1989), 2.

22. Ibid.

23. Ibid. 108.

24. Ibid.

25. Ibid.

26. Michael W. Apple, *Ideology and Curriculum* (New York: Routledge, 1979; 2nd ed., 1990); Michael W. Apple, *Education and Power* (New York: Routledge and Kegan Paul, 1982; rev. ARK ed. 1985); and Apple, *Teachers and Texts.*

27. By "level" I do not mean a hierarchy, signifying top and bottom. Perhaps a better word would be *site,* each with its own relatively autonomous practices.

28. See, for example, the discussion of needs and needs discourses in Fraser, *Unruly Practices.*

29. This is discussed in more detail in Michael W. Apple, "Is There a Curriculum Voice to Reclaim?" *Phi Delta Kappan* 71 (March 1990): 526–30.

30. Some of these alternatives can be found in Susan Gushee O'Malley, Robert C. Rosen, and Leonard Vogt, eds., *The Politics of Education: Essays From Radical Teacher* (Albany: State University of New York Press, 1990).

CHAPTER 2: THE POLITICS OF COMMON-SENSE: WHY THE RIGHT IS WINNING

1. Stuart Hall, "The Toad in the Garden: Thatcherism Among the Theorists," in Cary Nelson and Lawrence Grossberg, eds., *Marxism and the Interpretation of Culture* (Urbana: University of Illinois Press, 1988), 42.

2. Ibid.

3. Michael W. Apple, *Teachers and Texts: A Political Economy of Class and Gender Relations in Education* (New York and London: Routledge 1988).

4. Hall, "The Toad in the Garden," 35.

5. Ibid., 36.

6. See Apple, *Teachers and Texts,* and Henry Giroux, "Public Philosophy and the Crisis in Education," *Harvard Educational Review* 54 (May 1984): 186–94.

7. Michael W. Apple, *Education and Power* (New York: Routledge, 1985), and Apple, *Teachers and Texts.*

8. Herbert Gintis, "Communication and Politics," *Socialist Review* 10 (March-June 1980): 193.

9. Ibid., 196.

10. Ibid., 197.

11. Ibid.

12. Ibid., 194. See also Samuel Bowles and Herbert Gintis, *Democracy and Capitalism* (New York: Basic Books, 1986).

13. Apple, *Teachers and Texts.*

14. Mary Anderson, "Teachers Unions and Industrial Politics," (Ph.D. diss., Macquarie University, 1985), 6–8.

15. Ann Bastian, Norm Fruchter, Marilyn Gittell, Colin Greer, and Kenneth Haskins, *Choosing Equality: The Case for Democratic Schooling* (Philadelphia: Temple University Press, 1986), 14.

16. I wish to thank my colleague Walter Secada for his comments on this point. See also Jonathan Kozol, *Savage Inequalities* (New York: Crown, 1991).

17. Michael W. Apple, "National Reports and the Construction of Inequality," *British Journal of Sociology of Education* 7, no. 2 (1986): 171–90.

18. Michael W. Apple, *Ideology and Curriculum,* 2nd ed. (New York: Routledge, 1990); and Jorge Larrain, *Marxism and Ideology* (Atlantic Highlands, NJ: Humanities Press, 1983).

19. Stuart Hall, "Authoritarian Populism: A Reply," *New Left Review* 151 (May/June 1985): 122.

20. See David Clark and Terry Astuto, "The Significance and Permanence of Changes in Federal Education Policy," *Educational Researcher* 15 (October 1986): 4–13; Frances Piven and Richard Cloward, *The New Class War* (New York: Pantheon, 1982); and Marcus Raskin, *The Common Good* (New York: Routledge and Kegan Paul, 1986).

21. Stuart Hall and Martin Jacques, "Introduction," in Stuart Hall and Martin Jacques, eds., *The Politics of Thatcherism* (London: Lawrence and Wishart, 1983), 13.

22. Stuart Hall, "Popular Democratic vs. Authoritarian Populism: Two Ways of Taking Democracy Seriously," in Alan Hunt, ed., *Marxism and Democracy* (London: Lawrence and Wishart, 1980), 160–61.

23. Ibid., 161.

24. I realize that there is a debate about the adequacy of this term. See Hall, "Authoritarian Populism" and Bob Jessop, Kevin Bonnett, Simon Bromley, and Tom Ling, "Authoritarian Populism, Two Nations, and Thatcherism," *New Left Review* 147 (September/October 1984): 33–60.

25. Michael Omi and Howard Winant, *Racial Formation in the United States* (New York: Routledge and Kegan Paul, 1986), 214.

26. Walter Dean Burnham, "Post-Conservative America," *Socialist Review* 13 (November/December 1983): 125.

27. Hall, "Authoritarian Populism," 117. For further discussion of this, see Michael W. Apple, "The Politics of Official Knowledge: Does a National Curriculum Make Sense?" (The John Dewey Lecture presented at the American Educational Research Association Annual Meeting, San Francisco, 1992); and Education Group II, *Education Limited* (London: Unwin Hyman, 1991).

28. Ibid., 119.

29. Hall, "Popular Democratic vs. Authoritarian Populism," 166.

30. Hall, "The Toad in the Garden," 55.

31. Stuart Hall, "The Great Moving Right Show," in Stuart Hall and Martin Jacques, eds., *The Politics of Thatcherism,* 19–39.

32. Apple, *Education and Power.*

33. Hall, "The Great Moving Right Show," 29–30.

34. Ibid., 36–37. For an illuminating picture of how these issues are manipulated by powerful groups, see Allen Hunter, "Virtue With a Vengeance: The Pro-Family Politics of the New Right," (Ph.D. diss., Brandeis University, 1984). It is interesting to note that it is still an open question as to whether or not there *is* such a crisis in "literacy." See, (for example, Carl Kaestle, et al., *Literacy in the United States* (New Haven: Yale University Press, 1991).

35. Apple, *Teachers and Texts.*

36. Jessop, et al., "Authoritarian Populism, Two Nations, and Thatcherism," 49.

37. Hall, "The Great Moving Right Show," 21.

38. Allen Hunter, "The Politics of Resentment and the Construction of Middle America," (Department of Sociology, University of Wisconsin, Madison, 1987, photocopy), 1–3.

39. Ibid., 9. Much of the discussion in this section is based on conversations with Allen Hunter. His work is essential for understanding rightist social movements. Special thanks also go to Geoff Whitty here.

40. Samuel Bowles, "The Post-Keynesian Capital-Labor Stalemate," *Socialist Review* 12 (September/October 1982): 51.

41. Hunter, "The Politics of Resentment and the Construction of Middle America," 12.

42. Omi and Winant, *Racial Formation in the United States,* 214–15.

43. Raskin, *The Common Good.*

44. Omi and Winant, *Racial Formation in the United States,* 215–16. See also Hunter, *Virtue with a Vengeance.*

45. Omi and Winant, *Racial Formation in the United States,* 220. For a more complete discussion of how this has affected educational policy in particular, see Clark and Astuto, "The Significance and Permanence of Changes in Federal Education Policy"; and Apple, *Teachers and Texts.*

46. Omi and Winant, *Racial Formation in the United States,* 221. I have claimed elsewhere, however, that some members of the new middle class—namely efficiency experts, evaluators, testers, and many of those with technical and management expertise—will form part of the alliance with the New Right. This is simply because their own jobs and mobility depend on it. See Apple, *Teachers and Texts.*

47. Omi and Winant, *Racial Formation in the United States,* 227.

48. Ibid., 164.

49. Ibid. The discussion in Bowles and Gintis, *Democracy and Capitalism,* of the "transportability" of struggles over person rights from, say, politics to the economy is very useful here. I have extended and criticized some of their claims in Michael W. Apple, "Facing the Complexity of Power: For a Parallelist Position in Critical Educational Studies," in Mike Cole, ed., *Rethinking Bowles and Gintis* (Philadelphia: Falmer, 1988), 112–30.

50. See Apple, *Education and Power,* and Apple, *Teachers and Texts.*

51. Omi and Winant, *Racial Formation in the United States,* 177–78.

52. Ibid.

53. Ibid., 180.

54. Ibid., 190.

55. Ibid.

56. Ibid.

57. Ibid., 252.

58. Ibid., 155.

59. Hunter, "The Politics of Resentment and the Construction of Middle America," 23.

60. Ibid., 30.

61. Ibid., 33.

62. Ibid., 34.

63. See Michael W. Apple and Linda Christian-Smith, eds., *The Politics of the Textbook* (New York and London: Routledge, 1991).

64. Ibid., 21.

65. See Rebecca E. Klatch, *Women of the New Right* (Philadelphia: Temple University Press, 1987).

66. Michael Kazin, "The Grass Roots Right," *American Historical Review* 91 (February 1992): 143.

67. Ibid., 144.

68. Ibid., 146.

69. Ibid., 147. We, of course, need to be very careful of words such as "traditional." They naturalize their objects. Whose "tradition" are we talking about? How does something get constructed as "traditional?"

70. Ibid., 37. The vision of the family that stands behind the rightist position naturalizes something that is very much a social construction that has changed over time. See, for example, Stephanie Coontz, *The Social Origins of Private Life* (New York: Verso, 1988).

71. See Apple, "National Reports and the Construction of Inequality," and Apple, *Teachers and Texts.*

72. Stuart Hall, "Popular Culture and the State," in Tony Bennett, Colin Mercer, and Janet Woollacott, eds., *Popular Culture and Social Relations* (Milton Keynes: Open University Press, 1986), 35–36.

73. Hall, "The Toad in the Garden," 40.

74. Ibid., 45.

75. Ibid.

76. Chantal Mouffe, "Hegemony and New Political Subjects: Toward a New Concept of Democracy," in Cary Nelson and Lawrence Grossberg, eds., *Marxism and the Interpretation of Culture* (Urbana: University of Illinois Press, 1988), 96.

77. Ibid. See also, Stanley Aronowitz, *The Politics of Identity* (New York: Routledge, 1992).

78. Omi and Winant, *Racial Formation in the United States,* 165.

79. Ibid., 166.

80. I say "new" here, but the continuity of, say, black struggles for freedom and equality also needs to be stressed. See the powerful treatment of the history of such struggles in Vincent Harding, *There Is a River: The Black Struggle for Freedom in the United States* (New York: Vintage, 1981).

81. For a discussion of this in relationship to class dynamics, see David Hogan, "Education and Class Formation," in Michael W. Apple, ed., *Cultural and Economic Reproduction in Education* (Boston: Routledge, and Kegan Paul, 1982), 32–78.

82. Omi and Winant, *Racial Formation in the United States,* 166.

83. Apple, "National Reports and the Construction of Inequality."

84. Apple, *Teachers and Texts;* Martin Carnoy, Derek Shearer, and Russell Rumberger, *A New Social Contract* (New York: Harper and Row, 1984); Gary Burtless, ed., *A Future of Lousy Jobs?* (Washington: The Brookings Institute, 1990); and Sheldon Danzinger and Daniel Weinberg, eds., *Fighting Poverty* (Cambridge: Harvard University Press, 1986).

85. Apple, "National Reports and the Construction of Inequality." For a comprehensive analysis of the logic of capitalism, one that compares it with other political and economic traditions, see Andrew Levine, *Arguing for Socialism* (Boston: Routledge and Kegan Paul, 1984).

86. Apple, *Education and Power,* and Apple, *Teachers and Texts.*

87. See Sara Freedman, Jane Jackson, and Katherine Boles, *The Effects of the Institutional Structure of Schools on Teachers* (Somerville, MA: Boston Women's Teachers' Group, 1982).

88. William Reese, *Power and the Promise of School Reform* (New York and London: Routledge, 1986).

89. Center for Law and Education, "Vocational Education Project: Vocational Opportunity for Community and Educational Development," (mimeo, Center for Law and Education, Cambridge, MA, 1990), 3.

90. Ibid.

91. Ibid., 1.

92. Ibid., 4.

93. Further information on the Vocational Education Project can be obtained by writing to the Center for Law and Education, 995 Massachusetts Ave., 3rd. Floor, Cambridge, MA 02139.

94. Patricia Burdell, "Thinking About Change in Schools: The At Risk Student Project," *New Futures* (Newsletter of the National Center on Effective Secondary Schools, University of Winconsin, Madison, 1989) 1: 4–7.

95. Michael W. Apple, "American Realities: Poverty, Economy, and Education," in Lois Weis, Eleanor Farrar, and Hugh Petrie, eds., *Dropouts from School* (Albany: State University of New York Press, 1989), 205–23.

96. Apple, *Teachers and Texts,* especially chapter seven.

97. I would like to thank James Ladwig for his assistance in writing this section of the description of progressive programs.

98. Material on *Rethinking Schools* can be obtained from Rethinking Schools, 1001 E. Keefe Ave., Milwaukee, WI 53212.

99. See Apple, *Ideology and Curriculum.*

100. For further discussions of other aspects of these possibilities, see Apple, *Teachers and Texts;* Bastian, et al., *Choosing Equality;* David Livingstone, ed., *Critical Pedagogy and Cultural Power* (South Hadley, MA: Bergin and Garvey, 1987); and Roger Simon, Don Dippo, and Arleen Schenke, *Learning Work* (New York: Bergin and Garvey, 1991).

101. Hall, "The Great Moving Right Show," 120.

102. Apple, *Ideology and Curriculum.*

103. See, for example, Margo Culley and Catherine Portuges, eds., *Gendered Subjects* (New York: Routledge 1985); Elizabeth Kamarck Minnich, *Transforming Knowledge* (Philadelphia: Temple University Press, 1990); and Chris Weedon, "Post-structuralist Feminist Practice," in Donald Morton and Mas'ud Zavarzadeh, eds., *Theory/Pedagogy/Politics* (Urbana: University of Illinois Press, 1991), 47–63.

104. These and similar attempts have a long history that needs to be brought to life again. See, for example, Kenneth Teitelbaum, "Contestation and Curriculum," in Landon Beyer and Michael W. Apple, eds., *The Curriculum: Problems, Politics and Possibilities* (Albany: State University of New York Press, 1988), 32–55; and Clyde Barrow, "Pedagogy, Politics and Social Reform," *Strategies* 2 (Fall 1989): 45–66.

105. See Elizabeth Ellsworth, "Why Doesn't This Feel Empowering?" *Harvard Educational Review* 59 (August 1989): 297–324; and Henry Giroux, *Border Crossing* (New York: Routledge, 1992).

106. Raymond Williams, *The Year 2,000* (New York: Pantheon, 1983), 268–69.

CHAPTER 3: CULTURAL POLITICS AND THE TEXT

1. This chapter is an expansion and refinement of the introductory chapter to Michael W. Apple and Linda Christian-Smith, eds., *The Politics of the Textbook* (New York: Routledge, 1991). Many of the essays in that volume are crucial to a more thorough understanding of the issues I raise here.

2. See John Willinsky, *The New Literacy* (New York: Routledge, 1990).

3. Janet Batsleer, Tony Davies, Rebecca O'Rourke, and Chris Weedon, *Rewriting English: Cultural Politics of Gender and Class* (New York: Methuen, 1985), 164–65. For an exceptional treatment of "political literacy" in theory and practice, see Colin Lankshear with Moira Lawler, *Literacy, Schooling and Revolution* (Philadelphia: Falmer, 1988).

4. John Fiske, Bob Hodge, and Graeme Turner, *Myths of Oz: Reading Australian Popular Culture* (Boston: Allen and Unwin, 1987), x.

5. John Fiske, *Reading the Popular* (Boston: Unwin Hyman, 1989), 149–50.

6. See, for example, Michael W. Apple and Lois Weis, eds., *Ideology and Practice in Schooling* (Philadelphia: Temple University Press, 1983).

7. For a current representative sample of the varied kinds of studies being done on the textbook, see Arthur Woodward, David L. Elliot, and Kathleen Carter Nagel, eds., *Textbooks in School and Society* (New York: Garland, 1988). We need to make a distinction between the generic use of "texts" (all meaningful materials: symbolic, bodily, physical, etc., created by human, and sometimes "natural," activity) and textbooks. My focus in this chapter is mostly on the latter, though many schools and many teachers use considerably more than standardized textbook material. Also, in passing, I am more than a little concerned that some people have overstated the case that the world is "only a text." See Bryan D. Palmer, *Descent into Discourse* (Philadelphia: Temple University Press, 1990).

8. Fred Inglis, *Popular Culture and Political Power* (New York: St. Martin's Press, 1988), 9.

9. Allan Luke, *Literacy, Textbooks and Ideology* (Philadelphia: Falmer, 1988), 27–29.

10. Michael W. Apple, *Ideology and Curriculum,* 2nd ed. (New York: Routledge, 1990); Michael W. Apple, *Education and Power* (New York: Routledge, rev. ARK ed., 1985); and Michael W. Apple, *Teachers and Texts: A Political Economy of Class and Gender Relations in Education* (New York and London: Routledge, 1988).

11. Michael W. Apple, "Redefining Equality: Authoritarian Populism and the Conservative Restoration," *Teachers College Record* 90 (Winter 1988): 167–84.

12. See, for example, Susan Rose, *Keeping Them Out of the Hands of Satan* (New York: Routledge, 1988).

13. Allen Hunter, *Children in the Service of Conservatism* (Madison: University of Wisconsin Institute for Legal Studies, 1988).

14. James Moffett, *Storm in the Mountains* (Carbondale: Southern Illinois University Press, 1988).

15. Raymond Williams, *The Long Revolution* (London: Chatto and Windus, 1961). See also Apple, *Ideology and Curriculum.*

16. Fred Inglis, *The Management of Ignorance: A Political Theory of the Curriculum* (New York: Basil Blackwell, 1985), 22–23.

17. Ibid., 23.

18. Miriam Schipper, "Textbook Controversy: Past and Present," *New York University Education Quarterly* 14 (Spring/Summer 1983): 31–36.

19. A. Graham Down, "Preface," in Harriet Tyson-Bernstein, *A Conspiracy of Good Intentions: America's Textbook Fiasco* (Washington, D.C.: The Council for Basic Education, 1988), viii.

20. Harriet Tyson-Bernstein, *A Conspiracy of Good Intentions,* 3.

21. Robert Darnton, *The Literary Underground of the Old Regime* (Cambridge: Harvard University Press, 1982), 199.

22. The social roots of such adoption policies will be discussed in chapter four.

23. The issues surrounding cultural imperialism and colonialism are nicely laid out in Philip Altbach and Gail Kelly, eds., *Education and the Colonial Experience* (New York: Transaction Books, 1984). For an excellent discussion of international relations over texts and knowledge, see Philip Altbach, *The Knowledge Context* (Albany: State University of New York Press, 1988).

24. See the analysis of such power relations in Bruce Fuller, *Growing Up Modern* (New York: Routledge, 1991) and Martin Carnoy and Joel Samoff, *Education and Social Transition in the Third World* (Princeton: Princeton University Press, 1990).

25. For some of the most elegant discussions of how we need to think about these "cultural silences," see Leslie Roman and Linda Christian-Smith with Elizabeth Ellsworth, eds., *Becoming Feminine: The Politics of Popular Culture* (Philadelphia: Falmer, 1988).

26. Marcus Raskin, *The Common Good* (New York: Routledge, 1986).

27. Inglis, *The Management of Ignorance,* 142.

28. Inglis, *Popular Culture and Political Power,* 4.

29. Ibid. I have placed "dark side" in quotation marks in the previous sentence because of the dominant tendency to unfortunately equate darkness with negativity. This is just one of the ways popular culture expresses racism. See Michael Omi and Howard Winant, *Racial Formation in the United States* (New York: Routledge 1986); and Edward Said, *Orientalism* (New York: Pantheon, 1978).

30. Darnton, *The Literary Underground of the Old Regime,* 13.

31. Batsleer, Davies, O'Rourke, and Weedon, *Rewriting English: Cultural Politics of Gender and Class.*

32. Lankshear with Lawler, *Literacy, Schooling and Revolution.*

33. Batsleer, et al. *Rewriting English,* 5.

34. James W. Fraser, "Agents of Democracy: Urban Elementary School Teachers and the Conditions of Teaching," in Donald Warren, ed., *American Teachers: Histories of a Profession at Work* (New York: Macmillan, 1989), 128.

35. Apple, *Teachers and Texts.*

36. For further discussion of deskilling and reskilling, see Apple, *Education and Power.*

37. Margaret Haley, quoted in Fraser, "Agents of Democracy," 128.

38. Haley, quoted in Fraser, "Agents of Democracy," 138.

39. Tony Bennett, "Introduction: Popular Culture and 'the Turn to Gramsci,'" in Tony Bennett, Colin Mercer, and Janet Woollacott, eds., *Popular Culture and Social Relations* (Philadelphia: Open University Press, 1986), xvi.

40. The literature here is voluminous. For a more extended treatment see Apple, *Education and Power;* and Cameron McCarthy and Michael W. Apple, "Race, Class, and Gender in American Educational Research," in Lois Weis, ed., *Class, Race, and Gender in American Education* (Albany: State University of New York Press, 1989).

41. See Apple, *Ideology and Curriculum;* and Linda Christian-Smith, *Becoming a Woman Through Romance* (New York: Routledge, 1991).

42. Luke, *Literacy, Textbooks and Ideology,* 24.

43. Tyson-Bernstein, *A Conspiracy of Good Intentions,* 18.

44. Tony Bennett, "The Politics of the 'Popular' and Popular Culture," 19.

45. Ibid.

46. See Didacus Jules, "Building Democracy," in Michael W. Apple and Linda Christian-Smith, eds., *The Politics of the Textbook* (New York: Routledge, 1991), 259–87.

47. Stuart Hall, "The Toad in the Garden: Thatcherism Among the Theorists," in Cary Nelson and Lawrence Grossberg, eds., *Marxism and the Interpretation of Culture* (Urbana: University of Illinois Press, 1988), 44.

48. Ibid.

49. Allan Bloom, *The Closing of the American Mind* (New York: Simon and Schuster, 1987); and E. D. Hirsch, Jr., *Cultural Literacy* (New York: Houghton-Mifflin, 1986).

50. William Bennett, *Our Children and Our Country* (New York: Simon and Schuster, 1988), 9.

51. Ibid., 10.

52. Ibid.

53. Apple, "Redefining Equality."

54. Luke, *Literacy, Textbooks and Ideology,* 29–30. See also Allan Luke, "The Secular Word: Catholic Reconstructions of Dick and Jane," in Apple and Christian-Smith, eds., *The Politics of the Textbook,* 166–90.

55. Lawrence Grossberg and Cary Nelson, "Introduction: The Territory of Marxism," in Nelson and Grossberg, eds., *Marxism and the Interpretation of Culture,* 8.

56. Paulo Freire, *Pedagogy of the Oppressed* (New York: Herder and Herder, 1973).

57. See, for example, Paul Willis, *Learning to Labor* (New York: Columbia University Press, 1981); Angela McRobbie, "Working Class Girls and the Culture of Femininity," in Women's Studies Group, ed., *Women Take Issue* (London: Hutchinson, 1978), 96–108; Robert Everhart, *Reading, Writing and Resistance* (Boston: Routledge and Kegan Paul, 1983); Lois Weis, *Between Two Worlds* (Boston: Routledge and Kegan Paul, 1985); Bonnie Trudell, *Doing Sex Education* (New York: Routledge, in press); and Christian-Smith, *Becoming a Woman Through Romance.*

58. Tania Modleski, "Introduction," in Tania Modleski, ed., *Studies in Entertainment* (Bloomington: Indiana University Press, 1986), xi.

59. See Elizabeth Ellsworth, "Illicit Pleasures: Feminist Spectators and *Personal Best,*" in Roman, Christian-Smith, with Ellsworth, *Becoming Feminine,* 102–19; Elizabeth Ellsworth, "Why Doesn't This Feel Empowering?" *Harvard Educational Review* 59 (August 1989): 297–324; and Christian-Smith, *Becoming a Woman Through Romance.*

60. For an example of powerful and compelling literature for younger students, see the discussion in Joel Taxel, "Reclaiming the Voice of Resistance: The Fiction of Mildred Taylor," in Apple and Christian-Smith, eds., *The Politics of the Textbook,* 111–34.

61. Batsleer, et al. *Rewriting English,* 5.

62. This is discussed in more detail in the new preface to the second edition of Apple, *Ideology and Curriculum.*

63. Raymond Williams, *Resources of Hope* (New York: Verso, 1989), 37–38.

64. David Horne, *The Public Culture* (Dover, NH: Pluto Press, 1986), 76.

CHAPTER 4: REGULATING OFFICIAL KNOWLEDGE

1. "The Textbook Selection Process," *Interracial Books for Children Bulletin* 14 (no. 5, 1983): 17.

2. "Texas Battles Over Evolution," *EPIE gram* 12 (May 1984): 5.

3. "The Textbook Selection Process," 17.

4. Further economic information can be found in Michael W. Apple, *Teachers and Texts: A Political Economy of Class and Gender Relations in Education* (New York and London: Routledge, 1988); and Michael W. Apple and Linda Christian-Smith, eds., *The Politics of the Textbook* (New York and London: Routledge, 1991).

5. I shall differentiate between the *State* and the *state.* The first signifies the assemblage of publicly financed institutions, here meaning the government and

the institutions it supports in general. The second refers to a geographical entity, one of the fifty individual states in the United States.

6. Michael W. Apple, *Ideology and Curriculum,* 2nd ed. (New York and London: Routledge, 1990).

7. Ernest Mandel, "Foreword" in J. W. Freiberg, *The French Press: Class, State, and Ideology* (New York: Praeger, 1981), vii.

8. Ibid., viii.

9. Basil Bernstein, "On Pedagogic Discourse," in John G. Richardson, ed., *Handbook of Theory and Research for the Sociology of Education* (New York: Greenwood Press, 1986), 230.

10. See David Hogan, "Education and Class Formation," in Michael W. Apple, ed., *Cultural and Economic Reproduction in Education* (Boston: Routledge and Kegan Paul, 1982), 32–78; and Basil Bernstein, *Class, Codes and Control Volume 3,* 2nd ed., (Boston and London: Routledge and Kegan Paul, 1977).

11. See Martin Carnoy, *The State and Political Theory* (Princeton: Princeton University Press, 1984); Apple, *Teachers and Texts;* Martin Carnoy and Henry Levin, *Schooling and Work in the Democratic State* (Stanford: Stanford University Press, 1985); and Michael W. Apple, "Curriculum, Capitalism and Democracy," *British Journal of Sociology of Education* 7 (no. 3, 1986): 319–27.

12. Freiberg, *The French Press,* 13.

13. Ibid.

14. Apple, *Teachers and Texts.*

15. Margaret S. Archer, "Social Origins of Educational Systems," in John G. Richardson, ed., *Handbook of Theory and Research for the Sociology of Education* (New York: Greenwood, 1986), 31.

16. Bernstein, "On Pedagogic Discourse," 226–27.

17. Ibid., 227.

18. Ibid.

19. Nelson B. Henry, "Value of State Textbook Adoption is Debatable," *The Nation's Schools* 12 (December 1933): 19.

20. John G. Richardson, "Historical Sequences and the Origins of Common Schooling in the American States," in John G. Richardson, ed., *Handbook of Theory and Research for the Sociology of Education,* 36.

21. Ibid., 38.

22. Ibid., 47.

23. Ibid., stress added.

24. See Richardson, "Historical Sequence and the Origin of Common Schooling in the American States," for more detail on these regions.

25. Quoted in Marjory R. Kline, "Social Influences in Textbook Publishing," *Educational Forum* 48 (Winter 1984): 224.

26. Archer, "Social Origins of Educational Systems," 26. It is also the case that such state power is not always applied uniformly. Thus, it would be deceptive to assume that once a state had established uniform textbook legislation, that there was a guarantee that all students in all school districts would employ the same textbooks. In fact, for a period of time over half (15) of the states with such legislation also expressly exempted certain cities and school districts because of their specific sizes and race/class characteristics. Some, as well, gave local boards the right to select their own books if a majority of school board members voted in favor of such a move. See Clyde J. Tiswell, *State Control of Textbooks with Special Reference to Florida* (New York: Bureau of Publications, Teachers College Press, 1928), 21.

27. Henry, "Value of State Textbook Adoption is Debatable," 20.

28. Guy M. Whipple, "The Selection of Textbooks," *The American School Board Journal* 80 (May 1930): 51.

29. Quoted in Edgar Wallace Knight, *The Influence of Reconstruction on Education in the South* (New York: Teachers College, Columbia University Contributions to Education, no. 60, 1930; Arno Press, 1969), 80.

30. Ibid., 97.

31. H. L. Donovan, "How to Select Textbooks," *Peabody Journal of Education* 2 (July 1924); 2. It would be important to know whether the teachers being attacked here were women. Often, gender relations underpin the mistrust of teachers. See Apple, *Teachers and Texts*.

32. Henry, "Value of State Textbook Adoption is Debatable," 19.

33. Charles Judd, "Analyzing Textbooks," *The Elementary School Journal* 19 (October 1918): 145–46.

34. See John Franklin Brown, "Textbooks and Publishers," *The Elementary School Journal* 19 (January 1919): 382–88.

35. Judd, "Analyzing Textbooks," 143. This theme is echoed in a vast array of literature, in the press, and in professional publications from the middle of the nineteenth century onwards.

36. Ibid. By 1924, one educator forcefully declared that "the best textbooks are so well bound, so beautifully decorated, and so perfectly printed on the best of paper that it appears doubtful that notable further improvement along these lines will be achieved." The very fact that he even felt called upon to say this at the very outset of his essay on the text pointed to the serious problems, which sometimes came close to outright fraud, about the physical conditions of textbooks that had existed earlier. See Donovan, "How to Select Textbooks," 1.

37. Brown, "Textbooks and Publishers," 388.

38. Ibid.

39. J. B. Edmonson, "The Ethics of Marketing and Selecting Textbooks," in Guy Montrose Whipple, ed., *The Textbook in American Education* (Bloomington, IL.: Public School Publishing Co., 1931), 208–15.

40. See Tidwell, *State Control of Textbooks with Special Reference to Florida;* and Whipple, ed., *The Textbook in American Education.*

41. Robert H. Wiebe, *The Search for Order 1877–1920* (Cambridge, MA: Hill and Wang, 1967), 160.

42. Richard L. McCormick, "The Discovery that Business Corrupts Politics," *American Historical Review* 86 (April 1981): 251.

43. Ibid., 255.

44. Ibid., 262.

45. Ibid., 260.

46. Ibid., 257.

47. Ibid., 259.

48. Ibid., 265.

49. Ibid., 267.

50. Ibid., 268.

51. Dewey W. Grantham, *Southern Progressivism: The Reconciliation of Progress and Tradition* (Knoxville: University of Tennessee Press, 1983), 416.

52. Ibid., 275.

53. Ibid., 276. Clyde Barrow argues that progressivism provided a uniquely "conservative" program of reform that on the one hand improved labor's material condition, regulated "fair business practices," and yet generally preserved the basic economic framework of private property, markets, and the emphasis on individual achievement. Meanwhile, it introduced a concept of democracy in which the professional middle-class "expert" assumed the leading role as social engineer, reformer, legislator, and technical advisor to business, government, and labor. See Clyde Barrow, *Universities and the Capitalist State* (Madison: University of Wisconsin Press, 1990).

54. Grantham, *Southern Progressivism,* 301–302. For further discussion of regional differences, see Richardson, "Historical Sequences and the Origins of Common Schooling in the American States."

55. Richardson, "Historical Sequences and the Origins of Common Schooling in the American States," 47.

56. Theodore Mitchell, *Political Education in the Southern Farmers' Alliance 1887–1900* (Madison: University of Wisconsin Press, 1987), 25.

57. Ibid., 40.

58. Ibid., 80.

59. Ibid., 88.

60. Ibid., 46. This was not limited to agrarian movements. In California, for instance, the Workingmen's Party—also resentful of the power of the railroads and of corruption—won nearly one-third of the delegates to the second constitutional convention in 1878. Among other things, the delegates proposed state

printing of free textbooks and weekly school lectures on the importance of labor. They too, like the Farmers' Alliance later on, attacked the "textbook ring" and the "unethical practices" of publishers. By 1884, their position had influenced all major parties and an amendment was passed—the Perry Schoolbook Amendment—that established state printing and regulation of textbooks. For further discussion of California, see James A. Lufkin, "A History of the California State Textbook Adoption Program" (Ph.D. diss., University of California, Berkeley, 1968).

61. Mitchell, *Political Education in the Southern Farmers' Alliance,* 70.

62. Ibid., 52.

63. Ibid., 71. In the process, the Alliance also built its own educational materials, in essence a series of "counter-texts," organized around its own sense of class politics. For further examples of such "counter-texts" in, say, the socialist movement, see Kenneth Teitelbaum, "Schooling for Good Rebels" (Ph.D. diss., University of Wisconsin, Madison, 1985); and Kenneth Teitelbaum, "Critical Lessons from Our Past," in Apple and Christian-Smith, *The Politics of the Textbook,* 135–65.

64. Mitchell, *Political Education in the Southern Farmers' Alliance,* 123.

65. Ibid., 128–29.

66. Ibid., 74. Anger over northern textbooks was widespread as well and had a long history. See Marjory R. Kline, "Social Influences in Textbook Publishing," 224.

67. Mitchell, *Political Education in the Southern Farmers' Alliance,* 76. This, of course, has a very long history. For instance, in much of the South there was a very real fear of northern "cosmopolitan" beliefs about race, a fear that even affected such issues as postal rates. Indeed, in the years immediately preceeding the Civil War, there was considerable debate in Congress over eliminating postal charges, especially for newspapers. The champions of a "quiet, stable, localized, face-to-face society, simple in form and manageable" saw a very real threat in the cosmopolitan and usually northern publications such as large circulation newspapers. Newspapers (and books, pamphlets, etc.) from northern cities were "dangerous." Cheaper printing costs and minimal postal charges were creating a situation where "northern ideas" about the economy, about politics and culture, and especially about abolition and race relations were spreading. The structures of social and cultural control would then shift from local elites to metropolitan centers. Thus, postal rates should be correlated with, say, the distance a newspaper travelled, thereby making it too expensive for northern material to find an easy market in the South. See Richard B. Kielbowitz, "Modernization, Communication Policy, and the Geopolitical News, 1820–1860," *Critical Studies in Mass Communications* 3 (March 1986): 21–35.

It was not unheard of as well for northern literature to be burned in public bonfires. Thus, for example, in 1835 in Charleston, South Carolina, a group of people broke into the U.S. Post Office and carried off a number of mailbags that had just arrived from New York City. The bags were "stuffed with abolitionist tracts, magazines and newspapers." Crowds of white Charlestonians watched and cheered as the material was put to the torch. For more on these and similar instances, see David Paul Word, "The Evangelical Origins of Mass Media in America, 1815–1835," *Journalism Monographs* 88 (May 1984): 1–30.

68. Mitchell, *Political Education in the Southern Farmers' Alliance*, 77.

69. Ibid., 170.

70. Ibid., 148.

71. McCormick, "The Discovery that Business Corrupts Politics," 272–73.

72. Ibid., 273.

73. Grantham, *Southern Progressivism*, 4.

74. Ibid., 7.

75. Ibid., xxi.

76. Mitchell, *Political Education in the Southern Farmers' Alliance*, 186.

77. Quoted in Ibid., 190.

78. Ibid.

79. Ibid., 190–92.

80. Grantham, *Southern Progressivism*, xvii-xviii.

81. Ibid., 176.

82. Ibid., 231–33. The historic struggles by African-Americans against these pressures is discussed in Vincent Harding, *There Is a River: The Black Struggle for Freedom in the United States* (New York: Vintage, 1981).

83. Alwyn Barr, *Reconstruction to Reform: Texas Politics, 1876–1906* (Austin: University of Texas Press, 1971), 74.

84. Ibid., 241–42.

85. Grantham, *Southern Progressivism*, 31.

86. Ibid., 125–26.

87. Ibid., 213.

88. Ibid., xx. See also William Reese, *Power and the Promise of School Reform* (New York and London: Routledge and Kegan Paul, 1986) for his discussion of women's political activity in educational and social reform movements. See also Barr, *Reconstruction to Reform*, 230.

89. This is an important point. There were contradictory results from the movement to centralize authority. What may often have been retrogressive in class and race terms could at one and the same time have been partly progressive in gender terms. See Cameron McCarthy and Michael W. Apple, "Race, Class, and Gender in American Educational Research," in Lois Weis, ed., *Class, Race, and Gender in American Education* (Albany: State University of New York Press, 1988), 9–39. I do not wish to slight the immense accomplishments of African-American

women, especially women teachers. Their struggles with the local government over respect, resources, and even schooling itself is a crucial part of the history of the African-American battle for freedom. For further analysis of black teachers, see Linda M. Perkins, "The History of Blacks in Teaching," in Donald Warren, ed., *American Teachers* (New York: Macmillan, 1989), 344–69.

90. Grantham, *Southern Progressivism,* 13.

91. Ibid., 145.

92. Charles William Dabney, *Universal Education in the South Volume 1* (Chapel Hill: University of North Carolina Press, 1936; New York: Arno Press, 1969), 417.

93. Ibid., 418.

94. *The Constitution of the State of Texas: An Annotated and Comparative Analysis Volume 2* (Austin: Texas State Printing Office, n.d.), 506.

95. Dabney, *Universal Education in the South Volume 1,* 421.

96. Grantham, *Southern Progressivism,* 155. There *were* differences among the southern and southwestern states in the political, cultural, and economic dynamics that led to such a regulatory impulse. Yet the overall patterns are similar.

97. Ibid., 99–100.

98. Ibid., 103.

99. Ibid., 146.

100. Ibid., 14.

101. Ibid., 157.

102. Ibid., xvii.

103. Michael W. Apple, "Social Crisis and Curriculum Accords," *Educational Theory* 38 (Spring 1988): 191–201.

104. Grantham, *Southern Progressivism,* 418–19.

105. Ibid., 421.

106. Edmonson, "The Ethics of Marketing and Selecting Textbooks," 218.

107. Nelson B. Henry, "The Problems of Publishers in Making and Marketing Textbooks," in Whipple, ed., *The Textbook in American Education,* 182. Of course, the state may have a different interpretation of this. It is in the state's economic interest to have uniformity of textbooks controlled by the state, "since a state adoption involves a large number of books over a comparatively long period, all publishers will compete vigorously to secure contracts, and to that end they will offer their books at lower prices than they would if competition were less necessary." See Tidwell, *State Control of Textbooks with Special Reference to Florida,* 45.

108. "Political Attorney and Textbook Adoption," unsigned editorial, *The Elementary School Journal* 28 (November 1927): 162–63.

109. "State Adoption of Textbooks," unsigned letter from a textbook publisher, *The Elementary School Journal* 28 (February 1928): 403.

110. While I have pointed to it earlier in this chapter, I realize that I have not gone into the role played by organized groups of *teachers* here in the debates over state regulation. This would be essential if we were to more completely understand the internal dynamics and the politics of state regulation of education. A further discussion of the complex politics of race and region, with the North establishing centralized control over the South in the years after the Civil War would be essential as well, as would a much more detailed analysis of the constant attempts by African-Americans and Latinos/Latinas to use the State (and transform it) to enhance their children's lives.

CHAPTER 5: CREATING THE CAPTIVE AUDIENCE: CHANNEL ONE AND THE POLITICAL ECONOMY OF THE TEXT

1. Michael W. Apple, *Ideology and Curriculum,* 2nd ed., (New York: Routledge, 1990), and Michael W. Apple, *Education and Power* (New York: Routledge, rev. ARK ed., 1985).

2. Michael W. Apple, *Teachers and Texts* (New York: Routledge, 1988).

3. See Michael W. Apple and Linda Christian-Smith, eds., *The Politics of the Textbook* (New York and London: Routledge, 1991).

4. Carl Kaestle, Helen Damon-Moore, Lawrence C. Stedman, Katherine Tinsley, and William Vance Trollinger, Jr., *Literacy in the United States* (New Haven: Yale University Press, 1991).

5. Apple and Christian-Smith, *The Politics of the Textbook.*

6. For further discussion of this, see Apple, *Education and Power,* especially chapter six.

7. Madeleine Arnot, "Schooling for Social Justice," (Paper presented at the Twelfth National Conference of the New Zealand Association for Research in Education, Auckland, New Zealand, 1990), 2.

8. Ibid., 3.

9. Marcus Raskin, *The Common Good* (New York: Routledge, 1986).

10. Apple, *Teachers and Texts.*

11. William Celis, "School Districts Reeling in Weakened Economy," *The New York Times,* 5 June 1991, B10.

12. William Celis, "Schools Lose Money in Business Tax Breaks," *The New York Times,* 22 May 1991, A1.

13. Ibid., B9.

14. Ibid.

15. Ibid.

16. Ibid.

17. Ibid.

18. Celis, "School Districts Reeling in Weakened Economy," B10.

19. Ibid.

20. Larry Hoffman, "The Meanings of Channel One," (Paper presented at the American Educational Research Association Annual Meeting, Chicago, 1991), 20.

21. Ibid., 1.

22. Ann Marie Barry, "Channel One: Controversial Partnership of Business and Education," (Department of Communications and Theater, Boston College, 1991, photocopy), 2.

23. Hoffman, "The Meanings of Channel One," 31.

24. Ibid., 4.

25. Quoted in Ibid., 32.

26. Eileen R. Meehan, "Conceptualizing Culture as a Commodity," *Critical Studies in Mass Communications* 3 (December 1986): 448–57.

27. Barry, "Channel One," 1.

28. Ibid., 7.

29. Ibid.

30. Ibid.

31. Ibid., 2.

32. Ibid., 9–10.

33. Ibid., 5.

34. Ibid., 18.

35. Ibid., 17.

36. Ibid., 25.

37. Ibid., 23.

38. Ibid., 13.

39. See Apple, *Teachers and Texts.*

40. Richard Johnson, "What Is Cultural Studies Anyway?" (Occasional paper, Centre for Contemporary Cultural Studies, University of Birmingham, England, 1983).

41. John Fiske, "Television and Popular Culture," *Critical Studies in Mass Communications* 3 (June 1986): 200.

42. Ibid., 201.

43. Ibid.

44. Ibid.

45. Ibid.

46. Ibid.

47. Ibid., 202.

48. Ibid., 204.

49. Kevin M. Caragee, "Defining Solidarity," *Journalism Monographs* 119 (February 1990): 4.

50. Klaus Bruhn Jensen, "Qualitative Audience Research," *Critical Studies in Mass Communications* 4 (March 1987): 23.

51. Apple, *Education and Power.* See also, Michael W. Apple and Lois Weis, eds., *Ideology and Practice in Schooling* (Philadelphia: Temple University Press, 1983).

52. Kathleen Hall Jamieson and Karlyn Kohrs Campbell, *The Interplay of Influence* (Belmont, CA: Wadsworth, 1983), 38–39.

53. John Fiske, *Television Culture* (New York: Methuen, 1987), 284.

54. Apple, *Ideology and Curriculum.*

55. Fiske, *Television Culture,* 284.

56. Ibid., 284–85.

57. Ibid., 285, and Apple, *Ideology and Curriculum.*

58. Herbert Gans, *Deciding What's News* (New York: Pantheon, 1979), 10–13.

59. Michael R. Real. "Demythologizing Media," *Critical Studies in Mass Communications* 3 (December 1986): 474.

60. Steve M. Barkin and Michael Gurevitch, "Out of Work and On the Air," *Critical Studies in Mass Communications* 4 (March 1987): 10.

61. Ibid., 9–10.

62. Ibid., 15–16.

63. Ibid., 17.

64. Ibid.

65. I place the word "minority" in quotation marks to emphasize the fact that it is an ideological construction. White people have the power in schools and in the media to construct people of color as "the other." Yet, white people are a minority in the world and it would have a salutary effect on our understanding of the world if the word minority was reserved for *them.* On the issue of race as a social construction and how specific ideological constructions of it are given official sanction, see Michael Omi and Howard Winant, *Racial Formation in the United States* (New York: Routledge, 1986).

66. Jo Ellen Fair, "Comparative Perspectives on Black-on-Black Violence: Gangs and Tribes in News Discourses," (School of Journalism, University of Wisconsin, Madison, 1990, photocopy), 1.

67. Ibid., 2.

68. Ibid., 3.

69. James Larson, Emile McAnany, and J. Douglas Storey, "News of Latin Amer-

ica on Network Television," *Critical Studies in Mass Communications* 3 (June 1986): 176.

70. Ibid., 180.

71. Caragee, "Defining Solidarity," 34.

72. Ibid., 35.

73. Ibid., 36. Of course, there were conservative, liberal, and various kinds of socialist elements intermixed in the Solidarity program, but very few of the strongly egalitarian positions were reported. See Ibid., 37–39.

74. Ibid., 41.

75. Ibid., 40.

76. Ibid., 41.

77. I want to thank my colleague Ann De Vaney for first bringing this point to my attention.

78. See, for example, Peter Dahlgren, "Tuning in the News," in Jose Vidal-Beneyto and Peter Dahlgren, eds., *The Focused Screen* (Strasbourg: Council of Europe, 1987), 1–90. See also the chapters by Ann Celsing, "Seeing Is Believing," 93–138; and David Althiede, "The Format of T.V. Network News," 141–80, in the same volume.

79. Althiede, "The Format of T.V. Network News," 167. See also Pamela Shoemaker with Elizabeth K. Mayfield, "Building a Theory of News Content," *Journalism Monographs* 103 (June 1987): 1–36.

80. Raymond Williams, *Television* (New York: Schocken, 1974).

81. For more discussion of the codes of television, see Fiske, *Television Culture*, and Ann De Vaney, "A Grammar of Educational Television," in Dennis Hlynka and John Belland, eds., *Paradigms Regained* (Englewood Cliffs, NJ: Educational Technology Publications, 1991), 241–83.

82. Fair, "Comparative Perspectives on Black-on-Black Violence," 3–4.

83. John Fiske, "Television: Polysemy and Popularity," *Critical Studies in Mass Communications* 3 (December 1986): 394.

84. Fiske, "Television and Popular Culture," 214.

85. Ibid., 209.

86. Ibid., 203.

87. Ibid.

88. Paul Willis, *Common Culture* (Boulder, CO: Westview, 1990).

89. See Robert Hodge and David Tripp, *Children and Television* (Cambridge: Polity Press, 1986), and Fiske, "Television and Popular Culture," 204.

90. Fiske, "Television and Popular Culture," 204.

91. Ibid., 201. See also Linda Christian-Smith, *Becoming a Woman Through Romance* (New York: Routledge, 1991).

92. Basil Bernstein, *Class, Codes and Control, Volume 3,* 2nd ed., (New York and London: Routledge, 1977).

93. Barry, "Channel One," 8.

94. I am again indebted to Ann De Vaney for this point.

95. Peter Stallybrass and Allon White, *The Politics and Poetics of Transgression* (Ithaca: Cornell University Press, 1986).

96. Fiske, "Television and Popular Culture," 212.

97. See Cameron McCarthy and Michael W. Apple, "Race, Class, and Gender in American Educational Research," in Lois Weis, ed., *Class, Race, and Gender in American Education* (Albany: State University of New York Press, 1988), 9–39.

98. Apple, *Teachers and Texts,* chapter two.

99. Andrew Gitlin, "School Structure and Teachers' Work," in Apple and Weis, *Ideology and Practice in Schooling,* 193–212.

100. Thus, in many ways, the students' collective joy in playing with the commercials is equivalent to the machinists' creation of "homers," pieces of informal art that they make from scraps of metal left over when their production quota is completed. Such "homers" are often aesthetically and personally interesting, but they do not interfere with management's control of the content and process of the labor process. For further discussion of this, see Apple, *Education and Power.*

101. Apple, *Teachers and Texts,* and Apple and Christian-Smith, *The Politics of the Textbook.*

102. Basil Bernstein, *The Structuring of Pedagogic Discourse* (New York: Routledge, 1990).

103. Ann Bastian, Norm Fruchter, Marilyn Gittell, Colin Greer, and Kenneth Haskins, *Choosing Equality: The Case for Democratic Schooling* (Philadelphia: Temple University Press, 1986).

104. Apple, *Teachers and Texts.*

105. See Apple, *Education and Power.*

106. Stuart Hall, "Popular Culture and the State," in Tony Bennett, Colin Mercer, and Janet Woollacott, eds., *Popular Culture and Social Relations* (Milton Keynes: Open University Press, 1986), 35–36.

107. It is important to note, however, that capital is not united in its support of Channel One and this may give us some reason for optimism. There is a split in the business community on this proposal, one brought on by both a fear of an expanding sphere of competition and a dislike for what might happen to students. Thus, the president of Macdonalds in the United States, in arguing against programs such as Channel One, asks, "Do we want the classroom to become the new battleground for our companies? . . . The right thing to do is to give schools the audio-visual equipment for education, not for competitive advantage," See Barry, "Channel One," 16.

108. Quoted in David Horne, *The Public Culture* (Dover, NH: Pluto Press, 1986).

109. John Bunzel, ed., *Challenge to American Schools* (New York: Oxford University Press, 1985); and Apple, *Teachers and Texts.*

110. I am indebted to Paul Willis for this point.

111. Willis, *Common Culture*, 2–29.

CHAPTER 6: WHOSE CURRICULUM IS THIS ANYWAY?

1. See Michael W. Apple, *Teachers and Texts: A Political Economy of Class and Gender Relations in Education* (New York and London: Routledge, 1988), and Michael W. Apple, "Redefining Equality: Authoritarian Populism and the Conservative Restoration," *Teachers College Record* 90 (Winter 1988): 167–84.

2. Michael W. Apple, *Education and Power* (New York: Routledge, ARK ed., 1985).

3. Stephen Ball, "Staff Relations During the Teachers' Industrial Action: Context, Conflict and Proletarianization," *British Journal of Sociology of Education* 9 (no. 3, 1988): 290.

4. The issue of the "proletarianization" of teachers is a complicated one. For further discussion, see Apple, *Education and Power*, 135–64; and Apple, *Teachers and Texts*, 31–78. Some of the complexities are nicely articulated in Jenny Ozga and Martin Lawn, "Schoolwork: Interpreting the Labour Process of Teaching," *British Journal of Sociology of Education* 9 (no. 3, 1988): 323–336. Much of the next section is based on Michael W. Apple and Kenneth Teitelbaum, "Are Teachers Losing Control of Their Skills and Curriculum?" *Journal of Curriculum Studies* 18 (no. 2, 1986): 177–84.

5. Apple, *Education and Power*, 66–90, and Apple, *Teachers and Texts*, 31–78.

6. As many of you may know, Tayloristic strategies have a long history of use in education. For further discussion, see Herbert Kliebard, *The Struggle for the American Curriculum* (New York: Routledge, 1986); Michael W. Apple *Ideology and Curriculum*, 2nd. ed. (New York and London: Routledge, 1990); and Apple, *Education and Power*, 71–73, 135–64.

7. Apple, *Education and Power*, 71–73.

8. Apple, *Teachers and Texts*, 56–58.

9. Ibid., 54–78.

10. Lawrence Stedman and Marshall Smith, "Recent Reform Proposals for American Education," *Contemporary Education Review* 2 (Fall 1983): 85–104; and Apple, *Teachers and Texts*, 128–49.

11. The negative impact of such testing and reductive objectives-based curriculum and evaluation strategies is a major problem. It is nicely documented in Andrew Gitlin, "School Structure and Teachers' Work," in Michael W. Apple and Lois Weis, eds., *Ideology and Practice in Schooling* (Philadelphia: Temple Uni-

versity Press, 1983), 193–212. See also Linda McNeil, *Contradictions of Control* (New York: Routledge, 1986).

12. Apple, *Teachers and Texts*, 54–78.

13. Ibid. We are, of course, here making a "functional" argument, not necessarily an "intentional" one. Managers, policy experts, neo-liberals, neo-conservatives, and others need not consciously plan to specifically control the work of women for it to have this effect. For further discussion of the logic of functional explanations, see Daniel Liston, *Capitalist Schools: Explanation and Ethics in Radical Studies of Schooling* (New York: Routledge, 1988), 75–101.

14. Apple, *Education and Power.*

15. The economics and politics of textbook publishing are analyzed in much greater depth in Apple, *Teachers and Texts*, especially chapter four, and Michael W. Apple and Linda Christian-Smith, eds., *The Politics of the Textbook* (New York and London: Routledge, 1991).

16. See, for example, Richard Edwards, *Contested Terrain* (New York: Basic Books, 1979), and David Gordon, Richard Edwards, and Michael Reich, *Segmented Work, Divided Workers* (New York: Cambridge University Press, 1982).

17. Gordon, Edwards, and Reich, *Segmented Work;* and Apple, *Education and Power*, 38–90.

18. Some of this data is reviewed in Sheldon Danziger and Daniel Weinberg, eds., *Fighting Poverty* (Cambridge: Harvard University Press, 1986); Erik Olin Wright, *Classes* (New York: Verso, 1985); and Michael W. Apple, "American Realities: Poverty, Economy, and Education," in Lois Weis, Eleanor Farrar, and Hugh Petrie, eds., *Dropouts from School* (Albany: State University of New York Press, 1989), 205–23.

19. For a more detailed elaboration of the process and results of intensification, see Apple, *Teachers and Texts*, especially chapter two.

20. Gitlin, "School Structure and Teachers' Work," 193–212.

21. Ozga and Lawn, "Schoolwork," 333. On the issue of gendered dispositions and values in teaching, see Madeleine Grumet, *Bitter Milk* (Amherst: University of Massachusetts Press, 1988, and JoAnne Pagano, *Exiles and Communities* (Albany: State University of New York Press, 1990).

22. Whether such "literacy" is in fact necessary in the way its proponents propose and the possible educational, social, and economic effects of such technology are examined in greater depth in Apple, *Teachers and Texts*, 150–74.

23. Stuart Hall, "Variants of Liberalism," in James Donald and Stuart Hall, eds., *Politics and Ideology* (Philadelphia: Open University Press, 1986), 35.

24. Most of the material in this section is taken from Susan Jungck, "Doing Computer Literacy," (Ph.D. diss., University of Wisconsin, Madison, 1985). The research and presentation of this study were negotiated with the participants.

25. For further discussion of the references on this important point, see Apple, *Teachers and Texts*, and Daniel Liston and Kenneth Zeichner, *Teacher Education and the Social Conditions of Schooling* (New York: Routledge, 1991).

26. See Michael W. Apple, "Do the Standards Go Far Enough?" *Journal of Research in Mathematics Education*, in press.

27. This response, with all of its contradictions, is similar historically to the calls by teachers in the latter part of the nineteenth century for the provision of standardized textbooks. As I noted in chapter two, many teachers, especially young women, rightly felt exploited by low pay, poor working conditions, and an expanding curriculum for which they felt either ill prepared to teach or, more usually, had insufficient time for which to prepare quality lessons. The standardized text was one way to solve parts of this dilemma, even though it may actually have undercut some of their emerging autonomy at the same time. Some elements of this story are told in Marta Danylewycz and Alison Prentice, "Teachers, Gender, and Bureaucratizing School Systems in Nineteenth Century Montreal and Toronto," *History of Education Quarterly* 24 (Spring 1984): 75–100.

28. See, for example, Carol Gilligan, *In a Different Voice* (Cambridge: Harvard University Press, 1982), even though it has been challenged as essentialist. For a general discussion of the issue of gender and experience, see R. W. Connell, *Gender and Power* (Stanford: Stanford University Press, 1987); and Leslie Roman and Linda Christian-Smith, with Elizabeth Ellsworth, eds., *Becoming Feminine: The Politics of Popular Culture* (Philadelphia: Falmer, 1988).

29. Sandra Acker, "Teachers, Gender and Resistance," *British Journal of Sociology of Education* 9 (no. 3, 1988): 314. See also, Apple, *Teachers and Texts*. As Connell puts it, "No matter how attractive a proposal is in principle, if it makes it more difficult for you to manage a classroom, if it increases the emotional pressure on you, if it adds to the workload, then you don't do it." R. W. Connell, *Teachers' Work* (Boston: Allen and Unwin, 1985), 181.

30. Acker, "Teachers, Gender and Resistance," 307.

31. For a review of some of this literature, see Apple, *Education and Power*, 66–90; and Alice Kessler-Harris, *Out to Work* (New York: Oxford University Press, 1982).

32. Apple, *Teachers and Texts*, 128–49 and Apple, "Redefining Equality." For a more general theoretical discussion of the process of commodification and what conceptual resources might be necessary to understand it in all of its complexity, see the dense but important book by Philip Wexler, *Social Analysis and Education* (New York: Routledge, 1988).

CHAPTER 7: "HEY MAN, I'M GOOD": THE ART AND POLITICS OF CREATING NEW KNOWLEDGE IN SCHOOLS

1. See Michael W. Apple, *Ideology and Curriculum*, 2nd. ed. (New York: Routledge, 1990); Michael W. Apple, *Education and Power* (New York: Routledge, rev. ARK ed., 1985); and Michael W. Apple, *Teachers and Texts: A Political Economy*

of Class and Gender Relations in Education (New York and London: Routledge, 1988).

2. See, for example, Dwayne Huebner, "Curriculum Language and Classroom Meaning," in James B. Macdonald and Robert R. Leeper, eds., *Language and Meaning* (Washington, D.C.: Association for Supervision and Curriculum Development, 1966); and Dwayne Huebner, "The Tasks of the Curricular Theorist," in William F. Pinar, ed., *Curriculum Theorizing* (Berkeley: McCutchan, 1975).

3. See Colin Lankshear with Moira Lawler, *Literacy, Schooling and Revolution* (Philadelphia: Falmer, 1988); Janet Batsleer, Tony Davies, Rebecca O'Rourke, and Chris Weeden, *Rewriting English* (New York: Methuen, 1985); Allan Luke, *Literacy, Textbooks and Ideology* (Philadelphia: Falmer, 1988); and John Willinsky, *The New Literacy* (New York: Routledge, 1990).

4. Herbert Kohl, *36 Children* (New York: Signet, 1967).

5. See Michael W. Apple and Linda Christian-Smith, eds., *The Politics of the Textbook* (New York and London: Routledge, 1991), especially chapter one; and Lankshear with Lawler, *Literacy, Schooling and Revolution.*

CHAPTER 8: THE POLITICS OF PEDAGOGY AND THE BUILDING OF COMMUNITY

1. For further discussion of the politics of this issue, see Michael W. Apple, *Teachers and Texts: A Political Economy of Class and Gender Relations in Education* (New York and London: Routledge 1988).

2. The politics of a pedagogy that has to take all of this into account and some of the difficulties involved are laid out well in Elizabeth Ellsworth, "Why Doesn't This Feel Empowering?" *Harvard Educational Review* 59 (August 1989): 297–324.

3. The conceptual problem of how we are to think through the *contradictory* nature of these relations is dealt with in Michael W. Apple and Lois Weis, "Ideology and Practice in Schooling," in Michael W. Apple and Lois Weis, eds., *Ideology and Practice in Schooling* (Philadelphia: Temple University Press, 1983), 3–33; and Cameron McCarthy and Michael W. Apple, "Race, Class, and Gender in American Educational Research," in Lois Weis, ed., *Class, Race, and Gender in American Education* (Albany: State University of New York Press, 1988), 9–39.

4. See Ellsworth, "Why Doesn't This Feel Empowering?" and Kathleen Casey, *I Answer With My Life* (New York: Routledge, 1993). Casey's volume is an outstanding example of the use of life histories to illuminate the political lives of teachers.

5. See, for example, Apple, *Teachers and Texts;* McCarthy and Apple, "Race, Class, and Gender in American Educational Research"; and especially, Michael Omi and Howard Winant, *Racial Formation in the United States* (New York: Routledge, 1986).

6. Ernesto Laclau and Chantal Mouffe, *Hegemony and Socialist Strategy* (London: Verso, 1985), 87.

7. Ibid., 142.

8. Ibid. I have argued against some of the tendencies within postmodern theory that go much too far in uncritically accepting the logic of these arguments. See Michael W. Apple, "Education, Culture, and Class Power," *Educational Theory* 42 (Spring 1992): 127–45. See also Steven Best and Douglas Kellner, *Postmodern Theory* (London: Macmillan, 1991); and John Clarke, *New Times and Old Enemies* (London: Harper-Collins, 1991).

9. On the implications of what has been called the nonsynchronist parallellist position, see McCarthy and Apple, "Race, Class, and Gender in American Educational Research."

10. Philip Wexler, *Social Analysis of Education* (New York: Routledge and Kegan Paul, 1988).

11. Laclau and Mouffe, *Hegemony and Socialist Strategy,* 12.

12. For more detailed discussion of the importance of these larger struggles, see Michael W. Apple, *Education and Power* (New York: Routledge and Kegan Paul, rev. ARK ed., 1985).

13. The question of who benefits from research has of course been deliberated for quite some time. One of the very best discussions, from a feminist point of view, can be found in Leslie Roman, "Punk Femininity," (Ph.D. diss., University of Wisconsin, Madison, 1988). See also Leslie G. Roman and Michael W. Apple. "Is Naturalism a Move Away From Positivism?" in Elliot Eisner and Alan Peshkin, eds., *Qualitative Inquiry in Education* (New York: Teachers College Press, 1990), 38–73.

14. See the discussion of the politics of authorship in Kathleen Casey, *Teacher As Author,* (Ph.D. diss., University of Wisconsin, Madison, 1988).

APPENDIX: EDUCATION, POWER, AND PERSONAL BIOGRAPHY: AN INTERVIEW

1. Pierre Bourdieu, *In Other Words: Essays Toward a Reflexive Sociology* (Stanford: Stanford University Press, 1990), viii.

2. Ibid.

3. See, for example, Donna Haraway, *Primate Visions* (New York: Routledge, 1989); Nancy Tuana, ed., *Feminism and Science* (Bloomington: Indiana University Press, 1989); and Donna Haraway, *Simians, Cyborgs, and Women* (New York: Routledge, 1991). A provocative analysis of what this means for research and pedagogy in education, women's studies, and other areas can be found in Patti Lather, *Getting Smart* (New York: Routledge, 1991).

BIBLIOGRAPHY

Acker, Sandra. "Teachers, Gender and Resistance." *British Journal of Sociology of Education* 9, no. 3 (1988): 307–22.

Altbach, Philip. *The Knowledge Context.* Albany: State University of New York Press, 1988.

Altbach, Philip, and Gail Kelly, eds. *Education and the Colonial Experience.* New York: Transaction Books, 1984.

Anderson, Mary. "Teachers Unions and Industrial Politics," Ph.D. diss., Macquarie University, 1985.

Apple, Michael W. *Ideology and Curriculum.* Boston: Routledge, 1979.

———. *Education and Power.* Boston: Routledge, 1982.

———. *Education and Power.* New York: Routledge, rev. ARK ed., 1985.

———. "Curriculum, Capitalism and Democracy," *British Journal of Sociology of Education* 7, no. 3 (1986): 319–27.

———. "National Reports and the Construction of Inequality," *British Journal of Sociology of Education* 7, no. 2 (1986): 171–90.

———. "Facing the Complexity of Power: For a Parallelist Position in Critical Educational Studies." In Mike Cole, ed., *Rethinking Bowles and Gintis,* 112–30. Philadelphia: Falmer, 1988.

———. "Redefining Equality: Authoritarian Populism and the Conservative Restoration." *Teachers College Record* 90 (Winter 1988): 167–84.

———. "Social Crisis and Curriculum Accords," *Educational Theory* 38 (Spring 1988): 191–201.

———. *Teachers and Texts: A Political Economy of Class and Gender Relations in Education.* New York and London: Routledge, 1988.

———. "American Realities: Poverty, Economy, and Education." In Lois Weis, Eleanor Farrar, and Hugh Petrie, eds., *Dropouts from School,* 205–23. Albany: State University of New York Press, 1989.

———. *Ideology and Curriculum,* 2nd ed. New York and London: Routledge, 1990.

————. "Is There a Curriculum Voice to Reclaim?" *Phi Delta Kappan* 71 (March 1990): 526–30.

————. "Education, Culture, and Class Power." *Educational Theory* 42 (Spring 1992): 127–45.

————. "The Politics of Official Knowledge: Does a National Curriculum Make Sense?" The John Dewey Lecture presented at the American Educational Research Association Annual Meeting, San Francisco, 1992.

————. "Do the Standards Go Far Enough?" *Journal of Research in Mathematics Education.* in press.

Apple, Michael W., and Linda Christian-Smith, eds. *The Politics of the Textbook.* New York and London: Routledge, 1991.

Apple, Michael W., and Kenneth Teitelbaum, "Are Teachers Losing Control of Their Skills and Curriculum?" *Journal of Curriculum Studies* 18, no. 2 (1986): 177–84.

Apple, Michael W., and Lois Weis, eds., *Ideology and Practice in Schooling.* Philadelphia: Temple University Press, 1983.

Archer, Margaret S., "Social Origins of Educational Systems." In John Richardson, ed. *Handbook of Theory and Research for the Sociology of Education.* 3–33. New York: Greenwood, 1986.

Arnot, Madeleine. "Schooling for Social Justice." Paper presented at the Twelfth National Conference of the New Zealand Association for Research in Education, Auckland, New Zealand, 1990.

Aronowitz, Stanley. *The Politics of Identity.* New York: Routledge, 1992.

Ball, Stephen. "Staff Relations During the Teachers' Industrial Action: Context, Conflict, and Proletarianization," *British Journal of Sociology of Education* 9, no. 3 (1988): 289–306.

Barkin, Steve M., and Michael Gurevitch. "Out of Work and On the Air." *Critical Studies in Mass Communications* 4 (March 1987): 1–15.

Barr, Alwyn. *Reconstruction to Reform: Texas Politics, 1876–1906.* Austin: University of Texas Press, 1971.

Barrow, Clyde. "Pedagogy, Politics and Social Reform." *Strategies* 2 (Fall 1989): 45–66.

————. *Universities and the Capitalist State.* Madison: University of Wisconsin Press, 1990.

Barry, Ann Marie. "Channel One: Controversial Partnership of Business and Education." Department of Communications and Theater, Boston College, 1991. Photocopy.

Bastian, Ann, Norm Fruchter, Marilyn Gittell, Colin Greer, and Kenneth Haskins. *Choosing Equality: The Case for Democratic Schooling.* Philadelphia: Temple University Press, 1986.

Batsleer, Janet, Tony Davies, Rebecca O'Rourke, and Chris Weedon. *Rewriting English: Cultural Politics of Gender and Class.* New York: Methuen, 1985.

Bennett, Tony. "Introduction: Popular Culture and the 'Turn to Gramsci.'" In Tony Bennett, Colin Mercer, and Janet Woollacott, eds. *Popular Culture and Social Relations,* xi–xix. Philadelphia: Open University Press, 1986.

————. "The Politics of the 'Popular' and Popular Culture." In Tony Bennett, Colin

Mercer, and Janet Woollacott, eds. *Popular Culture and Social Relations,* 6–21. Philadelphia: Open University Press, 1986.

Bennett, William. *Our Children and Our Country.* New York: Simon and Schuster, 1988.

Bernstein, Basil. *Class, Codes and Control Volume 3,* 2nd ed. Boston and London: Routledge, 1977.

———. "On Pedagogic Discourse." In John G. Richardson, ed. *Handbook of Theory and Research for the Sociology of Education,* 205–40. New York: Greenwood Press, 1986.

———. *The Structuring of Pedagogic Discourse.* New York: Routledge, 1990.

Best, Steven, and Douglas Kellner. *Postmodern Theory.* London: Macmillan, 1991.

Beyer, Landon, and Michael W. Apple, eds. *The Curriculum: Problems, Politics and Possibilities.* Albany: State University of New York Press, 1988.

Bloom, Allan. *The Closing of the American Mind.* New York: Simon and Schuster, 1987.

Bourdieu, Pierre. *In Other Words: An Essay Toward a Reflexive Sociology.* Stanford: Stanford University Press, 1990.

Bowles, Samuel. "The Post-Keynesian Capital-Labor Stalemate." *Socialist Review* 12 (September/October 1982): 45–72.

Bowles, Samuel, and Herbert Gintis. *Democracy and Capitalism.* New York: Basic Books, 1986.

Bromley, Hank, "Identity Politics and Critical Pedagogy." *Educational Theory* 39 (Summer 1989): 207–23.

Brown, John Franklin. "Textbooks and Publishers." *The Elementary School Journal* 19 (January 1919): 382–88.

Bunzel, John, ed. *Challenge to American Schools.* New York: Oxford University Press, 1985.

Burdell, Patricia. "Thinking About Change in Schools: The At Risk Student Project." *New Futures* (Newsletter of the National Center on Effective Secondary Schools, University of Wisconsin, Madison) (no. 1, 1989): 4–7.

Burnham, Walter Dean. "Post-Conservative America." *Socialist Review* 13 (November/December 1983): 123–32.

Burtless, Gary, ed. *A Future of Lousy Jobs?* Washington: The Brookings Institution, 1990.

Caragee, Kevin M. "Defining Solidarity." *Journalism Monographs* 119 (February 1990): 1–63.

Carnoy, Martin. *The State and Political Theory.* Princeton: Princeton University Press, 1984.

Carnoy, Martin, and Henry Levin. *Schooling and Work in the Democratic State.* Stanford: Stanford University Press, 1985.

Carnoy, Martin, and Joel Samoff. *Education and Social Transition in the Third World.* Princeton: Princeton University Press, 1990.

Carnoy, Martin, Derek Shearer, and Russell Rumberger, *A New Social Contact.* New York: Harper and Row, 1984.

Casey, Kathleen. "Teacher As Author." Ph.D. diss., University of Wisconsin, Madison, 1988.

————. *I Answer With My Life.* New York: Routledge, 1993.

Celis, William. "Schools Lose Money in Business Tax Breaks." *The New York Times* 22 May 1991, A1.

————. "School Districts Reeling in Weakened Economy." *The New York Times,* 5 June 1991, B10.

Center for Law and Education. "Vocational Education Project: Vocational Opportunity for Community and Educational Development." (Mimeo, Center for Law and Education, Cambridge, MA, 1990).

Christian-Smith, Linda. *Becoming A Women Through Romance.* New York: Routledge, 1991.

Clark, David, and Terry Astuto. "The Significance and Permanence of Changes in Federal Education Policy." *Educational Researcher* 15 (October 1986): 4–13.

Clarke, John. *New Times and Old Enemies.* London: Harper-Collins, 1991.

Connell, R. W. *Teachers' Work.* Boston: Allen and Unwin, 1985.

Connell, R. W. *Gender and Power.* Stanford: Stanford University Press, 1987.

The Constitution of the State of Texas: An Annotated and Comparative Analysis Volume 2. Austin: Texas State Printing Office, n.d.

Coontz, Stephanie. *The Social Origins of Private Life.* New York: Verso, 1988.

Culley, Margo, and Catherine Portugues, eds. *Gendered Subjects.* New York: Routledge, 1985.

Dabney, Charles William. *Universal Education in the South Volume 1.* Chapel Hill: University of North Carolina Press, 1936; New York: Arno Press, 1969.

Dahlgren, Peter. "Tuning in the News." In Jose Vidal-Beneyto and Peter Dahlgren, eds. *The Focused Screen,* 1–90.

Strasbourg: Council of Europe, 1987.

Dale, Roger. *The State and Education Policy.* Philadelphia: The Open University Press, 1989.

Danylewycz, Marta, and Alison Prentice. "Teachers, Gender, and Bureaucratizing School Systems in Nineteenth Century Montreal and Toronto." *History of Education Quarterly* 24 (Spring 1984): 75–100.

Danziger, Sheldon, and Daniel Weinberg, eds. *Fighting Poverty.* Cambridge: Harvard University Press, 1986.

Darnton, Robert. *The Literary Underground of the Old Regime.* Cambridge: Harvard University Press, 1982.

De Vaney, Ann. "A Grammar of Educational Television." In Dennis Hlynka and John Belland, eds. *Paradigms Regained,* 241–83. Englewood Cliffs, NJ: Educational Technology Publications, 1991.

Donovan, H. L. "How to Select Textbooks." *Peabody Journal of Education* 2 (July 1924): 1–11.

Down, A. Graham. "Preface." In Harriet Tyson-Bernstein, *A Conspiracy of Good Intentions: America's Textbook Fiasco.* Washington: The Council for Basic Education, 1988.

Edmonson, J. B. "The Ethics of Marketing and Selecting Textbooks." In Gary Montrose Whipple, *The Textbook in American Education,* 199–234. Bloomington, IL: Public School Publishing Co., 1931.

Education Group II. *Education Limited.* London: Unwin-Hyman, 1991.

Edwards, Richard. *Contested Terrain.* New York: Basic Books, 1979.

Ellsworth, Elizabeth. "Illicit Pleasures: Feminist Spectators and *Personal Best.*" In Leslie Roman and Linda Christian-Smith with Elizabeth Ellsworth, eds. *Becoming Feminine.* 102–19. Philadelphia: Falmer, 1988.

Ellsworth, Elizabeth. "Why Doesn't This Feel Empowering?" *Harvard Educational Review* 9 (August 1989): 297–324.

Everhart, Robert. *Reading, Writing and Resistance.* Boston: Routledge and Kegan Paul, 1984.

Fair, Jo Ellen. "Comparative Perspectives on Black-on-Black Violence: Gangs and Tribes in News Discourses." School of Journalism, University of Wisconsin, Madison, 1990. Photocopy.

Fiske, John. "Television and Popular Culture." *Critical Studies in Mass Communications* 3 (June 1986), 200–220.

———. "Television: Polysemy and Popularity." Critical Studies in Mass Communications 3 (December 1986): 390–408.

———. *Television Culture.* New York: Methuen, 1987.

———. *Reading the Popular.* Boston: Unwin Hyman, 1989.

Fiske, John, Bob Hodge, and Graeme Turner. *Myths of Oz: Reading Australian Popular Culture.* Boston: Allen and Unwin, 1987.

Fraser, James W. "Agents of Democracy: Urban Elementary School Teachers and the Conditions of Teaching." In Donald Warren, ed. *American Teachers: Histories of a Profession at Work,* 118–56. New York: Macmillan, 1989.

Fraser, Nancy. *Unruly Practices.* Minneapolis: University of Minnesota Press, 1989.

Freedman, Sara, Jane Jackson, and Katherine Boles. *The Effects of the Institutional Structure of Schools on Teachers.* Somerville, MA: Boston Women's Teachers' Group, 1982.

Freire, Paulo. *Pedagogy of the Oppressed.* New York: Herder and Herder, 1973.

Fuller, Bruce. *Growing Up Modern.* New York: Routledge, 1991.

Gans, Herbert. *Deciding What's News.* New York: Pantheon, 1979.

Gates, Henry Louis Jr. "What Is Patriotism?" *The Nation* 253 (15–22 March 1992): 91.

Gilligan, Carol. *In a Different Voice.* Cambridge: Harvard University Press, 1982.

Gintis, Herbert. "Communication and Politics." *Socialist Review* 10 (March/June, 1980): 189–232.

Giroux, Henry. "Public Philosophy and the Crisis in Education." *Harvard Educational Review* 54 (May 1984). 186–94.

———. *Border Crossings.* New York: Routledge, 1992.

Gitlin, Andrew. "School Structure and Teachers' Work." In Michael W. Apple and Lois Weis, eds. *Ideology and Practice in Schooling,* 193–212. Philadelphia: Temple University Press, 1983.

Gordon, David, Richard Edwards, and Michael Reich. *Segmented Work, Divided Workers* New York: Cambridge University Press, 1982.

Grantham, Dewey W. *Southern Progressivism: The Reconciliation of Progress and Tradition.* Knoxville: The University of Tennessee Press, 1983.

Grossberg, Lawrence, and Cary Nelson. "Introduction: The Territory of Marxism." In Cary Nelson and Lawrence Grossberg, eds. *Marxism and the Interpretation of Culture,* 1–13. Urbana: University of Illinois Press, 1988.

Grumet, Madeleine. *Bitter Milk.* Amherst: University of Massachusetts Press, 1988.

Hall, Stuart. "Popular Democratic vs. Authoritarian Populism: Two Ways of Taking Democracy Seriously." In Alan Hunt, ed. *Marxism and Democracy.* 150–170. London: Lawrence and Wishart, 1980.

Hall, Stuart. "The Great Moving Right Show." In Stuart Hall and Martin Jacques, eds. *The Politics of Thatcherism.* 19–39. London: Lawrence and Wishart, 1983.

———. "Authoritarian Populism: A Reply." *New Left Review* 151 (May/June 1985): 115–124.

———. "Popular Culture and the State." In Tony Bennett, Colin Mercer, and Janet Woollacott, eds. *Popular Culture and Social Relations,* 22–49. Milton Keynes: Open University Press, 1986.

———. "Variants of Liberalism." In James Donald and Stuart Hall, eds. *Politics and Ideology.* Philadelphia: Open University Press, 1986.

———. "The Toad in the Garden: 'Thatcherism Among the Theorists.'" In Cary Nelson and Lawrence Grossberg, eds. *Marxism and the Interpretation of Culture* 35–57. Urbana: University of Illinois Press, 1988.

Hall, Stuart, and Martin Jacques. "Introduction." In Stuart Hall and Martin Jacques, eds. *The Politics of Thatcherism,* 9–16. London: Lawrence and Wishart, 1983.

Haraway, Donna. *Primate Visions.* New York: Routledge, 1989.

———. *Simians, Cyborgs, and Women.* New York: Routledge, 1991.

Harding, Vincent. *There Is a River: The Black Struggle for Freedom in the United States.* New York: Vintage, 1981.

Henry, Nelson B. "The Problems of Publishers in Making and Marketing Textbooks." In Guy Montrose Whipple, ed. *The Textbook in American Education,* 175–98. Bloomington, IL: Public School Publishing Co., 1931.

———. "Value of State Textbook Adoption is Debatable." *The Nation's Schools* 12 (December 1933): 19–20.

Hirsch, E. D., Jr. *Cultural Literacy.* New York: Houghton-Miflin, 1986.

Hodge, Robert, and David Tripp. *Children and Television.* Cambridge: Polity Press, 1986.

Hoffman, Larry. "The Meanings of Channel One." Paper presented at the American Educational Research Association Annual Meeting, Chicago, 1991.

Hogan, David. "Education and Class Formation." In Michael W. Apple, ed. *Cultural and Economic Reproduction in Education,* 32–78. Boston: Routledge and Kegan Paul, 1982.

Horne, David. *The Public Culture.* Dover, NH: Pluto Press, 1986.

Huebner, Dwayne. "Curricular Language and Classroom Meanings." In James B. Macdonald and Robert Leeper, eds. *Language and Meaning.* 8–26. Washington DC: Association for Supervision and Curriculum Development, 1966.

———. "The Tasks of the Curricular Theorist." In William F. Pinar, ed. *Curriculum Theorizing,* 250–70. Berkeley: McCutchan, 1975.

Hunter, Allen. "Virtue With a Vengeance: The Pro-Family Politics of the New Right." Ph.D. diss., Brandeis University, 1984.

————. "The Politics of Resentment and the Construction of Middle America." Department of Sociology, University of Wisconsin, Madison, 1987. Photocopy.

————. *Children in the Service of Conservatism*. Madison: University of Wisconsin Institute for Legal Studies, 1988.

Inglis, Fred. *The Management of Ignorance: A Political Theory of the Curriculum*. New York: Basil Blackwell, 1985.

————. *Popular Culture and Political Power*. New York: St. Martin's Press, 1988.

Jamieson, Kathleen Hall, and Karlyn Kohrs Campbell. *The Interplay of Influence*. Belmont, CA: Wadsworth, 1983.

Jensen, Klaus Bruhn. "Qualitative Audience Research." *Critical Studies in Mass Communications* 4 (March 1987): 16–39.

Jessop, Bob, Kevin Bonnett, Simon Bromley, and Tom Ling. "Authoritarian Populism, Two Nations, and Thatcherism." *New Left Review* 147 (September/October 1984): 33–60.

————. *Thatcherism*. New York: Polity Press, 1988.

Johnson, Richard. "What Is Cultural Studies Anyway?" Occasional paper, Centre for Contemporary Cultural Studies, University of Birmingham, England, 1983.

Judd, Charles. "Analyzing Textbooks." *The Elementary School Journal* 19 (October 1918): 143–54.

Jules, Didacus. "Building Democracy." In Michael W. Apple and Linda Christian-Smith, eds. *The Politics of the Textbook*, 259–87. New York: Routledge, 1991.

Jungck, Susan. "Doing Computer Literacy." Ph.D. diss., University of Wisconsin, Madison, 1985.

Kaestle, Carl, Helen Damon-Moore, Lawrence C. Stedman, Katherine Tinsley, and William Vance Trollinger, Jr. *Literacy in the United States*. New Haven: Yale University Press, 1991.

Katz, Michael B. *The Undeserving Poor*. New York: Pantheon, 1989.

Kazin, Michael. "The Grass Roots Right." *The American Historical Review* 91 (February 1992): 136–55.

Kessler-Harris, Alice. *Out to Work*. New York: Oxford University Press, 1982.

Kielbowitz, Richard B. "Modernization, Communication Policy, and the Geopolitical News, 1820–1860." *Critical Studies in Mass Communications* 3 (March 1986): 21–35.

Klatch, Rebecca E. *Women of the New Right*. Philadelphia: Temple University Press, 1987.

Kliebard, Herbert. *The Struggle for the American Curriculum*. New York: Routledge, 1986.

Kline, Marjory R. "Social Influences in Textbook Publishing." *Educational Forum* 48 (Winter 1984). 223–34.

Knight, Edgar Wallace. *The Influence of Reconstruction on Education in the South*. New York: Teachers College, Columbia University Contributions to Education, no. 60, 1930; New York: Arno Press, 1969.

Kohl, Herbert. *36 Children*. New York: Signet, 1967.

Kozol, Jonathan. *Savage Inequalities*. New York: Crown, 1991.

Laclau, Ernesto, and Chantal Mouffe. *Hegemony and Socialist Strategy*. London: Verso, 1985.

Lanksheer, Colin, with Moira Lawler. *Literacy, Schooling and Revolution.* Philadelphia: Falmer, 1988.

Larrain, Jorge. *Marxism and Ideology.* Atlantic Highlands, NJ: Humanities Press, 1983.

Larson, James, Emile McAnany, and J. Douglas Storey. "News of Latin America on Network Television." *Critical Studies in Mass Communications* 3 (June 1986): 170–191.

Lather, Patti. *Getting Smart.* New York: Routledge, 1991.

Levine, Andrew. *Arguing for Socialism.* Boston: Routledge and Kegan Paul, 1984.

Liston, Daniel. *Capitalist Schools: Explanation and Ethics in Radical Studies of Schooling.* New York: Routledge, 1988.

Liston, Daniel, and Kenneth Zeichner. *Teacher Education and the Social Conditions of Schooling.* New York: Routledge, 1991.

Livingstone, David, ed. *Critical Pedagogy and Cultural Power.* South Hadley, MA: Bergin and Garvey, 1987.

Lufkin, James A. "A History of the California State Textbook Adoption Program." Ph.D. diss., University of California, Berkeley, 1968.

Luke, Allan. *Literacy, Textbooks and Ideology.* Philadelphia: Falmer, 1988.

———. "The Secular Word: Catholic Reconstructions of Dick and Jane." In Michael W. Apple and Linda Christian-Smith, eds. *The Politics of the Textbook,* 166–90. New York: Routledge, 1991.

Mandel, Ernest. "Foreword." In J. W. Frieberg. *The French Press: Class, State and Ideology.* New York: Praeger, 1981, iii–xiv.

McCarthy, Cameron, and Michael W. Apple. "Race, Class, and Gender in American Educational Research." In Lois Weis, ed. *Class, Race, and Gender in American Education,* 9–39. Albany: State University of New York Press, 1988.

McCormick, Richard L. "The Discovery that Business Corrupts Politics." *American Historical Review* 86 (April 1981): 247–74.

McNeil, Linda. *Contradictions of Control.* New York: Routledge, 1986.

McRobbie, Angela. "Working Class Girls and the Culture of Femininity." In Women's Studies Group, ed. *Women Take Issue,* 96–108. London: Hutchinson, 1978.

Meehan, Eileen R. "Conceptualizing Culture as a Commodity." *Critical Studies in Mass Communications* 3 (December 1986): 448–57.

Minnich, Elizabeth Kamarck. *Transforming Knowledge.* Philadelphia: Temple University Press, 1990.

Mitchell, Theodore. *Political Education in the Southern Farmers' Alliance 1887–1900.* Madison: The University of Wisconsin Press, 1987.

Modleski, Tania. "Introduction." In Tania Modleski, ed. *Studies in Entertainment,* ix–xix. Bloomington: Indiana University Press, 1986.

Moffett, James. *Storm in the Mountain.* Carbondale: Southern Illinois University Press, 1988.

Mouffe, Chantal. "Hegemony and New Political Subjects." In Cary Nelson and Lawrence Grossberg, eds. *Marxism and the Interpretation of Culture,* 89–101. Urbana: University of Illinois Press, 1988.

O'Malley, Susan Gushee, Robert C. Rosen, and Leonard Vogt, eds. *The Politics of Education: Essays From Radical Teacher.* Albany: State University of New York Press, 1990.

Omi, Michael, and Howard Winant. *Racial Formation in the United States.* New York: Routledge, 1986.

Ozga, Jenny, and Martin Lawn. "Schoolwork: Interpreting the Labour Process of Teaching." *British Journal of Sociology of Education* 9, no. 3 (1988): 323–36.

Pagano, Jo Anne. *Exiles and Communities.* Albany: State University of New York Press, 1990.

Palmer, Bryan D. *Descent into Discourse.* Philadelphia: Temple University Press, 1990.

Perkins, Linda M. "The History of Blacks in Teaching." In Donald Warren ed. *American Teachers,* 344–69. New York: Macmillan, 1989.

Piven, Frances, and Richard Cloward. *The New Class War.* New York: Pantheon, 1982.

"Political Attorney and Textbook Adoption." unsigned editorial, *The Elementary School Journal* 28 (November 1927: 162–63.

Raskin, Marcus. *The Common Good.* New York: Routledge and Kegan Paul, 1986.

Real, Michael R. "Demythologizing Media." *Critical Studies in Mass Communications* 3 (December 1986): 459–86.

Resse, William. *Power and the Promise of School Reform.* New York and London: Routledge, 1986.

Richardson, John G. "Historical Sequences and the Origins of Common Schooling in the American States." In John G. Richardson, ed. *Handbook of Theory and Research for the Sociology of Education,* 35–63. New York: Greenwood Press, 1986.

Roman, Leslie. "Punk Femininity." Ph.D. diss., University of Wisconsin, Madison, 1988.

Roman, Leslie, and Linda Christian-Smith, with Elizabeth Ellsworth, eds. *Becoming Feminine: The Politics of Popular Culture.* Philadelphia: Falmer, 1988.

Roman, Leslie, G., and Michael W. Apple. "Is Naturalism a Move Away From Positivism?" In Elliot Eisner and Alan Peshkin, eds. *Qualitative Inquiry in Education,* 38–73. New York: Teachers College Press, 1990.

Rose, Susan. *Keeping Them Out of the Hands of Satan.* New York: Routledge, 1988.

Said, Edward. *Orientalism.* New York: Pantheon, 1978.

Schipper, Miriam. "Textbook Controversy: Past and Present." *New York University Education Quarterly* 14 (Spring/Summer 1983): 31–36.

Shoemaker, Pamela, with Elizabeth K. Mayfield. "Building a Theory of News Content." *Journalism Monographs* 103 (June 1987): 1–36.

Simon, Roger, Don Dippo, and Arleen Schenke. *Learning Work.* New York: Bergin and Garvey, 1991.

Smith, Adam. *The Wealth of Nations.* Oxford: Clarendon, 1976.

Stallybrass, Peter, and Allon White. *The Politics and Poetics of Transgression.* Ithaca: Cornell University Press, 1986.

"State Adoption of Textbooks." unsigned letter from a textbook publisher, *The Elementary School Journal* 28 (February 1928): 403.

Stedman, Lawrence, and Marshall Smith. "Recent Reform Proposals for American Education." *Contemporary Education Review* 2 (Fall 1983): 85–104.

Taxel, Joel. "Reclaiming the Voice of Resistance: The Fiction of Mildred Taylor." In

Michael W. Apple and Linda Christian-Smith, eds. *The Politics of the Textbook,* 111–34. New York: Routledge, 1991.

Teitelbaum, Kenneth. "Schooling for Good Rebels." Ph.D. diss., University of Wisconsin, Madison, 1985.

———. "Contestation and Curriculum." In Landon Beyer and Michael W. Apple, eds. *The Curriculum: Problems, Politics and Possibilities,* 32–55. Albany: State University of New York Press, 1988.

———. "Critical Lessons from Our Past." In Michael W. Apple and Linda Christian-Smith, eds. *The Politics of the Textbook,* 135–65. New York: Routledge, 1991.

"Texas Battles Over Evolution." *EPIE gram* 12 (May 1984): 17.

"The Textbook Selection Process." *Interracial Books for Children Bulletin* 14, no. 5 (1983): 17.

Tidwell, Clyde J. *State Control of Textbooks with Special Reference to Florida.* New York: Bureau of Publications, Teachers College, Columbia University, 1928.

Trudell, Bonnie. *Doing Sex Education.* New York: Routledge, in press.

Tuana, Nancy, ed. *Feminism and Science.* Bloomington: Indiana University Press, 1989.

Turner, Graeme. *British Cultural Studies.* Boston: Unwin and Hyman, 1990.

Tyson-Bernstein, Harriet. *A Conspiracy of Good Intentions: America's Textbook Fiasco.* Washington: The Council for Basic Education, 1988.

Weedon, Chris. "Post-structuralist Feminist Practice." In Donald Morton and Mas'ud Zavarzadeh, eds. *Theory/Pedagogy/Politics,* 47–63. Urbana: University of Illinois Press, 1991.

Weis, Lois. *Between Two Worlds.* Boston: Routledge and Kegan Paul, 1985.

Wexler, Philip. *Social Analysis of Education.* New York: Routledge, 1988.

Whipple, Guy M. "The Selection of Textbooks." *The American School Board Journal* 80 (May 1930): 51–53, 158.

Wiebe, Robert H. *The Search for Order 1877–1920.* Cambridge, MA: Hill and Wang, 1967.

Williams, Raymond. *The Long Revolution.* London: Chatto and Windus, 1961.

———. *Television.* New York: Schocken, 1974.

———. *The Year 2,000.* New York: Pantheon, 1983.

———. *Resources of Hope.* New York: Verso, 1989.

Willinsky, John. *The New Literacy.* New York: Routledge, 1990.

Willis, Paul. *Learning to Labor.* New York: Columbia University Press, 1981.

———. *Common Culture.* Boulder, CO: Westview, 1990.

Woodward, Arthur, David L. Elliot, and Kathleen Carter Nagel, eds. *Textbooks in School and Society.* New York: Garland, 1988.

Word, David Paul. "The Evangelical Origins of Mass Media in America, 1815–1835." *Journalism Monographs* 88 (May 1984): 1–30.

Wright, Erik Olin. *Classes.* New York: Verso, 1985.

Index